UNIVERSITY OF NORTH CAROLINA AT CHAPEL HILL
DEPARTMENT OF ROMANCE LANGUAGES

NORTH CAROLINA STUDIES
IN THE ROMANCE LANGUAGES AND LITERATURES

ESSAYS; TEXTS, TEXTUAL STUDIES AND TRANSLATIONS; SYMPOSIA

Founder: URBAN TIGNER HOLMES

NORTH CAROLINA STUDIES IN THE
ROMANCE LANGUAGES AND LITERATURES

Number 149

THE DRAMATIC WORKS OF
ÁLVARO CUBILLO DE ARAGÓN

THE DRAMATIC WORKS
OF
ÁLVARO CUBILLO DE ARAGÓN

BY

SHIRLEY B. WHITAKER

CHAPEL HILL

NORTH CAROLINA STUDIES IN THE ROMANCE
LANGUAGES AND LITERATURES
U.N.C. DEPARTMENT OF ROMANCE LANGUAGES
1975

Library of Congress Cataloging in Publication Data

Whitaker, Shirley B.
  The dramatic works of Álvaro Cubillo de Aragón.
  (North Carolina Studies in the Romance Languages and Literatures; no. 149)

  Bibliography: p. 169.
  1. Cubillo de Aragón, Álvaro, d. 1661 — Criticism and interpretation. I. Title. II. Series.
  PQ6388.C8Z96   862'.3   74-26586

ISBN: 978-0-807-89149-0

DEPÓSITO LEGAL: V. 3.293 - 1975

ARTES GRÁFICAS SOLER, S. A. - JÁVEA, 28 - VALENCIA (8) - 1975

TABLE OF CONTENTS

	Page
PREFACE	9
I. LIFE AND POSTHUMOUS REPUTATION	13
II. PLAYS FROM HISTORY AND LEGEND	25

1. *El conde de Saldaña, primera parte.* 2. *El conde de Saldaña, segunda parte (Los hechos de Bernardo del Carpio).* 3. *El conde Dirlos.* 4. *El rayo de Andalucía y genízaro de España, primera parte.* 5. *El rayo de Andalucía y genízaro de España, segunda parte.* 6. *La corona del agravio.* 7. *La manga de Sarracino y buen término de amor.* 8. *La mayor venganza de honor.* 9. *La tragedia del duque de Verganza.* 10. *Entre los sueltos caballos.* 11. *La honestidad defendida de Elisa Dido, reina y fundadora de Cartago.* 12. *El vencedor de sí mismo.* 13. *Del engaño hacer virtud.*

III. COMEDIAS DE COSTUMBRES	97

1. *Añasco el de Talavera.* 2. *El amor cómo ha de ser.* 3. *Perderse por no perderse.* 4. *La perfecta casada: Prudente, sabia y honrada.* 5. *Las muñecas de Marcela.* 6. *El señor de Noches Buenas.* 7. *El invisible príncipe del Baúl.*

IV. RELIGIOUS PLAYS	129

1. *El justo Lot.* 2. *El mejor rey del mundo y templo de Salomón.* 3. *Los desagravios de Christo.* 4. *Ganar por la mano el juego.* 5. *El bandolero de Flandes.* 6. *Los triunfos de San Miguel.* 7. *Ciento por uno: Auto de Nuestra Señora del Rosario.* 8. *Auto sacramental de la muerte de Frislán.*

V. CONCLUSION	166
BIBLIOGRAPHY	169

PREFACE

With the increase of scholarship in the Spanish *comedia,* our view of the theater of the Golden Age has been greatly enlarged. Nevertheless, few serious students would fail to recognize that many areas remain insufficiently explored. Among these one must surely include the dramatic production of minor writers. Though the modest scope and pretensions implicit in studies devoted to secondary playwrights are a recognized deterrent to their being undertaken, their potential usefulness in providing a broader foundation for works of synthesis can scarcely be disputed.

Upon turning to the minor dramatist Álvaro Cubillo de Aragón, one finds that a number of his works are unavailable in readily accessible editions and that commentary on individual plays, where it exists at all, is for the most part confined to brief plot summaries and an occasional line or paragraph of critical opinion. The aim of the present study is to offer a more comprehensive treatment, including an examination of sources and a review of previous criticism.

Two studies published earlier in this century have been of great value in the preparation of this monograph. Emilio Cotarelo y Mori's preliminary survey of Cubillo's theater has furnished indispensable biographical and bibliographical data; Ángel Valbuena Prat's introduction to an edition of two of Cubillo's *comedias, Las muñecas de Marcela* and *El señor de Noches Buenas,* contains the most complete study of Cubillo as a dramatic craftsman hitherto available, together with a table suggesting the major sources of twenty-one *comedias.*

Twenty-eight dramatic works (twenty-six *comedias* and two *autos*) have formed the basis of the present study. Of these, ten *comedias* appeared in *El enano de las musas,* a miscellany assembled by Cubillo and printed under his name in 1654: *La honestidad defendida de*

Elisa Dido; El rayo de Andalucía y genízaro de España, primera parte; El rayo de Andalucía y genízaro de España, segunda parte; Los desagravios de Christo; El invisible príncipe del Baúl; Las muñecas de Marcela; El señor de Noches Buenas; El amor cómo ha de ser; La tragedia del duque de Verganza; and *Los triunfos de San Miguel.*

The remaining plays to which attention is given include thirteen that were seen by Cotarelo and accepted by him as authentic: *El conde de Saldaña, primera parte; El conde de Saldaña, segunda parte (Los hechos de Bernardo del Carpio); La mayor venganza de honor; El vencedor de sí mismo; Añasco el de Talavera; Perderse por no perderse; La perfecta casada: Prudente, sabia y honrada; El bandolero de Flandes; Ganar por la mano el juego; El justo Lot; El mejor rey del mundo y templo de Salomón; Ciento por uno (auto);* and *La muerte de Frislán (auto).* Also included are four *comedias* which were not accessible to Cotarelo but which he mentions as having been printed under Cubillo's name: *La corona del agravio, La manga de Sarracino, Entre los sueltos caballos,* and *Del engaño hacer virtud.*

The present writer has been unable to examine the text of *El hereje,* an *auto* by Cubillo performed in Granada in 1640. Emilio Orozco Díaz announced in 1938 that he had discovered it and was planning to publish it, even though in his opinion its interest was slight. Whether or not Orozco Díaz carried out his intention is not known to the present writer.

Several other *comedias* and *autos* ascribed to Cubillo have either disappeared or have been proved to be the work of other dramatists. Three *autos* which he wrote for performance at the feast of Corpus Christi in Seville — *San Juan de la Palma, Mudarra,* and *Duelos con pan son buenos* — are known only by title. Another *auto, El mayor desempeño,* was for a time preserved in manuscript in the Salvá Collection, but its present location is unknown. Four works ascribed to Cubillo in Medel's *Índice* (1735) — *El rey Seleuco del Asia (auto), Las amazonas de España, Los casados por fuerza,* and *Mentir por razón de estado* — are also unknown.

Three other *comedias* have been rejected on the basis of evidence supplied by Cotarelo. *Galantear a todas y no amar a ninguna,* ascribed to Cubillo in a list at the end of the 1734 printing of *Las muñecas de Marcela,* was identified by Medel, and later by La Barrera, as the work of a certain Fulgencio Rodríguez de Esquivel. *La suerte y la industria*, which came out under Cubillo's name in an undated eighteenth-century *suelta*, is Juan Ruiz de Alarcón's *La industria y la suerte*. *El tramposo con las damas y castigo merecido*, printed under Cubillo's name in *Jardín ameno de comedias* (1734), is Alonso Jerónimo de Salas Barbadillo's *El galán tramposo y pobre*, which Salas Barbadillo himself said he wrote and which was printed posthumously in 1635 in his *Las coronas del Parnaso*.

Obscurity surrounding the date of composition of many of Cubillo's works makes a chronological order of presentation impracticable in this study. Instead, a division has been made on the basis of subject matter. The spelling and punctuation of quotations from the plays have been modernized, except where a change would distort the metric pattern.

Professor Sturgis E. Leavitt gave assistance and advice from the earliest stages of this project. Mrs. Bobbie Shuping uncomplainingly typed the manuscript under extremely trying conditions.

CHAPTER I

LIFE AND POSTHUMOUS REPUTATION

Besides those seventeenth-century playwrights who lived and wrote in Madrid as they competed for recognition by the most fickle of Spanish audiences, there were others who acquired their reputations while living far from the capital. One such dramatist was Álvaro Cubillo de Aragón, an "hijo de Granada" who continued to live in Andalusia after he began to write for the theater. For Cubillo, the opportunity to come to the attention of Madrid theatergoers must have been provided by *autores de comedias* who, as they traveled throughout Spain with their companies, sought *comedias* that were likely to please in Madrid and elsewhere. This indeed may explain how Cubillo became known outside his native Andalusia, for all evidence is that he continued to live there until well after his plays were being performed in Madrid, on occasion even before Philip IV.

The date of Cubillo's birth is unknown, although it is likely that he was born in Granada towards the end of the sixteenth century. Cotarelo, the chief authority on the facts of the playwright's life, conjectures c. 1596.[1] Several decades after Cotarelo conducted his investigations, Antonio Gallego Morell examined parish registers in Granada for baptismal records of literary figures believed to be natives of the city. Although his efforts were in many cases rewarded, his search for a document recording Cubillo's baptism was fruitless.[2]

---

[1] Emilio Cotarelo y Mori, "Dramáticos españoles del siglo XVII: Álvaro Cubillo de Aragón," *Boletín de la Real Academia Española*, 5 (1918), 2. Unless otherwise indicated, I follow Cotarelo's account of Cubillo's life.

[2] Antonio Gallego Morell, "Treinta partidas de bautismo de escritores granadinos," *Boletín de la Real Academia Española*, 34 (1954), 234; *Sesenta*

The only clue to the playwright's youthful activities is contained in a few lines in the "Prólogo al lector" in *El enano de las musas*:

> Hiciéronme conocido
> cuando muchacho, las clases,
> cuando joven, las audiencias,
> cuando adulto, los corrales. [3]

As Cubillo speaks of having received a formal education, Cotarelo infers that he was born into a middle-class family. His association with "las audiencias" was as an *escribano de provincia*, a modest post he retained even after he took up a literary career.

Beginning in 1622, documents furnish more precise data. On 2 February of that year Cubillo censored Mira de Amescua's *comedia El mártir de Madrid* for the Archbishop of Granada. On 2 November 1623 he became the father of a son by Doña Inés de la Mar, who is identified as his legal wife, although the date of the marriage is unknown. Early in 1625 the couple's first daughter was baptized. Family obligations must have eventually imposed a heavy burden, for eleven children were born of the marriage.

A verse composition entitled *Curia leónica*, published in Granada in 1625 with an *aprobación* dated 10 April 1623,[4] was Cubillo's first literary effort, as indicated by a statement in the dedicatory lines addressed to the Conde de Olivares. The poem, which takes the form of an allegory in which various personages of the court of Philip IV appear in the guise of members of the animal kingdom, deals chiefly with the program of the Junta de Reformación sponsored by Olivares.

During the decade following the composition of the *Curia leónica*, Cubillo moved towards a more active role in literary circles. The date when he began writing for the theater is a matter of conjecture, but if one accepts Menéndez y Pelayo's assertion that a manuscript

---

escritores granadinos con sus partidas de bautismo (Granada: Caja de Ahorros de Granada, 1970), p. 13.

[3] Álvaro Cubillo de Aragón, *El enano de las musas* (Madrid: María de Quiñones, 1654; rpt. Hildesheim: Georg Olms, 1971).

[4] Álvaro Cubillo de Aragón, *Curia leónica* (Granada: Martín Fernández, 1625). On the title page Cubillo is described as "vezino de Granada y Alcayde perpetuo de la cárcel Real de Calatrava." Cotarelo believes that the office of *alcaide perpetuo* was an honorary one and that its duties were discharged by a substitute. There is no evidence that Cubillo was ever in Calatrava.

of his *comedia La mayor venganza de honor* is in the handwriting of Andrés de Claramonte, who died on 19 September 1626, then he must have entered that intensely competitive world by the mid-1620's.[5] Cubillo described in a *relación* the elaborate festivities organized by the city of Granada to celebrate the birth of Prince Baltasar Carlos on 17 October 1629.[6] The printed text is undated, but it must have appeared shortly after the birth of the royal heir.

Cubillo's activity as a playwright in the 1630's is beyond dispute, as shown by external evidence. By 1632 his reputation was sufficiently established for Juan Pérez de Montalbán to say in the *Para todos* (fol. 357) that "Álvaro Cubillo, bizarro poeta, hace excelentes comedias, como lo fueron en esta corte y en toda España las dos de Mudarra" [the two *partes* of *El rayo de Andalucía*]. On 1 June 1634 Roque de Figueroa's company acted *El señor de Noches Buenas* for Philip IV.[7] In 1635 Cubillo was paid 500 *reales* for three *autos* written for the feast of Corpus Christi in Seville. These works, all of which have been lost, are *San Juan de la Palma*, *Mudarra*, and *Los duelos con pan son buenos*.[8] On 19 February 1636 *Las muñecas de Marcela* appears in a list of dramatic works that were being performed by *autores* who had not purchased them.[9] On 23 December payment was made to Alonso de Olmedo for presenting *La corona del agravio* and *La perfecta casada* before Philip IV.[10] On 25 March 1637 Olmedo listed Cubillo's *auto La muerte de Frislán* as one of several plays belonging to his company that had been performed without his authorization.[11]

---

[5] See below, p. 67.

[6] For the text of the *relación*, see Emilio Orozco Díaz, "Unas páginas desconocidas de Cubillo de Aragón," *Boletín de la Universidad de Granada*, 10 (1938), 24-28.

[7] N. D. Shergold and J. E. Varey, "Some Palace Performances of Seventeenth-Century Plays," *Bulletin of Hispanic Studies*, 40 (1963), 237.

[8] José Sánchez Arjona, *Noticias referentes a los anales del teatro en Sevilla desde Lope de Rueda hasta fines del siglo XVII* (Sevilla: Imprenta de E. Rasco, 1898), pp. 300-01, restores to Cubillo these three *autos*, which a misreading of a document had earlier led him to assign to a certain Álvaro de Bustillos.

[9] Sánchez Arjona, pp. 309-10.

[10] Shergold and Varey, p. 222.

[11] Cristóbal Pérez Pastor, *Nuevos datos acerca del histrionismo español en los siglos XVI y XVII*, 1.ª serie (Madrid: Imprenta de la Revista Española, 1901), pp. 204-05.

That Cubillo was still serving as an *escribano* in Granada in 1636 is indicated by two *cartas de pago* in which his name appears. In Madrid on 12 March 1637, payment was made of a debt that had been acknowledged by the actor Diego de Valdés Toral and his wife Bernarda de Castro, "por escritura otorgada ante Álvaro Cubillo de Aragón, escribano de su Magestad, vecino de Granada" on 3 June 1636.[12] A second *carta de pago,* dated Madrid, 1 December 1636, records that Valdés Toral paid 330 *reales* to a certain Toribio Ordóñez, "según obligación fecha en Granada ante Álvaro Cubillo, escribano de su Magestad."[13] The date when Valdés Toral appeared before Cubillo is not given; it may well be that both debts were incurred in the same year.

The year 1637 provides further documentation attesting to Cubillo's literary activity in the provinces. The first is an autograph manuscript of his *auto El mayor desempeño,* dated in Granada on 13 April 1637. In the same year he was again associated with the feast of Corpus Christi in Seville, as is borne out by the fact that the Comisión de la Fiesta del Corpus agreed to pay him 100 *reales.*[14] The reason for the payment is not specified; if it was for an *auto,* it was poor compensation.

In the spring of 1640 he composed in three days an *auto* entitled *El hereje* for performance at the religious celebrations which took place in Granada to redress an insult to the purity of the Virgin Mary contained in a *pasquín* found attached to the door of the cathedral. Padre Luis Paracuellos Cabeza de Vaca, who described these manifestations of religious fervor in a *relación* entitled *Triunfales celebraciones a honor de la pureza virginal de María,* is lavish in his praise of both Cubillo and Calderón, who also contributed an *auto.*[15]

By 1641 Cubillo was in Madrid, where he had purchased a post as *escribano.* About this time he was named an *escribano del ayun-*

---

[12] Cristóbal Pérez Pastor, *Nuevos datos acerca del histrionismo español en los siglos XVI y XVII,* 2.ª serie, publicada con un índice por Georges Cirot (Bordeaux: Feret et Fils, 1914), p. 98.

[13] Cristóbal Pérez Pastor, *Noticias y documentos relativos a la historia y literatura españolas* (Madrid: Imprenta de la Revista de Legislación, 1910-1926), I, 120.

[14] Sánchez Arjona, p. 306.

[15] Emilio Cotarelo y Mori, *Ensayo sobre la vida y obras de don Pedro Calderón de la Barca* (Madrid: Tip. de la "Rev. de Arch., Bibl. y Museos," 1924), p. 205.

tamiento de Madrid, an office he held until the end of his life. Newly arrived in Madrid, he received favorable mention in Luis Vélez de Guevara's *El diablo cojuelo* (1641). In Tranco IX of Vélez' work Don Cleofás and the Diablo Cojuelo visit a literary academy in Seville which has as its secretary "Álvaro Cubillo, ingenio granadino, que había venido a Sevilla a algunos negocios de su importancia, excelente cómico y gran versificador...." [16] Vélez' reference to Cubillo, though it appeared in 1641, of course reflects the latter's participation in literary circles before he came to Madrid. Whether he continued to supply *comedias* and *autos* after taking up residence in the capital in the quantity that he had earlier is an open question. The weight of evidence from his extant dramatic works is that he became less active as a playwright after leaving Andalusia.

The year 1654 marks the publication of *El enano de las musas,* which includes ten *comedias,* a long poem entitled *Las cortes del león y del águila* (pp. 1-40), and a large quantity of miscellaneous verse. In the dedication to Don Sebastián López Hierro de Castro, Cubillo elaborates on his purpose in having the volume published: "Avivó, puso espuelas a este intento el aver escrito, y sacado a las tablas más de cien comedias, y ver algunas impressas sin orden mía, llenas de errores."

Las cortes del león y del águila, a considerably expanded recasting of the *Curia leónica,* attests to Cubillo's continued interest in the topic that had engaged his attention in the earlier work. The reforms initiated at mid century under the ministry of Luis de Haro are the subject matter; the work was clearly designed to win the approval of the sponsors of the legislation, for it is filled with flattering allusions to Philip IV and Mariana de Austria (the *león* and *leona* of the allegory) and to Luis de Haro.

The miscellaneous verses were seemingly composed over a period of several years. Some are devotional; others are occasional poems addressed to members of the royal family and the aristocracy. It would appear that after Cubillo set up residence in Madrid he expended no little effort in attempting to attract the notice of illustrious personages.

---

[16] Luis Vélez de Guevara, *El diablo cojuelo,* edición y notas de Francisco Rodríguez Marín, Clásicos Castellanos, 34 (Madrid: Espasa-Calpe, S. A., 1941), p. 187.

Two festive compositions, "Carta del autor a un amigo suyo" (pp. 44-46) and "Retrato de un poeta cómico" (pp. 389-391), are worthy of more than passing attention as expressions of Cubillo's views on the *comedia*. In the "Carta del autor" he sets forth his conception of the *comedia* as *pasatiempo* and advises a would-be playwright to observe established techniques and fashions. Described in "Retrato de un poeta cómico" is the practice of refurbishing existing *comedias* and passing them off as new. As will be seen, Cubillo himself often followed the course which the anonymous playwright of the poem confesses that he has adopted.

During his last years Cubillo was still serving as an *escribano* and doing some writing, even if not for the theater. A document from the municipal archives of Madrid, dated 17 January 1657, attests that Cubillo, who is described as an "escribano del Rey nuestro señor, residente en su corte y provincia," certified that on 16-17 January 1657 the *autores* Diego Osorio and Pedro de la Rosa had not performed in the public theaters, "por estar ocupados en la fiesta que se hace a S. M. en la Zarzuela y ensayos della." On 6 February 1658 he entered a sonnet and a gloss in a *certamen* at the University of Alcalá. Dated 1659 are two published *relaciones* by Cubillo describing the reception of the Duc de Gramont, who had come to Madrid on behalf of Louis XIV to request the hand of the Infanta María Teresa.[17]

In 1660, the year before his death, Cubillo is known to have entered two *certámenes*. On 19 September 1660 he submitted verses in the competition held to celebrate the opening of a new chapel in Madrid dedicated to the Virgen de la Soledad. In Francisco de Avellaneda's account of this *certamen*, not published until 1664, Cubillo

---

[17] *Relacion breve de la solemne entrada que hizo en la villa de Madrid... el Excmo. Sr. Duque de Agramont, embajador extraordinario del Christianissimo Rey de Francia cerca de los felices casamientos de aquella Magestad con la serenissima infanta dona Maria Teresa de Austria...* Compuesta y escrita por Álvaro Cubillo de Aragón (Madrid: Andrés García de la Iglesia, 1659). *Relacion del convite y real banquete que, a imitacion de los persas, hizo en la corte de España el Excmo. Sr. D. Alonso Enriquez de Cabrera, Almirante de Castilla, al Excmo. Sr. Monsiur Duque de Agramont...* Compuesta y escrita por Álvaro Cubillo de Aragón (Madrid: Andrés García de la Iglesia, 1659). For the text of the *Relación breve*, see W. T. McCready and J. A. Molinaro, "La *Relación breve* de Cubillo de Aragón y la Paz de los Pirineos," *Bulletin Hispanique*, 62 (1960), 438-43.

is an "ingenio de alquitrán, por ser de Granada y por el fuego de sus obras, pues han dado tanta lumbre que corren muy válidas en la región del aire; porque en alas de cohetes han penetrado esas esferas azules." In October 1660 Cubillo entered some *octavas,* his last known work, in a poetic competition in Jaén.

Cubillo died in Madrid on 21 October 1661. At the time of his death he was living in the Calle de los Ministriles in the parish of San Sebastián, a section of the capital where many actors and playwrights lived.

* * *

During the eighteenth century a number of Cubillo's dramatic works were reprinted; and several, notably *El conde de Saldaña* (two *partes*), *El rayo de Andalucía* (two *partes*), and *Los desagravios de Christo,* continued in the repertory of acting companies. Even so, the playwright appears to have been largely ignored by eighteenth-century critics of the Golden Age theater, both its champions and its detractors. The sole exception seems to have been Ignacio de Luzán, the leading advocate of adherence to the neoclassical unities. Luzán points to Cubillo's *El conde de Saldaña* as exemplifying some of the features he finds most censurable in the *comedia* of the Golden Age:

> Es verdad que no es tan frecuente este defecto [falta de unidad de acción] como el de unidad de tiempo y de lugar. Las comedias de *Bernardo del Carpio,* del *Conde de Saldaña,* y otras semejantes han servido por esto de asunto de burla y mofa a un crítico Francés.[18] Y no sin bastante motivo, por ser absurdo intolerable que al principio salga Bernardo del Carpio niño, y antes de acabarse la comedia ya sea hombre hecho, y execute hazañas prodigiosas contra los Moros.[19]

---

[18] Ignacio de Luzán, *La poética, o reglas de la poesía* [Text of the first (1737) edition], con un estudio de Luigi de Filippo (Barcelona: Selecciones Bibliófilos, 1956), I, 131, quotes the well-known attack on the Spanish *comedia* from Boileau, *Art Poétique,* III:
> Un rimeur, sans péril, delà les Pyrenées,
> Sur la scène en un jour renferme des années.
> Là souvent le héros d'un spectacle grossier,
> Enfant au premier acte, est barbon au dernier.

[19] Luzán, II, 131. Luzán makes many changes in the second edition of his *Poética* (Madrid: Imprenta de D. Antonio de Sancha, 1789), but he retains (III, 245) the passages quoted above.

Beginning in 1826, one finds a few evidences of interest in Cubillo's work, but not until 1890, when Adolf Schaeffer devoted some fifteen pages to his theater in *Geschichte des spanischen Nationaldramas*,[20] does any assessment seem to reveal a careful reading of more than a handful of his plays. In the main, the first nineteenth-century scholars to take notice of Cubillo limited themselves to observations concerning a few *comedias*. In 1826 *Las muñecas de Marcela, La perfecta casada, El señor de Noches Buenas,* and *El amor cómo ha de ser* were published as the *Comedias escogidas* of Cubillo.[21] Each of these *comedias* is the subject of an *examen* containing pertinent comments by an anonymous editor; however, a broad view of the playwright's production does not emerge. In 1841, writing in *Lecciones de literatura española*, Alberto Lista remarks that "Cubillo tiene comedias muy buenas de capa y espada, como *El tramposo con las damas* y *Las muñecas de Marcela;* la primera parte del *Conde de Saldaña* tiene versos y escenas excelentes, y *La perfecta casada* es muy apreciable en el género ideal."[22]

Antonio Gil y Zárate, writing in 1844, seemingly bases his opinion on the *comedias* printed in the 1826 collection. He says that in his opinion the best of Cubillo's more than twenty-five dramatic works are *El amor cómo ha de ser, Las muñecas de Marcela,* and *La perfecta casada*. Of these he says that "sus planes son bastante arreglados y tienen fluidez en la versificación, moralidad y nobleza en los pensamientos."[23]

Ticknor, in his *History of Spanish Literature* (1849), makes brief mention of *El rayo de Andalucía, El señor de Noches Buenas, Los triunfos de San Miguel,* and *La perfecta casada*. In his view, "none of Cubillo's plays has high poetical merit, though several are pleasant, easy, and natural."[24]

---

[20] Adolf Schaeffer, *Geschichte des spanischen Nationaldramas* (Leipzig: F. A. Brockhaus, 1890), II, 90-105.
[21] Álvaro Cubillo de Aragón, *Comedias escogidas* (Madrid: Imprenta de Ortega y Compañía, 1826).
[22] Alberto Lista y Aragón, *Lecciones de literatura española* (Madrid: Nicolás Arias, 1841), II, 290.
[23] Antonio Gil y Zárate, *Manual de literatura: Resumen histórico de la literatura española* (Madrid: Boix, 1844), II, 480.
[24] George Ticknor, *History of Spanish Literature* (New York: Harper and Brothers, 1849), II, 412.

Count von Schack devotes several paragraphs to Cubillo, but one would suspect from the tenor of his observations that he knew the *comedias de costumbres* better than the historical and religious plays. Certainly his evaluation is primarily applicable to the first of these groups. His comments on Cubillo's skill in conveying the gentler emotions anticipate a direction given by Valbuena Prat to criticism of Cubillo's theater: "Álvaro Cubillo hubo de tener un carácter sensible, casi femenino, opuesto a la representación de pasiones enérgicas, pero conocedor de las más dulces del alma, especialmente de las de la mujer, y aficionado, por su propensión natural, a lo tierno y agradable, a la pintura del amor ferviente y lleno de abnegación." [25]

Mesonero Romanos, who in 1858 collected seven of Cubillo's *comedias* for inclusion in Volume 47 of the Biblioteca de Autores Españoles, [26] asserts that among Cubillo's dramatic works are to be found some which compare favorably with the most admired *comedias* written by Golden Age playwrights of the first rank. Mesonero, who considers the two *partes* of *El rayo de Andalucía* and *El conde de Saldaña* among the playwright's best works, goes on to say that in them, as in most of his other *comedias*, Cubillo displays skill in plot construction. Speaking of the *comedias de costumbres,* which he finds more regular than the heroic plays, he says that he finds them to have "intención moral, economía de acción, pintura viva de los caracteres, gracia y chiste en la elocución." He adds that he thinks Cubillo possessed "la *vis cómica* y el halagüeño colorido propio del drama de costumbres." [27]

Schaeffer, writing in 1890, sees Cubillo as a transitional dramatist who partakes of both the Lopean and the Calderonian manner. For this critic, who had studied eighteen of Cubillo's plays, the skill displayed in handling a variety of subject matter is a sign of a genuine talent for the theater. Although he acknowledges that Cubillo's achievement does not win him a place among Golden Age playwrights of

---

[25] Adolfo Federico, Conde de Schack, *Historia de la literatura y del arte dramático en España,* trans. Eduardo de Mier (Madrid: Imprenta y Fundición de M. Tello, 1885-1887), V, 172-73.

[26] The two *partes* of *El conde de Saldaña, La perfecta casada, Las muñecas de Marcela, El señor de Noches Buenas, El amor cómo ha de ser,* and *El invisible príncipe del Baúl.*

[27] Ramón de Mesonero Romanos, ed., *Dramáticos posteriores a Lope de Vega,* I, Biblioteca de Autores Españoles, 47 (Madrid: Librería de los Sucesores de Hernando, 1924), pp. xxi-xxiii.

the first rank, he maintains that in his dramatic works one generally finds poetic grace, nearly always a well-constructed plot, and frequently characters of great psychological depth. Among the principal defects to be found in some of the *comedias* are stilted versification, bombastic language, long speeches, and unattractively masculine women characters. [28]

Schaeffer's review was followed by Cotarelo's investigations, which were published in 1918. Though Cotarelo's study is more valuable for its biographical and bibliographical data than for its critical comments, the latter are the fruit of an examination of a larger number of Cubillo's works (24) than had served as the foundation of any previous study. Cotarelo, who places Cubillo among Lope's followers, finds his dependence on earlier plays to be all the more regrettable because when he devised his own plots, as in the second *parte* of *El rayo de Andalucía* and in *La perfecta casada,* he achieved success. In support of his assertion that Cubillo "no fue desgraciado" in character delineation, Cotarelo points to Bernardo del Carpio in the *Saldaña* plays, Enrique in *El señor de Noches Buenas,* Estefanía in *La perfecta casada,* Marfira in *El conde Dirlos,* Elvira in *El rayo de Andalucía, segunda parte,* and Marcela in *Las muñecas de Marcela.* Although Cotarelo scores Cubillo for sometimes employing pompous phraseology and lengthy descriptions, he appears to be excusing these defects to some degree when he says that it should not be forgotten that Cubillo was an Andalusian and that such "amplificaciones y recamos oratorios" are always agreeable to the Spanish ear. [29]

A complement to Cotarelo's study is Valbuena Prat's introduction to his edition in 1928 of *Las muñecas de Marcela* and *El señor de Noches Buenas.* Besides offering his views on twenty-one plays, Valbuena discusses at some length the question of Cubillo's position in relation to the Lopean and Calderonian cycles and devotes considerable attention to an analysis of his poetic style. [30] Rejecting Cotarelo's argument that Cubillo's reliance on models from the first cycle places

---

[28] Schaeffer, II, 104.
[29] Cotarelo, "Cubillo," pp. 279-80.
[30] Ángel Valbuena Prat, ed., *Las muñecas de Marcela. El señor de Noches Buenas,* by Álvaro Cubillo de Aragón, Clásicos Olvidados, III (Madrid: Compañía Ibero-americana de Publicaciones, 1928; rpt. Madrid: Ediciones Alcalá, 1966), pp. xix-xx.

him firmly within the Lopean group, Valbuena contends that the determining factor is not the subject matter itself but the manner in which it is treated.

Valbuena sees no sharp chronological division between the two modes, but rather a transitional period dating approximately from 1630 to 1645 in which they exist side by side and compete with each other. In his opinion, the playwrights most representative of these trends are Mira de Amescua and Cubillo, though each reacts somewhat differently to the changes in taste. He holds that Mira, although adopting Calderón's baroque poetic language, remains essentially faithful to Lope's technique of construction, while Cubillo, though he uses the heroic subject matter favored by Lope, "penetra en la fina trama y contextura perfecta del arte del segundo ciclo."

Valbuena thus divides into two groups the twenty-one *comedias* by Cubillo which he had studied. The first, which betrays influences of the Lopean cycle, especially Mira's early works, comprises those *comedias* in which, he says, the personality of the playwright is not fully manifested. The second group, much larger than the first, consists of those works in which the Calderonian technique is applied to material from the Lopean cycle.[31]

Valbuena, who adduces a number of examples as evidence of the influence of both Góngora and Calderón on Cubillo's poetic language, draws attention to a certain exquisiteness, a "labor de orfebrería," which he believes gives a distinctive cast to the latter's style. For Valbuena, Cubillo's best plays are his *comedias de costumbres*, in which the "labor de orfebrería" is most clearly discernible:

> Su deliciosa comedia de costumbres, en las obras más representativas... tiene que ser del agrado del hombre del novecientos, que fatigado de la descarga nerviosa del Greco y

---

[31] Valbuena Prat, *Las muñecas*, pp. xliii-xliv. The *comedias* of the first group are *Añasco el de Talavera, El amor cómo ha de ser, El bandolero de Flandes, Ganar por la mano el juego,* and *El vencedor de sí mismo*; those of the second group are *El justo Lot, El mejor rey del mundo y templo de Salomón, Los triunfos de San Miguel, La honestidad defendida de Elisa Dido, Los desagravios de Christo, El conde de Saldaña (primera parte), El conde de Saldaña (segunda parte), El rayo de Andalucía (primera parte), El rayo de Andalucía (segunda parte), La mayor venganza de honor, La tragedia del duque de Verganza, Perderse por no perderse, La perfecta casada, Las muñecas de Marcela, El señor de Noches Buenas,* and *El invisible príncipe del Baúl.*

de Wagner, se deleita, como en la fuente y el arroyo, en Giorgione y Mozart. Es algo de magia de "minuetto," de encanto de danza, lo que se siente en el teatro — en cierto modo de marionetas — de Cubillo y de Moreto. En esta superación de nuestro XVII está el preludio de toda la delicadeza de los jardines de Versalles y los palacios de Viena.[32]

Valbuena's view, which seems to owe something to Schack, has been given currency in histories of Spanish literature that have appeared since the publication of his study. Federico Carlos Sáinz de Robles takes it up in his *Teatro español: Historia y antología,* where one finds an amplification that is almost rapturous in tone.[33] Also dependent on Valbuena is Juan Luis Alborg, who in his *Historia de la literatura española* chooses Cubillo as representative of the minor dramatists of the Calderonian cycle.[34] Like Valbuena, he shows a preference for the *comedias de costumbres*. Although his observations on these *comedias* in the main follow Valbuena, he asserts his independence by rejecting the "labor de orfebrería" as applicable to all of Cubillo's *comedias de costumbres*.

From the critical comment which Cubillo's dramatic works have elicited since his death, one can infer that at no time has he enjoyed a greater reputation than the relatively modest one that was his lot during his lifetime. Although most scholars who have turned to his plays would acknowledge that some of them, especially the *comedias de costumbres,* have literary merit, and an occasional critic, notably Valbuena Prat, has professed to see elements of genuine beauty in his theater, no claim has ever been made that he should be regarded as more than a minor writer. That his name often goes unrecognized except by specialists in the theater of the Golden Age is testimony to his position as a lesser playwright.

---

[32] Valbuena Prat, *Las muñecas,* p. xx.
[33] Federico Carlos Sáinz de Robles, *Teatro español: Historia y antología* (Madrid: M. Aguilar, 1942-1943), III, 50-51.
[34] Juan Luis Alborg, "Dramaturgos menores del ciclo de Calderón: Álvaro Cubillo de Aragón," in *Época barroca,* Vol. II of *Historia de la literatura española* (Madrid: Editorial Gredos, S. A., 1967), pp. 804-10.

CHAPTER II

PLAYS FROM HISTORY AND LEGEND

Cubillo's extant *comedias* based on material from history and legend offer a wide range of subject matter. Most have their ultimate source in the national past; a few treat material that is non-Spanish in origin. Some of these *comedias* have survived in a single printing; others have been preserved in numerous editions. Several are known to have been extremely popular with theater audiences.

The historical plays furnish abundant material for analyzing Cubillo's procedure in recasting earlier *comedias,* since a number of his models have been identified. In some instances, however, he seems to have taken only scattered elements from other *comedias*. Elsewhere he appears not to have drawn directly from any previous dramatic work, but rather to have utilized other sources.

1. *El conde de Saldaña, primera parte*

In *El conde de Saldaña, primera parte* Cubillo makes use of subject matter deeply rooted in Spanish tradition, the legend of Bernardo del Carpio.[1] In brief, the account set down in the thirteenth century in the *Primera crónica general,*[2] which draws from the *Chronicon Mundi* of Lucas de Tuy, the *Historia Gothica* of Rodrigo Jiménez de Rada, and from "cantares et fablas," is as follows: King Alfonso el Casto of León, upon learning of the secret marriage of his

---

[1] For the historical elements in the legend, see Albert B. Franklin, "A Study of the Origins of the Legend of Bernardo del Carpio," *Hispanic Review,* 5 (1937), 286-303.

[2] *Primera crónica general de España,* I, Nueva Biblioteca de Autores Españoles, 5 (Madrid: Bailly-Baillière e Hijos, 1906), Chap. 617.

sister Jimena to the Conde San Díez de Saldaña and of a son, Bernardo, born of the union, sends the count in irons to the castle of Luna and orders Jimena to a convent. Bernardo, reared at court in ignorance of his parentage, some years later leads opposition to the childless king's offer of the succession to Charlemagne. After Alfonso repudiates the emperor, Bernardo plays a decisive part in defeating the French at Roncesvalles. Upon discovering the identity of his parents, he demands Saldaña's freedom of Alfonso, who banishes him from court. Having returned to court after the accession of Alfonso el Magno, he repeatedly asks for his father's release, which the king each time promises to grant. During a subsequent banishment, Bernardo builds near Salamanca the castle of El Carpio, which serves as the base from which he harasses the king. Seeking to end the strife, the Leonese nobles persuade Alfonso to free Saldaña in exchange for El Carpio. After receiving the keys to the castle, the king orders Saldaña set free. Informed of the count's death in prison, Alfonso directs that his body be propped on a horse to deceive Bernardo. Upon kissing the cold hand of the corpse, Bernardo realizes that he has been duped. Afterwards he leaves the Leonese court, never to return.

In *romances viejos* on Bernardo, one finds several modifications later utilized by playwrights. Perhaps the most striking is that every mention of Bernardo's possible French ancestry in the maternal line has vanished, leaving a thoroughly Spanish hero who occasionally acts with a rashness never attributed to him in the chronicle. Another change is the fusion of Alfonso el Casto and Alfonso el Magno into one king, Alfonso el Casto. "En los reinos de León" tells of a secret love affair between Saldaña and Jimena but makes no mention of a marriage. The incident of the blinding of Saldaña on Alfonso's orders seems to have its origin in the ballad "Antes que barbas tuviera," which has it that orders were given for the count to be handed over "sin ojos" to Bernardo.

Throughout the terse accounts set down in the chronicles and the more energetic *romances,* the heroic proportions of the conflict between sovereign and noble emerge more clearly than in dramatized versions, none of which achieves the primitive grandeur of the earlier narratives. The principal components of the legend — the marriage (or liaison) in violation of the code governing the relationship of vassal to king, the king's revenge, the innocent child who grows up unaware of his station, and the subsequent struggle between Bernardo and his sovereign — are, however, usually retained in the theater of the Golden Age. Because of the way the material is treated, a melodramatic tone is a common feature of nearly all these *comedias*.

The earliest dramatization of the legend is Juan de la Cueva's *Comedia de la libertad de España por Bernardo del Carpio*, first staged in Seville in 1579. In the main, Cueva's four-act play follows the *Primera crónica general* in a somewhat static reworking of the story of the secret marriage, Bernardo's birth, his discovery of the identity of his parents, Alfonso's offer of the crown to Charlemagne, and the defeat of the French at Roncesvalles. In the fashion so dear to Juan de la Cueva, the play ends with the appearance of a mythological figure when Mars steps forth to crown Bernardo as his successor in the arts of war. The appeal to patriotism inherent in the events at Roncesvalles, where Bernardo slays Roland, predominates over the Spaniard's efforts to win the freedom of his father.

A second *comedia* inspired by the legend is *Las mocedades de Bernardo del Carpio*, which is sometimes attributed to Lope de Vega.[3] The author retains the essential elements of the legend: the clandestine love affair, Bernardo's birth, his upbringing in ignorance of his parentage, and his long contest with the king. Among the new characters introduced are an unsympathetic Conde Rubio, Saldaña's rival in love and subsequently Bernardo's foster father, Benyúsef, a Moor who befriends Bernardo, and Félix Alba, a Moorish girl to whom Bernardo is attracted. By the addition of these and other minor characters, the author heightens the melodramatic features of the legend and provides a romantic interest for Bernardo, but the multiplicity of episodes prevents him from handling any of them in more than a perfunctory way. Nevertheless, the dignity of the poetic diction and the *romances* so aptly included compensate in large measure for the *comedia*'s structural deficiencies.

---

[3] S. Griswold Morley and Courtney Bruerton, in *The Chronology of Lope de Vega's "Comedias,"* Modern Language Association of America, Monograph Series, 11 (New York: Modern Language Association of America, 1940), p. 315, hold that Lope's authorship is doubtful, but that if the play is his, it was written between 1599 and 1608. J. B. Avalle-Arce, in "Dos notas a Lope de Vega," *Nueva Revista de Filología Hispánica*, 7 (1953), 426-29, adduces biographical evidence in support of his argument that the play is Lope's.

Cubillo's *El conde de Saldaña, primera parte*, a *refundición* of *Las mocedades de Bernardo del Carpio*, cannot be assigned to a specific year on the basis of available evidence. A *terminus ad quem* is provided by a *licencia* of 16 September 1641 appearing on the sole extant manuscript (Biblioteca Nacional MS. 16.720).[4] The words on the last folio, "Es de Lorenzo de Prado," show that it was at one time in the possession of the *autor de comedias* of that name.

El conde de Saldaña, primera parte has fared better at the hands of critics than most of Cubillo's other historical plays. The earliest observations were, however, conditioned by polemics between neoclassicists and nationalists. The harshest assessment of the *comedia* comes in the eighteenth century from Ignacio de Luzán, champion of neoclassicism, who attacks it for its disregard of the unities of time and place.[5] Mesonero Romanos, replying to Luzán in the mid-nineteenth century, argues that Spanish theatergoers of Cubillo's time would not have been troubled by the breaking of the unities of time and place. Mesonero singles out for special commendation the "magnífico diálogo" between the Moslem ambassador and Bernardo in which the two take the measure of each other. He argues that the author of such a scene "no era ciertamente un poeta vulgar" or a mere imitator of Rojas and Calderón.[6]

Since the time of Mesonero, critics who have expressed opinions concerning *El conde de Saldaña* have managed to consider the play more dispassionately. Adolf Schaeffer, writing in 1890, has little to say other than to note the absence of the poetic quality which pervades Lope's *comedias* on subjects from Spanish tradition. Menéndez

---

[4] The MS carries a second *licencia*, dated Valencia, 2 April 1641. At the end of Acts II and III appears the signature with *rúbrica*, "Don Álvaro Cubillo de Aragón." Antonio Paz y Melia, in *Catálogo de las piezas de teatro que se conservan en el departamento de manuscritos de la Biblioteca Nacional*, 2nd ed., I (Madrid: Blass, 1934), 57, says that a comparison of these signatures with Cubillo's handwriting as the censor of Mira de Amescua's play, *El mártir de Madrid*, suggests that neither is an autograph. Printed editions are as follows: N.p., n.d.; Madrid: Juan Sanz, n.d.; Sevilla, n.d.; Salamanca, n.d.; Madrid: Antonio Sanz, 1751; Barcelona: C. Sapera, 1769; Valencia: Joseph y Thomas de Orga, 1776; Barcelona, n.d.; Barcelona, n.d. (another edition); Madrid: Librería de Quiroga, 1791; Valencia: Laborda, n.d.; in BAE, 47 (Madrid: M. Rivadeneyra, 1858).

[5] See above, p. 19.

[6] Mesonero Romanos, I, xxii. Mesonero's comments on specific plays by Cubillo are taken throughout from the work cited.

y Pelayo, principally concerned with the relative merits of Cubillo's play and *Las mocedades,* says that Cubillo produced "una refundición muy atinada," in which, even if he did not retain the energy of the original, he managed to eliminate many defects contained in the earlier play. After observing that Cubillo's tightening of the plot makes the breaking of the unities of action and time less noticeable, Menéndez y Pelayo points out that this results in a *comedia* that is more dramatic but less epic in spirit than its model.[8]

For Cotarelo, *El conde de Saldaña* "es de valor en todos los aspectos que se le considere" and much superior to *Las mocedades.* In particular, Cotarelo praises two scenes for revelation of character. Original with Cubillo is one in which Bernardo struggles to show respect to his foster father Don Rubio, despite the shabby treatment he has received. The recognition scene between father and son, derived from *Las mocedades,* Cotarelo calls "tierna y bien dispuesta."[9]

Valbuena Prat, the most recent critic to study *El conde de Saldaña,* terms it Cubillo's best *comedia heroica,* with a "plan perfecto." Like Menéndez y Pelayo and Cotarelo, he finds Cubillo's tighter construction an improvement over the original. The elimination of scenes of dubious taste, such as those of the pregnant Infanta, the birth of Bernardo, and the blinding of Saldaña on stage, meets with his approval. Like previous critics, he admires the recognition scene.[10]

It is not the present writer's purpose to take exception to the generally held opinion that *El conde de Saldaña, primera parte,* though lacking brilliance, is an acceptable piece of dramatic craftmanship. Rather, some of its features will be examined more closely. In addition, attention will be directed to the importance of a device overlooked by earlier investigators.

---

[7] Schaeffer, II, 102. Schaeffer's comments on specific plays by Cubillo are taken throughout from the work cited.

[8] Marcelino Menéndez y Pelayo, ed., *Obras de Lope de Vega, publicadas por la Real Academia Española,* 15 vols. (Madrid: "Sucesores de Rivadeneyra," (1890-1913), VII, cxxxvii. Menéndez y Pelayo's comments on specific plays by Cubillo are taken throughout from his studies of *comedias* (in the work cited) which are related in subject matter to plays by Lope de Vega.

[9] Cotarelo, "Cubillo," p. 251. Cotarelo's comments on specific plays by Cubillo are taken throughout from the work cited.

[10] Valbuena Prat, p. lxxiv. Valbuena's comments on specific plays by Cubillo are taken throughout from the work cited.

Since the structure of Cubillo's *comedia* is dependent on that of *Las mocedades de Bernardo del Carpio*, it will be well to see how closely it follows its prototype. Compactness of plot is achieved by discarding much of the action of the earlier *comedia*. By introducing Bernardo as a young man, Cubillo eliminates many of the episodes of Act I of *Las mocedades*; however, a change in chronology leaves him with an improbable situation: Saldaña and the Infanta, whose liaison is not discovered until many years after Bernardo's birth, seem to have taken no interest in their son during his childhood. One can accept their having handed Bernardo over to Rubio, Saldaña's friend, in order to conceal him from the king, but not that they have made no effort to keep up with his progress. Lope avoids this improbability by having the parents placed in confinement during Bernardo's infancy. Saldaña, in prison, was in no position to communicate with his son; the Infanta, in a convent, was presumably kept under surveillance too.

By withholding Rubio's denunciation to the king until Act II, Cubillo adds an element of suspense not present in the first play. He retains the evil count as necessary to the movement of the plot but changes Rubio's reasons for betrayal. In *Las mocedades* Rubio is a disappointed suitor; in *El conde de Saldaña* he is jealous of Saldaña's friendship with the king. The device of a letter to the warden of Luna is also taken from Lope, but Cubillo lessens the effect of horror produced by the punishment by not having Saldaña blinded on stage.

Not until Act III of *El conde de Saldaña* does Bernardo go into exile, whereas in *Las mocedades* this incident occurs in Act II. The circumstances are similar, for in both cases Bernardo's hotheadedness offends the king. The arrival of the Moorish ambassador, who is also master of El Carpio, is in both plays, but Cubillo turns the interview into a contest of patriotic fervor when Bernardo rejects Abenyúsef's insinuation that Christians are less loyal Spaniards than are Moors.

In both plays the final scenes take place at the castle of Luna, where Bernardo finds his father. In Lope, Saldaña does not die; Bernardo's honor is restored by the king's promise to allow his parents to marry, thereby opening the way for *El casamiento en la muerte*. In contrast, Cubillo has Saldaña die in prison (rather absurdly, he just fades away) and reduces the "casamiento en la muerte" motif to the king's pledge to place Jimena's hand in the hand of the dead count.

Because he has excised much superfluous material, Cubillo is able to expand several situations and scenes with considerable feeling and skill. Examples are Bernardo's relationship with his foster father, a love scene between Jimena and Saldaña, and Saldaña's trip to the castle of Luna. In *El conde de Saldaña* Bernardo strives repeatedly to show respect for Rubio despite the latter's conduct toward him; in *Las mocedades* Bernardo is somewhat insolent to his foster father. A dialogue between Saldaña and Jimena, marred in the earlier play by indecorous attendant conditions, becomes in Cubillo's *comedia* a gracefully phrased reunion of the lovers. Unsure of each other's feelings after a separation of many years, each hesitantly reveals that his affection for the other is undiminished. Saldaña's arrival at the castle of Luna is more effective in Cubillo's play because the dramatist has inserted a preliminary scene showing the apprehensive count moving toward the castle and has expanded the dialogue between Saldaña and his reluctant jailer. As Saldaña approaches the castle, a song echoing his misgivings is heard. Welcomed as a distinguished guest, he pleads haste as an excuse for declining the warden's invitation to linger. Then the letter bearing the count's sentence is opened, and the portcullis is closed. Moved by Saldaña's resignation to his fate, the warden is loath to execute the order, but Saldaña insists that he do his duty. So it is that by careful preparation and skillful plotting, Cubillo closes Act II with heightened tension.

A recognition scene in Saldaña's cell is a high point of Act III in both *comedias*. Apparently Cubillo was satisfied with this scene as he found it in his model, for he makes no striking changes and even retains some of the *romance* fragments. The particulars of Saldaña's recollection of the events leading to his incarceration have been adjusted to fit Cubillo's presentation of that part of the count's life, but the arrangement and emotional content of the meeting are basically the same: Bernardo, exploring the reputedly haunted castle, hears sounds from a prisoner. Drawing near, he is invited to listen to an account of misfortunes. At the unfolding of the narrative, with its expression of Saldaña's still vivid memory of Jimena and his bitterness at having been forgotten by his son, Bernardo realizes that it is his father who is speaking.

Unlike *Las mocedades* is Cubillo's use of asides and cryptic allusions in Act I, a feature of the construction of *El conde de Saldaña* unnoticed by critics. The playwright's decision to introduce Bernardo as a young man and to postpone Rubio's treachery made it necessary to remind the audience of the circumstances of Bernardo's birth. By employing gradually more pointed asides and equivocal remarks, Cubillo achieves this goal and turns attention to Bernardo, but in so doing he reinforces the melodramatic rather than the heroic direction of the legend.

Cubillo has invested his principals with more fullness than has Lope in *Las mocedades*, though the stirring action is still paramount. For the taste of the present-day reader, Bernardo is too hotheaded (much more so than in *Las mocedades*), but it cannot be denied that his flamboyant role would appeal to an audience. Moreover, the playwright has given an explanation for his hero's impulsiveness: the youth's sensitivity to his ambiguous position and his desire to win recognition as a loyal vassal. In contrast to Lope, Cubillo portrays Saldaña as a mature nobleman whose dignified behavior balances his son's impetuosity. In Cubillo's play Saldaña's character is established in an original scene in Act I, where his manly presence, loyalty to the monarch, and generous nature impress Bernardo profoundly. By presenting the count as burdened by the indiscretions of his youth, the playwright has made him more than a wooden paragon of chivalric virtues.

In terms of lines spoken and interest generated, the role of King Alfonso falls behind those of Bernardo and Saldaña, yet it is important in advancing the plot. In this *comedia,* as in so many others of the Golden Age, much of the action hinges on a monarch whose character falls short of the demands of his office. In Act I Alfonso is established as an essentially good man conscious of his responsibilities but, as a king should not be, impulsive by nature. More than Lope, Cubillo stresses the contradictions in the king's character and takes pains to show the conflicting forces at work. For example, Alfonso's decision to imprison Saldaña is not motivated so much by his anger at the discovery of the love affair as by his chagrin that the ambassador from Barcelona has overheard Rubio's denunciation. In another fit of anger he names Charlemagne his successor, only to realize his grave error upon reflection. In Act II, in an impotent rage because no one will arrest Bernardo, he strikes out at the most defenseless person of all, Jimena, and orders her committed to a convent. Even in the final scene the king does not come out well, but in this there is a precedent in Lope: Alfonso accedes to Bernardo's demands only because the latter's troops have the upper hand.

By subordinating the female roles, Cubillo has succeeded in focusing attention on Bernardo's search for his identity and his efforts to win a place for himself. Doña Sol, Bernardo's beloved, is an episodic character, possibly included to prepare the audience for the more prominent role she plays in the *segunda parte*. Here, however, she does little more than give hints to Bernardo about his mysterious origin. The inclusion of Jimena was obligatory because of her connection with the legend, but only in the love scene with Saldaña is she more than mechanically introduced.

The language of *El conde de Saldaña* suffers by comparison with *Las mocedades,* for the ability to recapture the epic spirit of the traditional materials largely eludes Cubillo, who draws upon tradition through Lope rather than by going directly to *romances* and chronicles. Attempts to utilize the resources of the *estilo culto* are confined primarily to Act II. *Culteranismos* are most heavily concentrated in Saldaña's 191-line report to the king (181b-182a), the only point at which Cubillo succumbs to his fondness for long speeches. A valley between two mountain ranges is "una perla entre dos conchas," a lance becomes a "valiente fresno." In the same act Bernardo calls a sword a "cometa de dos filas" (182a).

Even though the poetic style of *El conde de Saldaña, primera parte* contributes little to infusing an epic spirit, in one notable respect the *comedia* is heroic. Like other Golden Age playwrights who used materials from the medieval past, Cubillo seems to have grasped that one of the functions of the public theater was to sustain in the popular mind a belief in Spain's greatness. Courage, tenacity of purpose, loyalty to the principle of monarchy even when sorely tried — all these had built the Spanish Empire. Cubillo's Bernardo, whose presence dominates the play throughout, exemplifies in abundant measure the qualities that had enabled Spain to rise to eminence. The *comedia* thus illustrates the playwright's ability to regularize the plot of an earlier work in order to concentrate on the major character, who is a dynamic figure at his hands. If Cubillo had had greater gifts as a poet, *El conde de Saldaña, primera parte* might well have been a first-rate historical play instead of merely a fairly good one.

2. *El conde de Saldaña, segunda parte (Los hechos de Bernardo del Carpio)*

In *Los hechos de Bernardo del Carpio,* Cubillo's sequel to *El conde de Saldaña, primera parte,* the action centers on Bernardo as the saviour of his country at Roncesvalles. As the legend evolved, Bernardo's part in opposing his sovereign's offer of a crown to Charlemagne and in commanding Spanish troops at Roncesvalles was greatly expanded until he was converted into a symbol of Spanish resistance to the French. Moreover, as he gradually took on the attributes of Roland, he became the Spanish reply to the French paladin. So it is that the events of a part of Bernardo's career occupying only a single chapter in the *Primera crónica general* (Ch. 619) eventually came to exert as great an attraction as those dealing with the purely local clash between vassal and king.

In outline, the account in the chronicle is as follows: Upon learning of Alfonso el Casto's offer to name Charlemagne his heir in return for help against the Moors, the *ricoshombres,* headed by Bernardo, threaten to depose the king. On being repudiated by Alfonso, Charlemagne demands that he swear fealty. Bernardo then seeks the aid of Charlemagne's enemy, Marsilio of Zaragoza. At this, the emperor breaks off his Moorish campaign. Alfonso, having assembled an army, goes out to meet Charlemagne, who has reached the Pyrenees. Leaving troops to guard the rear, the emperor moves up to a pass later named "Val de Carlos." In the *first* ranks are Roland and other peers. The Spanish forces, which include units under Marsilio and Bernardo, vanquish the invaders.

The anti-French sentiment of the chronicle is exploited in a number of sixteenth-century *romances* glorifying Bernardo. If one recalls the political situation of those years, in which Spain's emergence as a major European power brought her into frequent conflict with France, it is clear that Bernardo as the defender of his country at Roncesvalles was made to order for elaboration into a full-blown champion who would reflect Spain's attitude towards her neighbor to the north. For this reason, it is probably more than coincidental that a relatively large number of ballads on Bernardo as the epitome of Spanish solidarity date from the sixteenth century.

Some of the same animosity towards the French that characterizes many sixteenth-century ballads on Bernardo can be detected in Golden

Age *comedias* that dramatize his exploits at Roncesvalles. It has already been seen that in the first Bernardo play, Juan de la Cueva's *Comedia de la libertad de España por Bernardo del Carpio* (1579), the events at Roncesvalles take precedence over the struggle to effect Saldaña's liberation. Moreover, it will be recalled that in Cueva's play Bernardo slays Roland, an incident that became attached to the legend as Bernardo's feats were magnified.

Lope de Vega's *El casamiento en la muerte*[11] continues to exploit the popularity of the highly patriotic Bernardo. In this *comedia* Bernardo's expectation that a victory over the French will put the king in his debt links the patriotic elements with the main action, his efforts to expunge the stain on his honor by reuniting his parents. Lope's debt to ballads and chronicles is enormous, for characters, situations, and lines from Carolingian *romances* and *romances* on Bernardo are mingled with episodes drawn from the *Primera crónica general*. The play contains an inordinate number of diverse elements, not only in the Roncesvalles material but elsewhere; nevertheless, a powerful theme, attractive characters, and evocative language render it far more harmonious than an outline of its plot would suggest.

In Cubillo's *Los hechos de Bernardo del Carpio* the appeal to national pride which characterizes the two earlier plays on Bernardo is even more conspicuous. The earliest text of Cubillo's *comedia* is found in a 1660 collection,[12] but it seems plausible to assume that it was written shortly after *El conde de Saldaña, primera parte*, which was already being performed in 1641.[13] The propaganda value of *Los hechos de Bernardo del Carpio* would have been considerable in that year, for France was at war with Spain. Indeed, the intense

---

[11] Dated before 22 June 1597, probably 1595-97, by Morley and Bruerton, pp. 125-26.

[12] In *Comedias nuevas escogidas, parte trece* (Madrid: Mateo Fernández, 1660). Two manuscripts are known, neither of which appears to be earlier than the first printed edition. Biblioteca Nacional MS. 15.121 is in an eighteenth-century hand; Biblioteca Nacional MS. 15.387 is in a late seventeenth-century hand. Other printed editions are: Sevilla: Imprenta Real, n.d.; Madrid: Antonio Sanz, 1738; Madrid: Antonio Sanz, 1751; Salamanca, n.d.; Valencia: Imprenta de Joseph y Thomas de Orga, 1776; Murcia: Juan López, n.d.; Madrid: Librería de Quiroga, n.d.; Valencia: Ildefonso Mompié, 1822; Havana: Imprenta de R. Oliva, 1840; in BAE, 47 (Madrid: M. Rivadeneyra, 1858).

[13] See above, p. 28.

Franco-Hispanic rivalry reflected in the *comedia* would have had a special appeal as early as 1635, when France entered the Thirty Years War against Spain.

In brief, the plot of *Los hechos de Bernardo del Carpio* is as follows: Sent to Paris by King Alfonso of León, who seeks to withdraw his offer of the Leonese succession to Charlemagne, Bernardo learns of the emperor's determination to invade Spain if Alfonso refuses to acknowledge him as his heir. As Bernardo prepares to depart, Charlemagne disputes his assertion that Alfonso is the only king in the world. Acting as the emperor's champion, the French peer Roldán engages Bernardo in combat. Prevented by his sovereign from continuing the contest after being wounded, Roldán vows to seek redress in Spain. After Bernardo's return to León, the king gives him command of his army. Aided by a contingent under Bravonel, a Moorish general sent by Marsilio of Zaragoza, the Leonese defeat the French at Roncesvalles, where Bernardo slays Roldán. Bravonel then quarrels with Bernardo over the spoils of battle. After Bravonel's death at the hands of Bernardo consolidates the Christian gains, the victors set out for León.

The few critics who have commented on *Los hechos de Bernardo del Carpio* have been hard-pressed to find merit in it. For Schaeffer, one scene is impressive: that of a supernatural approbation of Bernardo by the statue of his father. Menéndez y Pelayo deplores the fact that Cubillo does not repeat "la gran situación imaginada por Lope" (the "casamiento en la muerte" theme), and that, by indulging in inappropriate elegance, he does not preserve the epic tone of his model. Also disparaging is the judgment accorded by Cotarelo, who terms unnecessary the episode of the death of the Conde Rubio and almost comic the appearance of Doña Sol, Bernardo's *dama,* and her female warriors at Roncesvalles. Moreover, he condemns the entire second act as superfluous in that it does not advance the action significantly. Valbuena Prat, though placing the *comedia* low on the scale of merit, finds some stylistic beauties in it and commends the delicacy with which certain heroic elements are treated. This latter commentary, in contrast to Menéndez y Pelayo, is perhaps a reflection of Valbuena's fondness for refinement of expression, even when it does not harmonize with the total effect. Yet despite these relatively charitable observations, a more merciless assessment could hardly be found than the one Valbuena makes of Act III, which he calls "completamente anodino."

Los hechos de Bernardo del Carpio owes much less to El casamiento en la muerte than does El conde de Saldaña, primera parte, to Las mocedades de Bernardo del Carpio. Since Lope links the Roncesvalles material with Bernardo's efforts to obtain his father's release, Cubillo, who kills off Saldaña at the end of his first play, can draw only a few situations from El casamiento en la muerte. In both comedias Bernardo, in mourning for Rubio, is ordered to undertake a mission to Charlemagne. The incidents in Paris are also similar. Act II of Los hechos de Bernardo del Carpio, which is given over largely to a subplot concerning Tancredo and Leonor, two lovers at the Leonese court, and to preparations for Roncesvalles, is nearly all of Cubillo's own invention. In Act III the arrangement of a few details of the battle of Roncesvalles recalls Lope's play.

In artistic merit Cubillo's play in no way competes with its model. Los hechos de Bernardo del Carpio contains no real dramatic tension or impressive scenes; its main plot is often absurdly motivated; the Tancredo-Leonor subplot, Cubillo's substitute for the ballad-inspired gallantries of El casamiento en la muerte, is uninteresting; its characters are superficially drawn and occasionally ridiculous. Among the most absurd of these is the warrior maiden, Doña Sol. Largely a concession to the public's taste for the *mujer vestida de hombre*, she is a cardboard figure devoid of the feminine attributes which would make plausible Bernardo's eulogies of her charms.

The language of the play, as critics have observed, lacks forcefulness. More than that, it sometimes deteriorates into bombast, especially in the lines spoken by Bernardo. In addition, mention should be made of the battle account included in Bernardo's 152-line report to Alfonso in Act II, with its strong similarities to others used by Cubillo. A horse, a "céfiro de nieve," becomes an "abrasada salamandra," and Roldán in the saddle is a "roca animada."

It is plain that in Los hechos de Bernardo del Carpio all other considerations are secondary to setting forth Bernardo's patriotic role. Besides expanding the encounter between Bernardo and Roland in Paris in an effort to show that they are equally matched, Cubillo contrives a series of incidents in Act III designed to exalt his hero. Captured by Roland, Doña Sol is released to that the French peer can demonstrate that he can be as generous as the Spanish champion, who has warned him of Ganalon's treachery. Bernardo has learned of this through the *gracioso* Pierres, introduced chiefly to reveal this information. Thus Cubillo is careful to inform his audience that betrayal plays no part in Bernardo's victory at Roncesvalles. As one would expect, the Spaniards are depicted more favorably than the French, but the latter are built up in order that the Spanish achievement may appear more impressive. Moreover, Cubillo does not content himself with overstating Spanish superiority to foreigners, for he devises an incident to show that those who profess another religion are untrustworthy: Bravonel, a Moorish ally, turns against Bernardo after Roncesvalles.

In essence, the Bernardo of *Los hechos de Bernardo del Carpio* is a personification of pride in being a Spaniard, an emotion that in Cubillo's time embraced confidence in the efficacy of Spanish arms, hostility towards foreigners, and antagonism towards adherents of other faiths. In no other play on Bernardo are the protagonist's exploits so highly colored; in no other play does the legend reach such a point of degeneration.

* * *

Despite their unevenness, Cubillo's Bernardo plays enjoyed a popularity unmatched by other Golden Age dramatizations of the legend.[14] Extant theatrical records disclose a large number of performances in the late seventeenth century and throughout the eighteenth. Both *comedias* continued in the repertory until the beginning of the Romantic period; the last documented performance was in 1834.[15]

---

[14] Besides the *comedias* already mentioned, two others by Golden Age dramatists are known: *Bernardo del Carpio, segunda parte,* known only through a *suelta* published under Lope de Vega's name, and *Bernardo del Carpio en Francia,* thought to be the work of Lope de Liaño, a native of Seville who composed *autos* for performance in that city in 1630. In the former play Bernardo and Roland meet in Rome, where they have been sent to petition the pope to arbitrate the dispute arising from Alfonso's offer to Charlemagne. The *comedia* ends with a mention of the coming conflict at Roncesvalles. In the latter play the action is set in the France of Louis the Pious amid disputes among the sovereign's children for their inheritance. Bernardo is portrayed as a champion who comes to the rescue of the empress and protects her family.

[15] I have found fifty-eight listings for the period between 1691 and 1834 (Madrid, Barcelona, Valladolid, Valencia, and Mexico City). In several instances variations in titles make it impossible to determine which of the two

3. El conde Dirlos

The story of the Conde Dirlos, brother of Durandarte in *romances* of the Carolingian cycle, is best known through the long ballad "Estábase el conde Dirlos." If one divests the ballad of its Carolingian setting, it becomes clear that the plot is old indeed, for it has been retold countless times since Homer sang of Odysseus and Penelope. According to the *romance*, Dirlos, ordered by Charlemagne to take an army into the lands of the Moorish king Aliarde, sets out after entrusting his estates to his bride, who is enjoined to wait seven years before marrying another. After fifteen years in the East, Dirlos assembles his army for the return march shortly after dreaming of seeing his wife in the arms of an Infante. When the count reaches his estate, the gatekeeper informs him that the Infante Celinos, having falsified letters reporting Dirlos' death, was about to be betrothed to the reluctant countess when news came that her husband was alive. Having slipped into Paris, Dirlos goes to his uncle Beltrán's house, where he is reunited with his wife. At the French court Charlemagne's effort to reduce the fifteen-year-old Celinos' action to the status of a youthful prank fails to appease the count, who asks for permission to settle the matter by combat. The emperor, fearing division among the peers, brings about a solution by eliciting Dirlos' acceptance of a compromise: Celinos, upon reaching the age of twenty, will be permitted to take up Dirlos' challenge. Until he is twenty-five, he will not be counted among the peers, nor will he be allowed at court when Dirlos and his lady are there. Harmony having been restored, Dirlos delivers to Charlemagne the spoils of the eastern campaign.

Before Cubillo's *El conde Dirlos* was written, the trials of Dirlos and his lady had already provided subject matter for two *comedias*: Guillén de Castro's *El conde de Irlos*, published in 1618, and Lope de Vega's *El conde Dirlos,* known only through the first *Peregrino* list (1604). Since Lope's play has been lost, any relation it may have had to the two later plays cannot be established; what can be shown,

---

plays was performed. Usually the *primera parte* was referred to as *El conde de Saldaña*, whereas the *segunda parte* was more commonly known by its subtitle, *Los hechos de Bernardo del Carpio,* or simply as *Bernardo del Carpio*. Nevertheless, such a listing as *Los hechos de Bernardo del Carpio, o el conde de Saldaña* shows that this distinction was not always preserved.

however, is the close connection between Castro's *comedia* and Cubillo's.

Castro preserves the outline of the *romance*, but his modifications in the plot and addition of many characters and episodes result in a diffuse work pervaded with an atmosphere of gallantry and extravagance. By presenting Dirlos as a suitor of Marfira (the playwright's substitute for the countess of the *romance*) and introducing Celinos as a rival for the lady's hand before the count's departure, Castro opens the way for a conventional romantic intrigue in Act I. Moreover, since Marfira remains unwed, later in the play the mounting pressure of Celinos' attentions is melodramatically set against the misfortunes that delay the count's return. The note of gallantry is sustained in the resolution of the plot, for Celinos is exonerated because of his love for Marfira.

The emphasis on gallantry and *lo novelesco* seen in the main characters and their relationships is expanded in the treatment of other characters and situations. Included are several pairs of Carolingian lovers from Spanish balladry as well as the magician Malgesí and the Saracen knight Rocandolfo from Italian chivalric romances. Such complications as an intricately plotted competition for Marfira's scarf, a Celinos-Leonora amorous subplot, Malgesí's scheme to destroy Dirlos, and the latter's madness are further indications of extravagant treatment.

The date of composition of Cubillo's *El conde Dirlos* is unknown. The only extant manuscript (Biblioteca Nacional MS. 16.823) offers no clues, nor does the sole printing, an undated *suelta*.[16] No record of performance has been found. The *comedia* may have been written in the late 1620's, for by that time some earlier *comedias* were being recast to provide occasions for greater use of stage machinery, as in *El conde Dirlos*. Moreover, by then Cubillo could have been influenced by the Calderonian stylistic devices which are prominent in the play. Nevertheless, it may have been written some years later, for Cubillo used many spectacular elements and highly metaphorical language in *comedias* written relatively late in his career. It is possible that the *gracioso* Landín's mention of a "jardín de Falerina" is an

---

[16] The only copy of this *suelta* that I have been able to locate is in the British Museum. The name "Álvaro Cubillo" appears not only on the title page but also in the customary plea for the indulgence of the *senado*.

allusion to one of Calderón's works of this title, either the lost *comedia* of 1636 or the *zarzuela* of 1648. On the other hand, it may be no more than a commonplace taken from Italian romances. Until the present study, Cubillo's *comedia* has received no critical attention other than mention of its debt to Castro's play.

In reworking Castro's play Cubillo eliminates much extraneous action by reducing the number of characters. The episodes concerning various enamoured couples (Roldán and Alda, Gaiferos and Melisendra, Durandarte and Belerma), which occupy so much attention in Act I, and to a lesser extent in Act II, of Castro's *comedia*, find no place in the *refundición*. Likewise, Cubillo excises the Moorish king from Act II. For the most part, however, in Acts I and II he follows Castro's arrangement of the action dealing with the count himself. In addition, he retains the Celinos-Leonora subplot. It is in Act III that the plots of the two plays diverge most noticeably. Castro, though he introduces new characters and episodes, follows the outline of the *romance* in bringing Dirlos back to the French court to sound out the situation before he reveals his identity. In Cubillo's *comedia* Dirlos' return and his confrontation with Marfira result from the machinations of the enchanter Malgesí. The expanded role of the magician in Cubillo's play underscores the chief difference between it and its model and offers a possible explanation for the discarding of several features of the original. Malgesí, who in Castro's play appears in only one scene, in Cubillo's *comedia* becomes the manipulator of the plot; many incidents which in Castro are attributed to natural causes become the work of Malgesí's magic.

Throughout *El conde Dirlos* Cubillo makes use of spectacle and music, which are negligible in Castro's play. Early in Act I three couples dance, each occupying the center of the stage in succession. At the same entertainment Malgesí is blown to the ground by a dark cloud. Later in Act I a musician steps out "con el rostro cubierto de un velo negro" and sings of Marfira's coming misfortunes. The same musician later controls Dirlos' nomination as general. As the stage directions put it, "húndase [la música] por un escotillón. Salgan llamas, y con ella una lanza, y en el hierro un cartel atravesado con el nombre del conde." In Act II Malgesí orders Galalón and Celinos to fix their gaze upon a "globo o espejo," revealed when a back curtain is drawn. In the same act "cae del teatro en el tablado un retrato pequeño," which is Dirlos' portrait of Marfira. When Celinos and Galalón wish to return to Paris from Malgesí's cave, "vanse por una tramoya." In this act the most elaborate device is a mountain that opens and closes to reveal Marfira being slain by Celinos. In Act III mechanical contrivances are not used, but Malgesí's activities are prominent in reuniting the lovers.

Despite the importance of magic in the play, Cubillo, probably not wishing to run afoul of the church, is careful to indicate the limitations of the art. Using Malgesí as his mouthpiece, he reminds spectators that divine will governs destiny:

> Ayudarte prometo en su querella,
> mas tiene el conde tan feliz estrella,
> que a vencerla no hay fuerza suficiente. (II)

Later Malgesí warns Celinos that it is folly to seek to know the future, "porque es secreto reservado al cielo, / y nunca le sabrá humano desvelo" (II). As the play draws to an end, Malgesí, speaking to Dirlos, once again makes the point that heaven's will is supreme.

Since Cubillo concentrates interest on Malgesí, a completely artificial figure, the other characters are mere stereotypes. Marfira, loyal and long-suffering, and Dirlos, the embodiment of moral excellence, are much the same as in Castro's play, though perhaps more woodenly virtuous. Against them stands Celinos, not the gallant of Castro's *comedia,* but a malevolent creature who is constantly spurred on by Galalón.

The poetic style of Cubillo's play is very different from that of its model. Castro, though he often strives for elegance through the use of long lines, keeps his speeches short and relatively free from adornment. Cubillo, in contrast, includes several long speeches and frequently resorts to lavish metaphorical language. In Act I of his play a courtly debate between Celinos and Dirlos on the relative merits of *dar* and *recibir* contributes to the slow start of the action. At the end of the same act Dirlos' sentimental testament does not demand the 134 lines it receives. Even longer (144 lines) is Rocandolfo's report to Charlemagne (III), with its inevitable description of clashing armies.

Highly figurative language and intricate syntax are sprinkled throughout the three acts. Some florid expressions are encountered in the *gracioso* Landín's description of Marfira (II), and Rocandolfo speaks of "pálidos jacintos, / purpúreos en roja sangre tintos" (I).

Malgesí, watching Celinos draw near, observes that "pisando nieve es un volcán de fuego" (II). These passages reveal that Cubillo was touched by Góngora, who influenced in some measure nearly all dramatists of the period. One passage in Act III, however, is specifically Calderonian in manner. Here Cubillo follows closely Calderón's formula for using the four elements in imagery. [17] Each of the creatures or inanimate objects catalogued in the first seven lines — *luces, aves, peces,* etc. — is native to a certain element listed either by its name — e.g. *agua* — or by a synonym — e.g. *viento*. In the third stage a specific quality or characteristic of the creature or object is given, as *eco* is of *montaña*. Finally, in typical Calderonian fashion, a recapitulation is made in the catalogue in the last two lines.

In summary, Cubillo's *El conde Dirlos* is an entertainment concocted to divert an audience by means of eye-filling spectacle and the activities of a crafty magician. The plot motivations are highly contrived; the characters are stereotyped; and the poetic style is ostentatious. The desire to concentrate attention on Malgesí's interventions in the fortunes of Dirlos is perhaps the chief reason for the elimination of many secondary characters found in the model and the radical divergence from Act III of the original. When one notices the number of mechanical devices mentioned in the stage directions, it seems clear that enchanter's expanded role was designed to exploit the elaborate stage machinery which had come into use after Castro wrote his play.

4. *El rayo de Andalucía y genízaro de España, primera parte*

El rayo de Andalucía, primera parte treats the exploits of Mudarra, the bastard who avenges the death of his half brothers, the Siete Infantes the Lara. [18] Set in the tenth century, the legend of the seven brothers is first documented in the thirteenth, when it appears in the *Primera crónica general* (Chs. 736-743, 751). The chronicle account, from which Menéndez Pidal reconstructs a "Cantar de los Infantes," can be summarized as follows: In Burgos, where Gonzalo Gustioz of

---

[17] For a discussion of this formula, see E. M. Wilson, "The Four Elements in the Imagery of Calderón," *Modern Language Review*, 31 (1936), 34-47.

[18] The standard study of the legend of the Siete Infantes is Ramón Menéndez Pidal, *La leyenda de los infantes de Lara*, 2nd ed. (Madrid: Centro de Estudios Históricos, 1934).

Salas, his wife Doña Sancha, and their seven sons have come to attend the wedding of Doña Sancha's brother, Ruy Velázquez, to Doña Lambra, cousin of Count Garci Fernández, a quarrel leads to the slaying of the bride's cousin by the youngest Infante, Gonzalo González. Not long after an apparent reconciliation, Gonzalo González unwittingly offends Doña Lambra, who sends a servant to throw a blood-soaked cucumber at him. At her refusal to surrender the servant, the Infantes kill him in her presence. Feigning acceptance of the Infantes' explanation, Ruy Velázquez takes his nephews into his service and sends Gonzalo Gustioz to Almanzor of Córdoba with a letter asking him to behead the emissary and attack a Christian force which the Infantes will accompany. Although Almanzor spares Gonzalo Gustioz and presents him with a high-born Moorish girl, the seven brothers are ambushed and slain. Moved by his prisoner's grief at the sight of the heads of the Infantes, Almanzor orders his release. Before leaving Córdoba, Gonzalo Gustioz tells his paramour that if the child she is expecting proves to be a son, she should send him to Salas with the half of a ring he leaves with her. The son, who is called Mudarra, grows up much beloved by Almanzor. Upon learning the identity of his father, he takes his mother's half of the ring and goes to Salas, where Gonzalo Gustioz receives him as a son. After an initial encounter with Ruy Velázquez at the Castilian court, Mudarra waylays and slays him in a remote spot. He completes his vengeance by hunting down and burning Doña Lambra at the stake.

The Mudarra episodes in the *Primera crónica general* are, as Menéndez Pidal observes, little more than an epilogue to the feud; in later accounts, however, the vengeance taken by the bastard son is elaborated into a full second part of the legend. The *Crónica de 1344,* in which Menéndez Pidal sees evidences of a second *cantar,* discloses a multiplicity of new episodes connected with Mudarra and a much greater preoccupation with violence and barbarous cruelty. Gonzalo Gustioz' liaison with the Moorish girl, so summarily treated in the *Primera crónica general,* is greatly expanded. One detects evidence of a conscious effort to link this situation with Mudarra's mission as the avenger of his family. Here the girl is Almanzor's sister, ordered to comfort Gonzalo Gustioz after he has seen the heads of his sons. New material also appears in the account of Mudarra's journey to Salas and his recognition there by his father. The savagery of the vengeance theme is most apparent, however, in the events occurring subsequent to Mudarra's meeting with Gonzalo Gustioz.

Perhaps the most striking feature of *romances* on the legend of the Siete Infantes is the absence of the episodes of unfeeling brutality which characterize Mudarra's vengeance in the *Crónica de 1344*. Although five *romances viejos* summarize the most vivid episodes, they do not reflect the expanded role assigned the bastard in the second *cantar*, for only one deals specifically with him: "A cazar va don Rodrigo," which relates the final encounter between Ruy Velázquez and Mudarra. Far more numerous than *romances viejos* are sixteenth- and early seventeenth-century *romances eruditos, semi-artísticos*, and *artísticos*. Because so many of these ballads owe a heavy debt to the *Primera crónica general*, in which Mudarra is not prominent, relatively few deal with him. By the end of the sixteenth century, *comedias* were keeping *romances* on the legend alive; many late sixteenth- and early seventeenth-century ballads contain details which reveal their authors were acquainted with dramatic versions of the legend. In those years, when composers of *romances* were drawing from *comedias*, ballads on Mudarra became more numerous.

When the legend reached the Spanish stage in the sixteenth century, playwrights began turning not only to *romances* but also to prose accounts indebted to early chronicles. Among the works most frequently consulted were *La estoria del noble cauallero el conde Fernan Gonzalez con la muerte de los siete infantes de Lara* (1511), based on the *Crónica de 1344*, and the *Valerio de las historias* (by 1472), a *refundición* of the *Crónica de 1344*. The *Primera crónica general* was known through Florián de Ocampo's edition (1541). Since the *romances* on Mudarra, though they were few in number, reached a much wider public than did the long prose accounts, they must have been instrumental in forming in the popular mind a conception of him as an attractive figure. In *comedias* one detects immediately a preference for the second part of the legend. In several plays the action does not begin until after the death of the brothers; even in those in which they appear, Mudarra plays a more important role.

The first dramatization of the legend, Juan de la Cueva's *Tragedia de los siete infantes de Lara* (1579), despite its title, deals only with events occurring after the death of the brothers. Cueva follows chiefly *La estoria del noble cauallero el conde Fernan Gonzalez* in his dramatization of Gonzalo Gustioz' imprisonment in Córdoba and liaison with Almanzor's sister, the presentation of the ring which will identify the child who is to be born, Mudarra's slaying of Ruy Velázquez, and the burning of Doña Lambra. Cueva, however, devitalizes the legend by using an erudite form abounding in classical allusions and long, turgid declamations.

An anonymous *comedia* of 1583, *Los famosos hechos de Mudarra,* reveals no trace of borrowings from Cueva's play. The three acts deal only with Mudarra's revenge, beginning with his discovery of his father's identity and following through to the death of Ruy Velázquez and Doña Lambra. The work betrays a debt to the *Valerio de las historias* and to a lesser extent to ballads. Like Cueva, the anonymous author fails to preserve the popular flavor of his sources.

Lope de Vega's *El bastardo Mudarra* (1612) brings to the theater for the first time the feud as well as Mudarra's revenge. Lope begins with the incidents at the wedding and carries the story through to the betrayal and death of the Infantes, the captivity of Gonzalo Gustioz (Lope's Gonzalo Bustos), his liaison with Almanzor's sister (Lope's Arlaja), the birth of Mudarra, and the slaying of Ruy Velázquez. Lope takes the outline of his plot from the *Primera crónica general* and adds material from the *Valerio de las historias* and numerous *romances,* both from the Infantes cycle and from others. The greatest use of original material is found in Mudarra's search for his victim. Unlike previous dramatizations, Lope's *comedia* retains the spirit and color of the legend through an adroit blending of diverse sources and use of traditional Spanish meters.

Lope's *comedia* was imitated by Alfonso Hurtado Velarde in *La gran tragedia de los siete infantes de Lara,* known to have been written by October 1614. The *comedia* shows that its author was also acquainted with the *Primera crónica general* and several *romances* not used in the model. Menéndez Pidal finds some merit in the treatment of the legend, although he contends that its effectiveness is diminished by deliberately archaic language.

Cubillo's *El rayo de Andalucía, primera parte* marks a return to dramatization of Mudarra's exploits alone. Both external and internal evidence indicate that the *comedia* is representative of a relatively early period in Cubillo's career. In 1632 Juan Pérez de Montalbán praised the play and its sequel, *El rayo de Andalucía, segunda parte,* in the *Para todos*.[19] Cubillo's statement in *El enano de las musas*, which contains the earliest dated text,[20] that both *comedias* were first performed by the company of [Alonso de] Olmedo proves that they could not have been acted before 1616, the year when Olmedo became an *autor de comedias*.[21] It seems probable, however, that they were written several years later; it will be recalled that Cubillo says in the *Curia leónica* (*aprobación*, 1623) that the latter work represents the "primicias de su ingenio."

Within the *primera parte*, the prominence given to the cult of Santiago directs attention to 1629 as a *terminus ad quem*. It may well be that this emphasis reflects the Santiago-Santa Teresa polemics which were so intense between 1618 and 1629.[22] Cubillo introduces

---

[19] See above, p. 15.

[20] Two manuscripts of the *primera parte* are known: Biblioteca Nacional MSS. 16.555 and 17.208. Paz y Melia says that the title of the first is in Cubillo's handwriting and raises the possibility that the text may be an autograph also. The second, which is dated 1667, appears to be a copy made from the printed text in *El enano de las musas*. Other editions are: Barcelona, n.d.; N.p., n.d.; Madrid: Antonio Sanz, 1734; Madrid, 1747; Madrid, 1747 (another edition); Salamanca, n.d.; Valencia: Imprenta de la Viuda de Joseph de Orga, 1770; Salamanca: Imprenta de la Santa Cruz, 1792; Barcelona: Francisco Suriá y Burgada, n.d.; Sevilla: Imprenta del Correo Viejo, n.d.

[21] Hugo A. Rennert, *The Spanish Stage in the Time of Lope de Vega* (New York: The Hispanic Society of America, 1909), p. 540. Cotarelo, interpreting Cubillo's statement ("Representóla Olmedo") to mean that Olmedo played the principal role, sets a *terminus a quo* of 1620, by which date he says Olmedo "ya hacía galanes." When, however, Cubillo states that a given person "representó" a play, he seems to mean that a company headed by the person named performed the play. For example, in speaking of certain *comedias* he says "representóla Roque [de Figueroa]" or "representóla [Bartolomé] Romero," a clear indication that he was referring to the companies of these *autores*, neither of whom played leading roles.

[22] Early in the seventeenth century the Discalced Carmelites began to make efforts to have Santa Teresa declared patroness of Spain. In 1618 these endeavors, which found the support of Philip III, culminated in Pope Paul V's naming her co-patroness with Santiago. The refusal of the partisans of Santiago to accept the papal decision is attested by a large number of works favoring their candidate which they put into circulation. A partial victory for their cause was achieved in 1629, when Pope Urban VIII decreed that the acceptance of Santa Teresa would not be obligatory (Américo Castro, *La realidad histórica de España* [México: Editorial Porrúa, 1954], pp. 190-96). The result of the revised papal decision, says Castro, in *The Structure of Spanish History*, trans. Edmund L. King (Princeton: Princeton University Press, 1954), p. 197, was that Santa Teresa's "equality of status with Santiago became a reality in the Carmelite convents and virtually nowhere else."

the Santiago material, which had not previously been associated with the legend of the Siete Infantes, by incorporating elements from the "Feudo de las Cien Doncellas." Set in the ninth century, the legend first appears in the thirteenth-century chronicles of Rodrigo Jiménez de Rada and Lucas de Tuy. Both of these sources are utilized in the account given in the *Primera crónica general* (Chs. 629-30) of Santiago's miraculous appearance at the battle of Clavijo, which brings a victory to King Ramiro of León and thereby frees him from an obligation to deliver an annual tribute of one hundred maidens to the Moors. The advocacy of Santiago that is so clear in Cubillo's play would have given it an added appeal to the majority of theatergoers, since the populace generally favored Santiago over Santa Teresa.

Since the time of Pérez de Montalbán, critics have been sparing in words of commendation for *El rayo de Andalucía, primera parte*. An anonymous critic who reviewed both parts in the *Memorial Literario* after they were performed in November 1784 has this to say:

> Estas dos comedias son muy desarregladas en tiempo y lugar, y aunque en la primera Jornada de la primera parte hay un vehemente y elegante exortacion del Rey Ramiro a que se animen a quitar el feudo de las cien Doncellas; no obstante en esto falta a la historia, pues este hecho es de D. Alonso el Casto su antecesor.[23]

Mesonero Romanos, though considering the *primera parte* an inferior play, contends that the spirited manner in which Mudarra is portrayed renders less noticeable some of its defects. Schaeffer does not comment on the two parts separately; he sees both as clearly youthful works in which the energetic language is weakened by excessive use of hyperbole and emphasis on detail in the long speeches. Menéndez y Pelayo deems the play of little merit, though he does call the poetic diction clear and correct. Cotarelo, who maintains that in the opening scenes "Mudarra se produce casi como un valentón de oficio," is more moderate in his enthusiasm for the character of the protagonist than

---

[23] Quoted in Ada M. Coe, *Catálogo bibliográfico y crítico de las comedias anunciadas en los periódicos de Madrid desde 1661 hasta 1819*, The Johns Hopkins Studies in Romance Literatures and Languages, Extra Vol. 9 (Baltimore: The Johns Hopkins Press, 1935), p. 192. I follow Coe throughout for quotations from the *Memorial Literario*.

is Mesonero. Nevertheless, he concedes that the "temperamento caballeresco de Mudarra [está] reflejado con acierto" and admires the dramatic qualities of the scene in which Mudarra and Gonzalo Bustos, unaware of their kinship, engage in a duel. Cotarelo terms the play undistinguished in plot structure, which he says is "un continuo paralelismo en la sucesión de escenas en la Corte de León y la del rey moro Almanzor, intercalando entre ellas dos o tres batallas campales." Valbuena Prat, while approving the sentiment expressed in the duel scene and paying tribute to the inclusion of some attractive imagery, concludes that the total effect is less impressive than Lope's treatment of the subject.

Although the action of *El rayo de Andalucia, primera parte* does not begin until Mudarra reaches manhood, Cubillo turns away from an emphasis on his traditional role as an avenger in order to focus on the problem of his identity, the answer to which is revealed to him during his service as commander of Almanzor's army. Aside from the bare outlines of the characters of Mudarra, Gonzalo Bustos, Almanzor, Ruy Velázquez, and Mudarra's mother, the *comedia* is connected with the legend of the Siete Infantes in only a few episodes. In Act II, when a captive musician at the Moorish court sings a song reminding Almanzor of the grotesque banquet served to Gonzalo Bustos, Cubillo recasts a late ballad of the Infantes cycle, "Yantando con Almanzor." Other traces of the legend are found in a few borrowings from Lope's *El bastardo Mudarra*. Cubillo's handling of a scene in which Mudarra threatens to kill his mother (called Arlaja in imitation of Lope) is very close to Lope's treatment, as is the episode of the slaying of Ruy Velázquez.

In his use of the legend of the hundred maidens, which distorts Mudarra's story so strikingly, Cubillo draws from the *Primera crónica general*, but he adds material from Lope's *Las doncellas de Simancas*, in which an army of women releases the Christians from further acknowledgments of submission. Besides introducing a band of female warriors, Cubillo employs the same names, Elvira and Leonor, for its leaders. He does, however, reverse their importance, for in Lope's *comedia* Elvira is the *segunda dama*, whereas in Cubillo's she is the *primera*. In addition, a speech in which Cubillo's Elvira excoriates the Christians for being too cowardly to move against the enemy is similar to a speech in Act III of *Las doncellas de Simancas*.

In Act I the legend is introduced as preparation for Santiago's intervention at Clavijo later in the *comedia*. It is in this act, after Elvira's squadron has been defeated by the Moorish force sent to collect the tribute, that Ramiro urges his subjects to unite against the invaders. Since much of Act II deals with the battle of Clavijo, the opportunities for reminding spectators of Santiago's contribution to the growth of the nation are numerous. The saint is first mentioned when Ramiro tells of a dream in which Santiago has promised victory. The act ends on a fervent note as the victors offer thanks for the favor extended to their cause.

In Act III Mudarra's lengthy account of the battle, with its highly emotional championing of the saint, is the culminating point of the Santiago motif. Later the Santiago motif is reintroduced to provide an explanation for Ramiro's unlikely presence at the place where Mudarra has just killed Ruy Velázquez. As Ramiro says, he is on his way to Burgos, where Santiago is to be proclaimed patron of Spain. Not wishing to omit a reference to another significant role the cult of Santiago played in Spanish history, Cubillo piles anachronism upon anachronism by having Ramiro announce that he will establish the Order of Santiago, which was not founded until the twelfth century.

From a structural point of view, the utilization of the two legends is unfortunate. To it is due the monotonous shifting back and forth from Córdoba to León. Moreover, much of the action is advanced by coincidences contrived in an effort to pull the two legends together. In Act I Mudarra, appearing as the leader of the army sent to collect the tribute, encounters Elvira and her female warriors. Later the two legends are brought together once more when Gonzalo Bustos, who conveniently happens to be passing through Ramiro's court in search of Ruy Velázquez, is appointed general of the expedition that meets Mudarra's troops at Clavijo. The vengeance theme, since it is introduced so late in the *comedia*, seems to be almost an afterthought.

Among the characters, Mudarra stands out above all others. Since Cubillo chooses to dwell upon the problem of the protagonist's identity, he devises situations in which the youth can be shown to possess all the virtues of a Christian nobleman, for this is what he will be revealed to be. Valiant in battle, generous and gallant in freeing Elvira, upright in his scorn of traitors, and loyal in serving Almanzor, he is moreover instinctively Christian, for his report of the battle of Clavijo reveals him as deeply moved at the sight of Santiago. The most carefully worked-out device for making him sympathetic is the *cri du sang*. Furthermore, suspense is melodramatically intensified by his repeated voicing of intuitive feelings which draw him towards his future station in life.

The other characters in the play are decidedly subordinate to Mudarra. Elvira, who provides the love interest, is just another Doña Sol leading an army of females. Once again a woman who is noticeably unfeminine in her actions arouses amorous response. Gonzalo Bustos is a conventionally noble old man. Almanzor is introduced as a dignified figure, but he becomes merely foolish when he so readily yields to Elvira's charms. The captive Nuño's chief function is choral: to provide hints about Mudarra's birth. Although he makes an occasional witty remark, he is not a real *gracioso*. Ruy Velázquez is portrayed as he is in chronicles and ballads: all evil, yet courageous as befits a man of noble birth.

The *comedia* includes several scenes (a melodramatic battlefield encounter between Gonzalo Bustos and Mudarra, and a rousing climax to the battle of Clavijo) which would have audience appeal, but only one, Mudarra's slaying of Ruy Velázquez, in which artistry of a high order is displayed. Only here does the playwright convey more than momentarily the spirit of the legend of the Siete Infantes. The episode is included in *El bastardo Mudarra,* but Cubillo's treatment is more adroit than Lope's and leaves more of an impression of the execution of swift, inexorable justice. It would seem that here Cubillo was not working exclusively from an earlier play but was also drawing directly from a lost version of "A cazar va don Rodrigo." The dialogue assigned to Mudarra and Ruy Velázquez gives the vengeance scene a somber, sharply incised quality absent elsewhere in the *comedia*. Yet because the main thread of the plot deals with Mudarra's identity, when that is disclosed, the vengeance motif seems somewhat anticlimatic. One wonders whether spectators would have been satisfied if the play had ended with Mudarra's announcement that, having found his father, he was ready to track down Ruy Velázquez. If this had occurred, the *comedia* would have one less awkwardly fused element; on the other hand, it would lose its best scene.

The poetic style of the play, other than in the scene of Ruy Velázquez' death, is not heroic in the epic manner, although it might be termed heroic in the seventeenth-century fashion. The *comedia* abounds in flamboyant speeches for the principals, especially for Mudarra. He is assigned the longest, a 142-line account of the battle of Clavijo (III, 23b-24b). Here, as elsewhere in the *comedia,* Cubillo employs some figurative language, but there are no long passages with an accumulation of complex imagery.

To the reader acquainted with Cubillo's plays set in medieval Spain, *El rayo de Andalucía, primera parte* cannot fail to bring to mind *El conde de Saldana, primera parte.* In language and structure his first *comedia* on Mudarra is weaker than his first on Bernardo del Carpio, yet in both he invests the central figure with a vitality that is felt throughout. From an actor's viewpoint, *El rayo de Andalucía, primera parte* is Mudarra's play. His character is conceived with more dash than depth, but youthful impetuosity combined with nobility of spirit make his role a showy one. The popularity of the play in the seventeenth century and afterwards suggests that Cubillo's Mudarra was highly acceptable to audiences, despite the fact that much of the plot has little or no relation to the legend of the Siete Infantes de Lara.

5. *El rayo de Andalucía y genízaro de España, segunda parte*

If the characters were renamed and a few lines eliminated, *El rayo de Andalucía, segunda parte* would be unrecognizable as a Mudarra play. Having exhausted the vengeance theme in the *primera parte,* Cubillo was unable to depend on the legend to furnish him with material. Hence the connection between the sequel and the legend is tenuous indeed, limited as it is primarily to the names of characters. Although the *comedia* contains a great many commonplaces of Golden Age drama, the weight of evidence is that it should be considered an original work.

The earliest extant text is preserved in *El enano de las musas* (1654), but the play, like the *primera parte,* was praised by Pérez de Montalbán in 1632. That it was composed shortly after the first play seems likely in view of passages in Act I in which references to Santiago link the sequel with the earlier *comedia*:

>   MUDARRA.   Fuera ya de aquel peligro
>   y precedida licencia,
>   día del apóstol Santiago,
>   a cuya espada y venera

> debéis la mayor victoria,
> y yo la mayor clemencia.
> Día, al fin, de Santiago
> aquel de la cruz bermeja,
> que en el caballo de nieve
> de muy soldado se precia,
> se celebró mi bautismo.[24] (I, 2a)

MUDARRA.   Seré ruina, y estrago
del escuadrón agareno
y elijo al hijo del trueno.
Ya es mi amigo Santiago;
de la deuda satisfago
de mi sangre esclarecida. (I, 7b)

Critical commentary on the *segunda parte* is confined to a few passing statements indicative of the low esteem in which it is held. As has been seen, both the anonymous critic of the *Memorial Literario* and Adolf Schaeffer dismiss it as worthy of little attention. Cotarelo, who rates it generally inferior to the *primera parte*, nevertheless judges it to be superior in versification and style. For him, the effect of the character of Mudarra, "algo bravucón en el lenguaje, pero noble y moderado en las obras," remains essentially unchanged, despite the decreased amount of action in comparison with Cubillo's first Mudarra play. Valbuena Prat approves Mudarra's expressions of rebellious spirit in King Ramiro's presence, though he too finds the play much inferior to the first part.

That the link between *El rayo de Andalucía, segunda parte* and the Mudarra legend is in the names of the characters rather than the action strongly suggests that Cubillo did not have a sequel in mind when he wrote the *primera parte*. Surely Mudarra's vengeance would not have been completed in the first play if a sequel had been planned at that time. It seems likely that a favorable reception of his first Mudarra *comedia* led him to offer a *segunda parte* barely related to the legend in the hope that the same characters would please the public once more.

---

[24] Citations are to the text in *El enano de las musas*. Other editions are: N.p., n.d.; Salamanca: Imprenta de la Santa Cruz, n.d.; Madrid: Antonio Sanz, 1734; Madrid: Antonio Sanz, 1747; Valencia: Imprenta de la Viuda de Joseph de Orga, 1770; Barcelona: Francisco Suriá y Burgada, n.d.

The final scene of the *primera parte,* in which Elvira is promised to Mudarra under King Ramiro's sponsorship, serves as the springboard to the action of the second play. After Mudarra enters Ramiro's service as a military commander, the king becomes attracted to Elvira. With Mudarra's departure to block the advance of Almanzor into Christian territory, Ramiro's attentions become more insistent. Besides the principal plot, there is a subplot concerned with Mudarra's attempts to free his mother, who is being held prisoner by Almanzor because of her desire to become a Christian. A second subplot deals with the efforts of Ruy Velázquez' son, Alfonso (a character grafted on to the legend by Cubillo) to avenge the death of his father.

In the main action Cubillo presses the didactic note instead of unfolding a real conflict. Since the king is portrayed as struggling to overcome his passion for Elvira, who is the epitome of matronly virtue, there is little doubt that the lady will preserve her honor. Rather than the emergence of a serious threat to Mudarra's honor, which would have been possible if the king had been depicted as licentious or if Elvira had seemed less steadfast, the play contains merely the presentation of a series of lessons whereby Elvira and (to a lesser extent) Mudarra cause the king to become so ashamed of his ignoble conduct that he determines to change.

In the secondary actions the outcome is clearly predictable. First, as Arlaja's freedom is dependent on Mudarra's vanquishing Almanzor, one can be confident that the Christian army will ultimately triumph. Second, Alfonso, Ruy Velázquez' son, is from the outset an ineffectual instrument of vengeance, for he is shown as a youth who has taken up his father's cause in a half-hearted way, more because it is expected of him than because of a desire for blood. There is even a touch of the ridiculous about him, as is evident when Nuño calls him a "figura."

The characterizations of the principals are for the most part unimpressive. Given the different tone of the second play, Mudarra would be more effective had he been endowed with less bravado. As it is, he is a cardboard figure of a valiant warrior. Elvira is no longer the Amazon of the *primera parte*; rather, she is a loving wife whose strength of character preserves her marriage. Even if one grants that she is more appealingly portrayed than in the first play, she is merely a conventional *esposa honesta.* The character of the king is conceived with more subtlety, but, as has been noted, the sympathetic manner in which he is portrayed reduces the element of conflict.

The play offers no individual scenes of great merit, though one rises slightly above the level of mediocrity. In Act II the king, after fighting his emotions for some time, finally confesses his love to Elvira. Though aware that she does not return his feelings, his desperation leads him to implore that she show pity for him by pretending to love him. By her reply, in which she shows the folly of assuming an emotion she does not have, Elvira appeals to the king's better nature.

The language of the play is more controlled than that of the *primera parte,* but it is not successful as dramatic poetry, for it does not convey tension in the scenes between the principals. Neither is it impressive lyrically. The two long speeches, Mudarra's 204-line account of his baptism and marriage (I, 1a-4a) and his 154-line report on the Andalusian campaign (III, 21a-21b), contain distracting details and inappropriate imagery. Except in these speeches designed to inflate the leading role, however, the poetic style is not pompous.

The total effect of the *segunda parte* is much less attractive than that of the *primera,* even though the plot contains fewer absurdities, the characters are less incongruous, and the language more restrained. The great amount of action by which the playwright sought to make the *primera parte* palatable to audiences is not present, but the void has not been filled in a significant way. Although there is a certain harmony in that the main action and the two minor actions all represent dangers to Mudarra's life and honor, none is convincingly developed. Despite these strictures, the fact remains that Mudarra is the leading character. And if audiences responded to him in the first play, they very probably found him to their liking in the second, for, as Cotarelo has pointed out, Cubillo sees him as fundamentally the same in both *comedias.*

* * *

Among Cubillo's works only the two Bernardo del Carpio plays appear to have exceeded the Mudarra *comedias* in popularity. That they enjoyed an early vogue is shown by the fact that the actor Pedro Manuel Castilla, known to have been a member of Alonso de Olmedo's troupe as early as 1631, acquired the sobriquet "Mudarra" as a result of his interpretation of the leading role.[25] The two parts must have

---

[25] Sánchez Arjona, p. 299.

still been familiar to playgoers in the 1640's, for the *gracioso* in the *Entremés del doctor Carlino* (c. 1642-c. 1648) says of a braggart: "¡Más arrogancias no tienen / las dos partes de Mudarra!"[26]

Beginning in 1694 and continuing until 1796, numerous performances have been documented. Records disclose that both parts, which were usually performed together, were played fairly frequently in Madrid and the provinces.[27] The two *comedias* reached the stages of the New World also; they were presented in Lima in 1791[28] and in Mexico City in 1792.[29] In 1796, when the two parts were given their last documented performance in Madrid, the leading roles were taken by Isidoro Máiquez and Antonia Prado,[30] before the former's preference for neoclassical tragedies had become firmly fixed.

6. *La corona del agravio*

In *La corona del agravio* Cubillo has interwoven a romantic intrigue between Count Ramón de Borgoña and the Infanta Urraca, daughter of Alfonso VI, with a pseudo-historical plot dealing with the outrage perpetrated by the Infantes de Carrión on the daughters of the Cid. No earlier *comedia* that might have served as a model is known. The only extant text is found in a *suelta* without date or place of publication which was printed under Cubillo's name.[31] Medel ascribes the play

---

[26] Quoted in Menéndez Pidal, pp. 468-69.

[27] I have found documentation for twenty-six performances in Madrid, Barcelona, Valladolid, and Valencia. Cubillo's *comedias* on Mudarra were outstripped in popularity by Juan de Matos Fragoso's *El traidor contra su sangre* (printed in 1658), based on Hurtado Velarde's *La gran tragedia de los siete infantes de Lara*. Cubillo himself, as has been seen, was the author of an *Auto de Mudarra*, written for performance in Seville in 1635. The popularity of the Siete Infantes in the theater gave rise to a *comedia burlesca*, *Los siete infantes de Lara*, written by Jerónimo Cáncer and Juan Vélez de Guevara. This play, of which Acts I and II parody Matos and Act III derives from Lope, is said by Menéndez Pidal (p. 154) to have been performed for Philip IV in 1650.

[28] Irving A. Leonard, "El teatro en Lima, 1790-93," *Hispanic Review*, 8 (1940), 108.

[29] Armando de María y Campos, *Guía de representaciones teatrales en la Nueva España, siglos XVI al XVIII* (México: B. Costa-Amic, n.d.), pp. 183, 191.

[30] Emilio Cotarelo y Mori, *Isidoro Máiquez y el teatro de su tiempo* (Madrid: Impr. de J. Perales y Martínez, 1902), p. 592.

[31] The only copy of this *suelta* that I have been able to locate is in the Bibliothèque Nationale, Paris.

to Cubillo, but there is no firm evidence that it has been studied until now.[32] Although the date of composition is not known, a *terminus ad quem* can be deduced from a record of payment made to Alonso de Olmedo on 23 December 1636 for a performance given for Philip IV.[33]

The attribution of *La corona del agravio* to Cubillo appears to be well founded. The *comedia* contains many features frequently encountered in his works: excessively long speeches, much ornate language, and a romantic intrigue that is more skillfully handled than is the historical plot. Furthermore, one finds a type of speech that is virtually Cubillo's trademark in plays containing historical or pseudo-historical elements: a long report, heavy with figurative language, made by a victorious general.

The action dealing with Ramón and Urraca is largely fictitious, for Ramón, though he did marry Urraca and thereby become the progenitor of a Burgundian dynasty in Spain, was betrothed to the Infanta in 1087, when the latter was barely seven years old. Chronicles and histories which were readily accessible to Cubillo, however, would have given little more than the fact that the marriage took place. Neither the *Crónica general,* which calls Urraca's husband "Remon, conde de Tolosa," or Mariana's *Historia de España,* which identifies him as "Ramón o Raemundo, hermano del conde de Borgoña," elaborates on the couple's relationship. Cubillo may have seen Mariana's account, since he calls Ramón a count of Burgundy, but he also knew that Alfonso VI made Ramón Conde de Galicia and that Ramón was Alfonso's kinsman, neither of which is mentioned in the *Crónica general* or in Mariana's history. On the other hand, the only record of Ramón's activities in war is a defeat by the Almorávides in 1094, not the resounding victory with which Cubillo credits him.

---

[32] Francisco Medel del Castillo, *Índice general alfabetico de todos los titulos de comedias que se han escrito por varios autores antiguos y modernos, y de los autos sacramentales y alegoricos, assi de D. Pedro Calderon de la Barca, como de otros autores clasicos* (Madrid, 1735), ed. J. M. Hill, *Revue Hispanique,* 75 (1929), 169. Mesonero Romanos includes the title in his catalogue of Cubillo's works; however, he may not have had access to the text, for he gives the play the subtitle of *El agravio satisfecho.* The only *comedia* known by this title, a work by Alonso de Castillo Solórzano based on Cervantes' *La fuerza de la sangre,* is unrelated in subject matter to *La corona del agravio.*

[33] Shergold and Varey, p. 222.

The treatment of the Afrenta de Corpes material, which Cubillo would have known through the *Crónica general* and *romances*, is fairly close to traditional accounts of the Infantes de Carrión's maltreatment of their wives, the Cid's challenge to the miscreants, the combat in which the Infantes are vanquished, and the subsequent marriage of the daughters to Infantes of Aragon and Navarre. In moving from the *Poema del Cid* to chronicles and ballads, this material underwent no substantial changes. A few details were modified, but the outlines remained essentially the same. Moreover, the climactic episode of these events in the *Poema del Cid* — the encounter between the Cid and the Infantes de Carrión at the Cortes de Toledo — continued to be the one given the greatest attention.

Cubillo follows the traditional sequence and gives emphasis to the challenge at the Cortes, but he makes some changes in order to link Ramón de Borgoña with these events from first to last. In Act I it is Ramón who rescues Sol and Elvira, whereas in the *Crónica general* and most of the *romances* Ordoño, a nephew of the Cid, comes to their aid. Only a few ballads retain Félez Muñoz as their deliverer, as he is in the *Poema del Cid*. Cubillo further enhances Ramón's role by having him drive off the Infantes, who in earlier accounts have disappeared by the time the sisters are set free.

In Act II Ramón participates also in the scene at the Cortes, not as a judge, but as a volunteer who offers to meet the Infantes in combat. In this scene Cubillo follows the *Crónica general* fairly closely, except that in the play the Infantes attempt to justify their repudiation of Sol and Elvira before the Cid appears. The speech in which the Cid demands justice includes lines from an anonymous ballad from the Cid cycle, "Medio día era por filo." Cubillo may have taken the detail of the *plazo* of three months from another *romance*, "Después que el Cid Campeador."

In Act III Ramón is still associated with the pseudo-historical plot in that he is present when the successful outcome of the combat is announced. By having the Cid present when the contest takes place, Cubillo once more departs from earlier accounts, all of which state that the Cid left for Valencia before his champions met the Infantes. Furthermore, according to tradition the combat took place in Carrión, not at Alfonso's court. Nevertheless, by making these two changes Cubillo maintains the link between Ramón and the insult given the Cid.

But despite the playwright's attempt to give a semblance of unity by stressing Ramón's role throughout, one cannot fail to perceive that *La corona del agravio* contains two actions, either of which could have been elaborated into a full-length play. As it is, the *comedia* has, not a main plot and a subplot, but two equally stressed, insufficiently developed situations. Consequently, one finds too great a division of interest between the light Ramón-Infanta intrigue and the more serious Afrenta de Corpes material. To bring these two dissimilar plots together, Cubillo is obliged to resort to highly artificial devices. In Act I he contrives an enchanted forest as the setting for Ramón's fortuitous encounter with the Infanta and for his rescue of the daughters of the Cid. Later the *comedia de enredo* and the pseudo-historical plot are brought together by having Doña Sol, one of the Cid's daughters, resemble the Infanta so closely that Ramón cannot distinguish between the two and by continuing to link Ramón with the Cid's dishonor in ways for which there was no precedent in tradition.

In the handling of the two situations, three manners are evident. An extravagant tone reminiscent of romances of chivalry characterizes the action in the forest, where both plots get underway. Afterwards, at the royal court the frivolous complications of the Ramón-Urraca intrigue alternate with the comparatively dignified, straightforward progress of the pseudo-historical plot.

The opening scenes in the enchanted forest, if they were not padded with tedious speeches, would be a delight, for Cubillo is obviously poking fun at *libros de caballerías*. In the most extravagant language, just about every motif which would evoke a setting befitting Amadís and his like is brought forth: a runaway horse, a beautiful lady, a shield of mysterious origin, dreams, strange prophecies, and damsels in distress. As if the fictional atmosphere were not already plain, the *gracioso* Carlín underscores it by spoofing its conventions. After witnessing the perplexing incidents that befall his master, Carlín observes: "Si ésta no es selva encantada, / no vio encantos Amadís" (I). Later, after Ramón has put to flight the Infantes de Carrión, he says:

> Con pies entramos en Castilla
> derecho a enderezar tuertos;
> mal año para el mejor
> libro de caballerías;
> pudo envidiar estos días
> el mismo Don Galaor.

....
Hoy a profesar empiezas
la caballería andante,
gloria del siglo pasado;
solamente te han faltado
un enano y un gigante. (I)

The *comedia de enredo* plot is replete with devices common to the form. All of the complications stem from Ramón's request that the Infanta not reveal her name, since he wishes to continue in the hope that she is the original of the portrait. Further misunderstandings occur when Ramón's use of the word *sol* in a metaphorical sense leads Urraca to believe he refers to Doña Sol. The elaboration of the intrigue, though it contains a few amusing scenes, does not bear careful scrutiny. For example, Ramón does not find the likeness between Sol and Urraca confusing until Act II, even though he has seen them together earlier.

In the pseudo-historical plot the subject matter is treated seriously, but its effectiveness is lessened by the unnecessary length of some of the speeches. Furthermore, the characters, with the exception of the Cid, are not conceived in a heroic mold. Ramón is a naive type who functions more successfully as the muddle-headed lover of the comedy of intrigue than as a heroic character. Bermudo, who in the first half of the play is Ramón's insipid, dull-witted rival for the Infanta's affections, is revealed upon the Cid's arrival to be Per Mudo, henceforth depicted as a warrior so skilled in arms that in a practice bout he overcomes the Cid. With the latter, Cubillo is more successful. Secondary figure though he is, the Cid has been endowed with *mesura* and magnanimity. The women characters are conventional *damas*. Urraca is a woman in love too proud to admit her initial mistake. Her foil is Doña Sol, who one is disconcerted to learn is also a victim of the outrage of Corpes. Elvira, the other daughter, has a minor role of no importance.

Three features of the style of the play merit comment: the number of long speeches, the reminiscences of Calderón in imagery and other rhetorical devices, and the heavy concentration of elaborate language in Act I. There is no justification for the several long speeches except that they offer the easiest way to reach the requisite number of lines and to give the actors showy parts. For example, in Act I the Infanta does not need 116 lines to ask Ramón who he is and to refuse to disclose her own identity. Likewise, Ramón could have told her the story of his early life in less than 236 lines. In Act II the Infanta takes 106 lines to rebuke the hapless Ramón for having abandoned her to go to the aid of Sol and Elvira. In the same act the Cid is given 103 lines to demand justice of the king. The last long speech, the campaign report so often used by Cubillo, takes Ramón 116 lines to deliver. That five speeches contain a total of 777 lines, nearly one-fourth of the play, points up the structural deficiencies of *La corona del agravio*.

Traces of Calderonian influence are found in the poetic diction. The old man who gives Ramón the mysterious shield is called an "esqueleto vivo." The portrait on the shield is a "breve sombra," a metaphor for a picture often employed by Calderón. Also reminiscent is the "hipogrifo del sol," the horse Ramón receives from the old man. Besides isolated phrases, longer passages also bring Calderón to mind. The use of anaphora and oxymoron in the lines below follows a technique he often uses:

> esta cifra misteriosa,
> esta verdad misteriosa,
> y esta obscura claridad,   (III)

Likewise Calderonian are the *versos multimembres* in which, after a horse has been compared with a *tigre*, a *pavón*, and a *garza*, the similarities are summed up:

> Tigre, pavón y garza parecía
> en fuerza, en presunción, y en bizarría.   (I)

The presence of numerous Calderonian passages in Act I suggests the greater extent to which ornate language is found there than in Acts II and III. It would seem that Cubillo did this purposely to heighten the extravagant mood. Moreover, in addition to specifically Calderonian influences, a general *culto* influence can be detected in a great many passages. Ramón, telling how he punished his mount, says:

> Castigué en lo desleal lo hermoso.
> Ambos pies le corté que ser pudieran,
> para el carro del sol veloces plumas;   (I)

Later he addresses the Infanta in lines showing a concentration of *palabras cultas* and hyperbaton:

> Hermoso palmo del mundo,
> invencible cazadora,
> muerte fatal de las fieras,
> dulce de las flores pompa,
> aliento peinado del alba aljófar,
> sendienta de búcaros bebe
> la púrpura de la rosa. (I)

Within Cubillo's total extant dramatic production, *La corona del agravio* occupies a very low position in terms of literary merit. It indeed shows a few signs of the aptitude for plotting a romantic intrigue that is displayed in some of his *comedias de costumbres,* but taken as a whole, its construction is clumsy and it lacks real dramatic focus. As much as anything, the *comedia* illustrates the pitfalls of the long rhetorical speeches that came more frequently into use in the period dominated by Calderón. A dramatic poet of the caliber of Calderón might on occasion incorporate several without detriment to the artistry of a work; for a playwright of Cubillo's stature, their fundamentally undramatic nature posed problems that were seldom resolved successfully.

7. *La manga de Sarracino y buen término de amor*

Relations between Moors and Christians, which in the sixteenth century had become idealized in a number of ballads and works of prose fiction, began to be treated in the same manner on the stage before the century had ended. [34] A relatively large number of *comedias* attesting to the popularity of idealized Moorish themes date from the period of Lope and his cycle; by the time that Calderón was achieving prominence, public acceptance appears to have declined, for few such *comedias* date from after the first third of the seventeenth century.

La manga de Sarracino y buen término de amor, which is ascribed to Cubillo in Medel's *Índice* (1735), has apparently survived in only

---

[34] For the idealized Moor in Spanish literature, see María Soledad Carrasco Urgoiti, *El moro de Granada en la literatura del siglo XV al XX* (Madrid: Revista de Occidente, 1956) and *Antonio de Villegas' "El abencerraje,"* ed. Francisco López Estrada and John Esten Keller, University of North Carolina Studies in Comparative Literature, No. 39 (Chapel Hill: The University of North Carolina Press, 1964), pp. 11-38.

one printing. This eighteenth-century *suelta,* which carries Cubillo's name, bears no date or place of publication.[35] Schaeffer, the only scholar who has studied the play, accepted it as an authentic work by Cubillo and, on the basis of the freshness and simplicity of its style, believed it to have been written early in the playwright's career, when the impact of Lope's manner was still being felt. Although the present writer has found nothing in the text which would dispute Schaeffer's attribution, the authorship cannot be proved without more impressive evidence than is now available. There is no evidence of the existence of an earlier *comedia* on the same subject matter that the playwright might have recast.

The plot, briefly, is as follows: Don Diego Girón, a knight of Calatrava, after being rejected by Doña Elvira, a lady he has long admired, volunteers to lead Christian troops against a Moorish raiding party. Elvira, having realized that she loves Diego, follows him without his knowledge. Captured in battle, the two are taken separately to Toledo, where they become slaves of Galiana, a maiden loved by Sarracino, a Moorish general. Upon meeting again in captivity, Diego (now known as Penar) and Elvira (now called Esperanza) are uncertain of each other's identity; after a time they recognize each other and confess their love. Diego, pretending to respond to the attentions Galiana shows him, finds her increasingly suspicious that the two slaves have formed an attachment. When she declares her love for him openly, he points out that her Moslem faith is an obstacle. Galiana then confesses her desire to become a Christian. Sarracino gallantly renounces her and offers to escort Elvira and Diego, for whom ransom has arrived, to Almagro. At this, Galiana makes known her intention of accompanying them, since she still wishes to be baptized. Upon seeing that this announcement has no effect on the the very evident bond between Diego and Elvira, she acknowledges her defeat and accepts Sarracino, who will also become a Christian.

Treating as it does the less awesome manifestations of love, *La manga de Sarracino* has no profound implications, yet it has the not inconsiderable attractions of a simple plot, lively incidents, engaging characters, and brisk dialogue, along with a graceful idealization of *lo morisco.* The germ of the plot is found in a well-known *romance*

---

[35] The only copy I have been able to locate is in the British Museum.

morisco, "Galiana está en Toledo," in which the happiness of the Moorish princess Galiana as she makes a "rica manga" for her suitor Sarracino is contrasted with the grief of a captive Christian maiden as she recalls how she had discouraged the suit of a knight of Calatrava until shortly before he was killed in battle. Cubillo incorporates almost the entire ballad into Act II of his *comedia.*

From the lines telling of the *cautiva*'s rejection of her suitor Cubillo takes the idea for Act I, in which Elvira's rejection of Diego causes him to seek his fortune in war. The playwright gives a new direction to the material taken from the ballad by having Elvira follow Diego and by having both presented as slaves to Galiana. Changing the death of the lover to a report that is eventually proved false gives the impulse to Act II, which deals largely with incidents leading to mutual recognition. In Act III Galiana becomes a more prominent figure when the flickerings of interest she has earlier evidenced in Diego become more pronounced. Most of the action of Act III thus arises from Diego's determination not to endanger his position (and Elvira's) by lukewarm responses to Galiana, while at the same time assuring Elvira that his love is reserved for her.

The Diego-Galiana relationship has strong parallels with the Ramón de Borgoña-Infanta Urraca courtship in *La corona del agravio.* Diego is not motivated by love, as is Ramón, but in both cases the *galanes* are handicapped by their inferior station in paying court to an imperious, capricious woman. Several dialogues are conducted along similar lines in both plays, yet the effect is dissimilar. Long speeches impede the dramatic movement of the advances and withdrawals made by Urraca and Ramón, whereas in *La manga de Sarracino* sprightly dialogue quickens the pace of the exchanges between Diego and Galiana. So it does also in those between Diego and Elvira, where the time-tested device of non-recognition is also aptly used.

The idealization of *lo morisco,* while it lends an aura of exoticism, is in fact incidental to a romantic triangle in which interest is created and sustained by devices largely extraneous to the Moorish theme. It is true that the Moors of the *comedia* are concerned primarily with love rather than with war and that, besides the *romance morisco,* such standard features of the *comedia de moros y cristiano*s as lavish costumes, *juegos de cañas,* and sudden conversions are incorporated. Nevertheless, the play is essentially a tale of love, devoid of the confrontation between Moor and Christian that is an integral feature of the full-fledged *comedia de moros y cristianos*.

8. *La mayor venganza de honor*

The legend of the Comendadores de Córdoba, which forms the subject matter of *La mayor venganza de honor*, was thought by many scholars to have little foundation in fact until Cotarelo uncovered a document which showed that the terrible revenge taken by a Veinticuatro de Córdoba upon learning of his wife's infidelity was based on an occurrence in the reign of Juan II:[36] the murder by a certain Don Fernán Alfonso, Veinticuatro de Córdoba and first Señor de Belmonte, of his wife Doña Beatriz de Hinestrosa, two female servants, Catalina and Beatriz, and two Comendadores de Calatrava, Don Fernando Alfonso de Córdoba and Don Jorge Solier, brothers of Don Pedro Solier, Bishop of Córdoba. An account of this bloodbath is set down in a legal document dated 28 November 1449, certifying that Fernán Alfonso had availed himself of the terms of a *privilegio rodado* issued on 20 February 1440, in which Juan II offered pardons for crimes to anyone who would enlist for a year and a day's service in the defense of Antequera. According to the document of 1449, the murders had occurred some twenty-one months earlier.

An anonymous "Cantar de los comendadores" is believed by Menéndez y Pelayo to have been composed shortly after the murders and to reflect accurately the situation that culminated in the terrible carnage. The song preserves several names identical with those mentioned in the legal document: Fernando, Veinticuatro de Córdoba, his wife Beatriz, and the two brothers, Comendadores de Calatrava, one of whom is called Jorge. The opening lines are assigned to Beatriz, who recalls the attraction exerted by Jorge at their first meeting, when he was a guest in her husband's house. The narrative then shifts to the third person as the account of the fatal assignation unfolds: Having learned of the Veinticuatro's absence on a hunting expedition, Jorge and his younger brother slip into the house for a rendezvous with

---

[36] The results of Cotarelo's investigations were published in *Cancionero de Antón de Montoro (El ropero de Córdoba), poeta del siglo XV, ordenado y anotado por D. Emilio Cotarelo y Mori* (Madrid, 1900), pp. 316-325, which Menéndez y Pelayo (XI, lix) acknowledges as the source of his summary of the historical antecedents of the legend.

Beatriz and her female servant. Caught *in flagrante,* the culprits are slain by the Veinticuatro, who in his frenzy also kills a slave cowering in a corner.

The legend inspired yet another fifteenth-century composition, Antón de Montoro's *octavas de arte mayor* "A la muerte de los dos hermanos comendadores," included in his *Cancionero.* It is possible that some of the details added by Montoro, a native of Córdoba, were based on fact. His version, which is of little artistic distinction, did not, however, take hold of popular imagination as did the anonymous poem.

That the legend lived on in popular memory is attested by the inclusion of fragments from the anonymous poem or allusions to it in several sixteenth-century works. Nevertheless, a new treatment of the entire legend did not appear until 1596, when Juan Rufo published his long *romance* on the Comendadores. Rufo preserves the gist of the narrative as it appears in the "Cantar de los comendadores," but he places the action in the time of the Catholic Sovereigns and adds new characters and incidents. The second Comendador, unnamed in the two fifteenth-century poems, is called Fernando; the latter's paramour is Ana, Beatriz' *secretaria.* Rufo adds Galindo, Jorge's servant, and the Veinticuatro's loyal slave Rodrigo, who confirms his master's suspicions by disclosing he has witnessed the comings and goings of the Comendadores. Fernando el Católico becomes a participant through Rufo's introduction of the ring motif: Having received a valuable ring from the king, the Veinticuatro bestows it upon his wife, who in turn gives it to Jorge. At the sight of the ring on Jorge's hand, the king grasps the situation at once. By intimating that the Veinticuatro should regain possession of the jewel, he serves as catalyst to the revenge. The violence of the outcome is greater than in previous versions, for the Veinticuatro kills every living creature in his house, even a monkey and a parrot. After the murders the Veinticuatro flees to France, where a pardon from the king reaches him. Ordered to return to Spain, he is received "con aplauso" and honored by the king's selection of a noble widow to be his second wife.

Rufo's poem is the chief source of the first treatment of the legend to reach the stage, Lope de Vega's *Los comendadores de Córdoba.* Thought by Morley and Bruerton to have been written between 1596 and 1598, it may be the *comedia* that Lope designates as *Los comendadores* in the first *Peregrino* list (1604), though it was not printed until 1609, when it was included in his *Parte segunda*. In the *comedia*, which Valbuena Prat calls "uno de los casos más felices de Lope," the close connection with Rufo's poem is patent in the names of the major and minor characters, the roles assigned to them, and the incidents of the plot, which Lope follows closely, even to such small details as the killing of the monkey and the parrot. At the hands of a less gifted playwright, the material acquired from Rufo, stressing as it does incident rather than character, might have been turned into merely another melodramatic play on conjugal honor. That *Los comendadores de Córdoba* rises above this is due chiefly to the striking characterizations of the principals. Beatriz and Jorge, the completely amoral adulterers, are propelled towards each other — and towards catastrophe — by a lust and carnality seldom treated with such boldness in the *comedia* of the Golden Age. In contrast to them is the Veinticuatro, whose devotion to his wife and deep feeling for his home, conveyed in the domestic scenes of Acts I and II, make the discovery of his loss even more shattering.

The only other dramatization of the legend is *La mayor venganza de honor*, based on Lope's *comedia*. The one known manuscript of *La mayor venganza de honor*, an autograph of Andrés de Claramonte in the Biblioteca Nacional (MS. Vv-711 [old style]), was first described by Menéndez y Pelayo, who was convinced that the *comedia* was not Claramonte's. This manuscript was identified as Cubillo's *La mayor venganza de honor* by Rennert and Castro,[37] who must have compared the manuscript with the single printed text, which appeared under Cubillo's name in *Parte décima* of the *Comedias nuevas escogidas de los mejores autores* (Madrid, 1658). The two texts contain only a few insignificant variants. Rennert and Castro's attribution is supported by the correct versification and by the way in which material from an earlier play is utilized. Furthermore, the *comedia* includes in Act I a type of speech much favored by Cubillo: a long description of a Christian victory over a Moorish army.

If one grants that the play is Cubillo's, then the manuscript in Claramonte's hand provides an important clue to the date of com-

---

[37] Hugo Albert Rennert and Américo Castro, *Vida de Lope de Vega* (Madrid: Imprenta de los Sucesores de Hernando, 1919), p. 470.

position. Since Claramonte died on 19 September 1626,[38] the play must have been one of Cubillo's early dramatic works. It is, in fact, the earliest for which documentation exists.

Specialists in the theater of the Golden Age have accorded *La mayor venganza de honor* a favorable rank among Cubillo's historical plays, though they have frequently cited its failure to sustain the forcefulness of *Los comendadores de Córdoba*. The most earnest apologist for Cubillo's version is Schaeffer, who finds it psychologically more convincing than Lope's, praises the logical, energetic movement of the plot, and applauds the vigorous language. More reserved is Menéndez y Pelayo's opinion that even though it is "muy notable" and composed with more reflection than Lope's play, it lacks the spontaneous beauties of the earlier work. Taking exception to Cubillo's portrayal of the lovers, Menéndez y Pelayo argues that "por lo mismo que los Comendadores se presentan tan urbanos y corteses, y tan morigerada Doña Beatriz hasta que repentinamente cambia de carácter, resulta ilógico el desarrollo de la pieza, y doblemente bárbara la catástrofe al recaer en personajes simpáticos." He nevertheless concedes that the *comedia,* although not equaling Lope's in interest and "brío poético," honors its author and deserves to be the subject of serious study.

Since the time of Menéndez y Pelayo, Cotarelo and Valbuena Prat have made brief comments. Cotarelo finds the plot of Cubillo's play more carefully ordered than that of its model but regards the movement of Acts I and II as slow and the outcome of Act III tumultuous. This imbalance in tempo, he contends, contrasts with the effect of passion and life present from the outset in *Los comendadores de Córdoba*. But despite these strictures, he calls Cubillo's play one of the best of its kind in the Spanish theater. Valbuena Prat adds little to earlier observations other than to argue that Cubillo's predilection for the delicate, exemplified in the detailed analysis of Beatriz' psychology, does not compensate for the absence of a broad interpretation of life — an interpretation which he finds in Lope's play.

Brief though previous commentary on *La mayor venganza de honor* is, it gives, in the main, a perceptive estimate of its merit. A closer look at the plot, characters, and poetic language of Cubillo's *comedia*

---

[38] Sturgis E. Leavitt, *The "Estrella de Sevilla" and Claramonte* (Cambridge, Mass.: Harvard University Press, 1931), p. 54.

will reveal a basis for the generally held opinion that it contains a number of commendable features, although it does not equal *Los comendadores de Córdoba* in dramatic power. Even a superficial comparison of the two plays discloses that Cubillo's *comedia* is not a slavish imitation of its model, for the setting has been changed, the plot structure modified, and several characters portrayed differently.

Cubillo is closer to the legend than is Lope in that he sets the events in the reign of Juan II and connects them with the siege of Antequera, but he departs from the legend (and from Lope) in devoting all of Act I to action leading up to the marriage of Beatriz and the Veinticuatro. His delineation of Beatriz takes a turn that is not suggested in any previous version of the legend, and he draws Juan II much more closely into the action than Rufo and Lope draw Fernando el Católico.

La mayor venganza de honor offers parallels with *Los comendadores de Córdoba* in the basic situation that is treated and in the names of the major and most of the minor characters. Cubillo retains the ring motif as a device to further the action and follows Lope in the outlines of the scenes in which the ring is prominent. Also reminiscent of *Los comendadores de Córdoba* is the Veinticuatro's farewell to his wife at the end of Act II. In both plays the dénouement is similar: The Veinticuatro overtakes the lovers in his own house.

The unsatisfying effect of Cubillo's play as compared with Lope's is occasioned in part by a more uneven distribution of the action. This defect is not so apparent in Act I, for though it deals exclusively with events prior to the marriage of Beatriz and the Veinticuatro, the emotional bond between Beatriz and Jorge is established, and the ring motif is set in motion. This is essentially what Lope accomplishes in Act I of his play, yet the fact that he allows his audience to witness the awakening of an unbridled passion is dramatically more convincing than Cubillo's presentation of a series of trite incidents whereby Beatriz and Jorge are prevented from marrying.

In Act II of Cubillo's play, where the plot should be advanced, it scarcely moves. This inertness is due largely to the fact that Jorge and Beatriz are kept apart during the entire act. Moreover, too much effort is expended on Beatriz' endeavors to shake off the memory of her affection for Jorge. The several lengthy scenes in which the young wife is shown resisting Jorge's attempts to communicate with her demonstrate that she can protect her virtue as long as she refuses to see her former suitor, but the major part of an entire act should not be required to accomplish this purpose. Not until the final scene, when the Veinticuatro gives his wife the king's ring, does the action get under way again; whereas in Act II of Lope's play the plot moves swiftly as the ring motif is carried to its conclusion amid the lovers' increasing heedlessness.

Because Cubillo lingers on the analysis of Beatriz at the expense of plot-furthering action in Act II, he is obliged to pack a heavy accumulation of incidents into Act III in order to bring the plot to a conclusion. Lope, who has more judiciously apportioned the action, leads up to the Veinticuatro's revenge through the inclusion of a dinner invitation issued to the brothers, a device drawn from traditional sources. Cubillo, however, can permit no refinements of preparations on the Veinticuatro's part, for before he can introduce some of the incidents that in Lope's play advance the plot as early as the beginning of Act II, he must bring Beatriz and Jorge together. Given the character of Beatriz that he has been so careful to establish, he is forced to contrive a ruse that will lead her to admit Jorge into her presence. Succeeding each other pell-mell are the king's *capa y espada* intervention pretending to be Jorge, Beatriz' presentation of the ring to Jorge, the Veinticuatro's recognition of the ring on Jorge's hand, and the final holocaust.

The key to many of the changes made by Cubillo is to be found in his approach to Beatriz, who, unlike the Beatriz of Lope's *comedia*, is portrayed sympathetically. His delineation of her is consonant with an attitude often reflected in the theater of the Golden Age: that woman is a frail creature who cannot withstand pressure indefinitely. In order to illustrate his thesis that even the most virtuous woman will eventually succumb, Cubillo must depict Beatriz in a way that will arouse sympathy. Hence he devises a new Act I, where Beatriz and Jorge are shown as a couple whose plans for marriage are thwarted, thus making possible a subsequent conflict in Beatriz' mind. The slower tempo of Act II, with the consequent necessity of jamming Act III with action, is the result of efforts to depict her as torn between her growing love for her husband and the memory of her affection for Jorge.

At the opening of Act II she, newly married, appears wearing black, which she calls "el color de mi ventura." Jorge is still in her thoughts, but, fighting her memory of him, she rebukes her servant for speaking his name. Her fear of the consequences she expresses metaphorically:

> El fuego que está cubierto,
> cuando más le solemnizas,
> su actividad sutilizas:
> déjame, no me hables más,
> que si otro soplo les das,
> quizá arderán las cenizas.[39]   (II, 187a^r)

Another obstacle to her virtue presents itself with a letter from Jorge handed over by the insidious Ana. Beatriz' reaction, to tear up the message without reading it, is motivated by distrust of her own emotions rather than by anger at the sender. Telling Ana that her love for Jorge has subsided, she reaffirms her attachment to her husband. Later, however, she becomes conscious that she has not entirely erased Jorge from her thoughts:

> ¡Ayudadme cielos!
> Que aunque yo quiero ayudarme,
> son flacas las fuerzas mías,
> y recelo que me falten.   (II, 188a^r)

In view of these preparations, Beatriz' surrender to Jorge does not appear as implausible as Menéndez y Pelayo would have it. The playwright is obliged to resort to a misunderstanding to bring Jorge into Beatriz' presence, but once he is there the outcome is not surprising, since Beatriz' words have previously made it clear that she can rely on her own strength only as long as she can keep the Comendador from her sight.

The other characters are less subtly analyzed than Beatriz, but the fundamental change in her portrayal brings about alterations in some of them also. By virtue of being the man Beatriz at first hopes to marry, Jorge is less despicable than in Lope's *comedia*. Whether he is *simpático,* as Menéndez y Pelayo would have it, is open to doubt; for though he, like his brother, is polished in manner and personally

---

[39] Citations are to *La mayor venganza de honor,* in *Comedias nuevas escogidas de los mejores autores, parte décima* (Madrid: Imprenta Real, 1658).

courageous, he seeks to infringe upon the code of honor just as deliberately as does the Jorge of *Los comendadores de Córdoba*.

Juan II, through personal ties with Beatriz and the Veinticuatro, is more intimately connected with the plot than Lope's Fernando el Católico, who gives impetus to the plot only through the ring episode. In Cubillo's play the enlargement of the king's role results from the playwright's decision to separate Beatriz and Jorge and to bring them together later. By spitefully awarding Beatriz to the Veinticuatro, Juan II unwittingly sets up the situation which leads to disaster; later, by pretending to be Jorge in an effort to protect the Veinticuatro's honor, he just as unwittingly causes the misunderstanding that reunites the lovers.

Ana, in Lope's play a naive young woman who seems to be included merely to be paired with the second Comendador, becomes in *La mayor venganza de honor* a calculating female bent upon bringing about Beatriz' moral downfall. By changing Ana's role, Cubillo increases the pressures that are brought to bear upon Beatriz.

The Veinticuatro remains essentially the same as the Veinticuatro of *Los comendadores de Córdoba,* a husband whose deep love for his wife makes the discovery of her betrayal produce a far greater dilemma than if he were depicted as merely the ruthless avenger of an insult. That Cubillo makes no substantial change in the Veinticuatro would seem to be yet another indication that the audience was expected to approve the husband's actions. Moreover, that the king condones the murders, as in Lope's play, is tantamount to the approbation of society.

It is likely that a seventeenth-century audience would have found the Veinticuatro's revenge in *La mayor venganza de honor* entirely acceptable, given the view of woman as an inferior being, a "caduco y frágil ser." For this reason, the present writer must take exception to Menéndez y Pelayo's contention that the punishment itself is not justified in Cubillo's play, because the husband's victims are "personajes simpáticos." The decision to convert Beatriz and (to a lesser extent) Jorge into sympathetic figures may well have proved a handicap to Cubillo, since it is more difficult to arouse interest out of the materials of virtue than of wickedness. Nonetheless, spectators of his day probably would have considered that the ties existing between Beatriz and Jorge prior to the former's marriage in no way justified their renewing them and that in so doing the two were undermining the very foundation of the social order, the sanctity of marriage, just as unpardonably as the Beatriz and Jorge of Lope's play.

The poetic style of *La mayor venganza de honor* is characterized by a dignified simplicity that contributes to the impact of the subject matter. In several scenes, notably the interview between Rodrigo and the Veinticuatro (III) and the Veinticuatro's farewell to his wife (II), the dialogue is particularly successful in conveying the attitudes of the speakers. Use of a more ornamental style is limited to two speeches typical of Cubillo: the Veinticuatro's 165-line report of the victory at Antequera and an idealized description of Beatriz given by the *gracioso* Galindo. In the first of these, Rodrigo de Narváez with sword in hand is a "muralla viva de acero"; a horse is a "mayorazgo del viento." The enumeration of Beatriz' attributes, since it is assigned to the *gracioso*, may have been intended for comic effect.

As a drama of conjugal honor attributed to Cubillo, *La mayor venganza de honor* is of particular interest. If it is his work and if it was written no later than 1626, as indicated by the acting copy in the handwriting of Claramonte, then it shows that early in his career he was capable of a maturity and reflection in the treatment of serious subjects that is not always evident in his later writing for the theater. (It will be recalled that in *El rayo de Andalucia, segunda parte,* he develops the conjugal honor theme routinely and unconvincingly.) It would be a mistake to attribute this outlook to the influence of Lope by way of *Los comendadores de Córdoba,* for it has already been seen that *La mayor venganza de honor* is not a close imitation. In the long run, the *comedia* attributed to Cubillo has very probably suffered unduly by being compared with one of Lope's finest plays. *La mayor venganza de honor* is a lesser work than *Los comendadores de Córdoba,* but it deserves recognition as a good drama of conjugal honor in its own right.

9. *La tragedia del duque de Verganza*

La tragedia del duque de Verganza takes as its subject matter a revolt against royal authority which occurred in Portugal during the reign of João II (1481-1495). The royal chronicler Rui de Pina relates the events as follows: [40] In November 1481 João, moving to consoli-

---

[40] Rui de Pina, *Crónica de el-rei D. João II,* nova edição com prefacio e notas de Alberto Martins de Carvalho (Coimbra: Atlântida, 1940), Chaps. iii-vi, viii-xiv *passim.*

date the power of the crown, summoned the Cortes to give assent to a new oath of fealty to be taken by the nobles. The latter, bent upon retaining the privileges which had accrued to them in the previous reign, protested against the act of homage, the terms of which they would be obliged to accept in writing. Particularly offensive to them was the provision that the administration of justice, even on private estates, be in the hands of the king and his officials.

Among the great nobles, the first to make known his dissatisfaction was João's kinsman the Duke of Braganza and Guimaraes. Shortly after the meeting of the Cortes, the ducal treasurer found among Braganza's papers several documents implicating him in treasonable activity with Castile. These documents were delivered to the king, who had them copied and returned without Braganza's knowledge. Holding proof that Castile was plotting against him, the sovereign endeavored to bring about the revocation of the Treaty of Moura, under the terms of which his son Alfonso was being held as a Castilian hostage.

When in 1483 the progress of negotiations with Castile made his son's release imminent, João made ready to proceed against Braganza. After confronting him with knowledge of the correspondence, the king expressed a willingness to overlook its implications in return for wholehearted support. Braganza responded with assurances of loyalty, but, interpreting the concession as a mark of weakness, he began, together with his brothers and the Duke of Viseo, to defy João more boldly. On 15 May 1483 a new treaty with Castile was signed, after which the king proceeded to Evora to meet his son. Braganza, deciding that this turn of events required a show of allegiance to the crown, met the prince at Portel and escorted him to Evora. As the duke prepared to return to his estates, the king drew him aside. Unmoved by protestations that the reports of treason were unfounded, João ordered him taken into custody. After a lengthy trial the judges handed down a death sentence in the presence of the king, who wept as the votes were cast. On 20 June 1483 Braganza, who during his incarceration and in the final moments of his life had conducted himself with exemplary fortitude, was beheaded in the main square of Evora.

The earliest dated text of Cubillo's *El duque de Verganza* is found in *El enano de las musas* (1654).[41] The closing lines of the play,

---

[41] Two *sueltas* are known: Salamanca: F. D. de Torres, n.d.; N.p., n.d.

however, which draw parallels between the Duke of Braganza portrayed in the tragedy and the Braganza of Cubillo's own day, direct attention to the early 1640's:

> Dé fin la trágica muerte
> del gran Duque de Verganza
> cuyo mayor descendiente
> siguiendo sus mismos pasos
> hoy a Castilla se atreve.[42]   (III, 478b)

Construing this passage as an allusion to the Portuguese rebellion against Spain which broke out in December 1640 under the titular leadership of the eighth Duke of Braganza, Cotarelo takes 1641 as the date of composition.[43] The assumption is plausible in that in 1641 a play capitalizing on the uprising would have been very timely. On the other hand, the line "hoy a Castilla se atreve" may be an allusion to a definite threat of invasion by Braganza's forces rather than to the rebellion in general. Before 1652, when the *aprobación* was issued for *El enano de las musas,* engagements between Spanish and Portuguese troops amounted to little more than a series of skirmishes, except in September 1643, when a sizable Portuguese force moved across the frontier to Badajoz, and in May 1644, when the Portuguese won the battle of Montijo. In light of these events, the play may have been written in late 1643 or in 1644.

Specialists in the theater of the Golden age, viewing *El duque de Verganza* primarily as a political drama written in support of the principle of royal authority or attracted to it because of its doctrinal resemblances to other political plays of the period, have made only a few observations concerning its literary qualities. Schaeffer praises it but nevertheless contends that it does not convey the deep feeling by which real tragedy transports and stirs. Menéndez y Pelayo, who thinks that the political aim resulted in a work that is "más grave y doctrinal" than Lope's *El duque de Viseo,* which he erroneously

---

[42] Citations are to the text in *El enano de las musas.*

[43] Bartolomé Romero, whose company Cubillo says (in *El enano de las musas*) acted the play, is known to have contracted for his troupe to perform in Lisbon from November 1640 to Shrovetide 1641 (Rennert, *The Spanish Stage,* p. 583). The outbreak of hostilities may have altered the conditions of Romero's trip, but if he did carry it out, his company could not have played *El duque de Verganza* until after Easter 1641.

assumed to be Cubillo's model, maintains that in poetic merit it is inferior because of Cubillo's lack of ease with heroic subject matter. As an illustration he cites the appearance of a ghost in Act III, which he deems so mechanically and inopportunely introduced that it contributes nothing to the tragic effect.

The comments made by Cotarelo, limited as they are, reveal a closer study of the play. He finds the characterizations of the king and Braganza "inmejorables" in the first half of the play; the second half, he says, is weaker because Cubillo could not express the emotions of tragedy with grandeur. Like Menéndez y Pelayo, Cotarelo thinks that the ghost scene is too rapid to be effective. He terms the dialogue between the duchess and the king (Act III), in which the former asks that her husband be spared, a "pueril juego de palabras" and dismisses the king's summing up in Act III as "vana palabrería." These reservations notwithstanding, Cotarelo calls the drama "uno de los buenos de su autor y aun muy estimable entre las joyas de nuestro gran drama histórico."

Valbuena Prat's observations add little to previous commentary. Valbuena merely points out the presence of numerous Gongoristic images and indicates his favorable opinion, in contrast to Cotarelo's, of the scene in which the duchess asks the king's mercy.

The chief source of the play, according to J. B. Avalle-Arce, is the account of Braganza's treason given in Chapters xxvii-xlvi of Garcia de Rezende's *Chorónica que trata da vida... do Christianíssimo dom João o Segundo deste nome* (Lisboa, 1607). [44] In support of his assertion Avalle-Arce cites passages in Cubillo's play which are little more than versifications of passages from Rezende. Rezende's chronicle was unavailable to the present writer, who has examined Rui de Pina's *Crónica de el-rei D. João II* (not published until 1792), from which Avalle-Arce says Rezende copies his text. [45] A comparison of *El duque de Verganza* with Rui de Pina's account shows that Cubillo follows the chronicle closely in his main plot, even if in some instances he compresses the action for dramatic purposes.

The rigorous historicity of the main action of *El duque de Verganza* precludes extensive borrowings from the only other play of

---

[44] Avalle-Arce, p. 430.

[45] A comparison of the passages from Rezende reproduced in Avalle-Arce's article with Rui de Pina's text reveals only a few insignificant variants.

related subject matter, Lope de Vega's *El duque de Viseo,* thought by Morley and Bruerton to have been written c. 1604-1610. In this latter work, which follows the career of Braganza's brother-in-law, the misfortunes which befall Braganza and Viseo result from the machinations of an envious underling, Don Egas. Braganza, called Guimarans by Lope, is a minor figure who is portrayed as completely innocent of designs against the throne. Menéndez y Pelayo, perhaps basing his assertion on the fact that Act II of *El duque de Viseo* ends with Guimarans' death, held that Cubillo drew his plot from the first two acts of Lope's play. This statement, taken up by Cotarelo and Valbuena Prat, loses validity when the two *comedias* are compared. A more accurate assessment of the relationship has been made by Avalle-Arce, who says that Cubillo's play bears no resemblance to Lope's except in the tragedy at the end. (The closing scene of Act II of Lope's play, in which the king seeks to impart a lesson to Viseo by showing him the corpse of Guimarans, is the same as the final scene in *El duque de Verganza.*) Beyond this, Cubillo may have had Lope's *comedia* in mind in one other scene. In Act III the Duquesa goes before the king to intercede for her husband, just as Doña Elvira, a young unmarried woman, pleads with the king to spare Guimarans in *El duque de Viseo* (Act II). Since this incident is not documented in the chronicle, Cubillo may have taken it from Lope.

The apparition scene in Act III of Cubillo's play recalls ghostly interventions in several other *comedias.* Schaeffer says that Cubillo had in mind a scene from Jiménez de Enciso's *La mayor hazaña de Carlos V*; Menéndez y Pelayo and Valbuena Prat contend that the ghost is from *El duque de Viseo.* Avalle-Arce, however, points out that in Lope's play the dead Guimarans appears to warn Viseo to be on guard against the king, whereas in Cubillo's play Braganza sees his own specter. Avalle-Arce thinks that this situation is closer to Lope's *El caballero de Olmedo,* in which Don Alonso is confronted by his own ghost. Out of this maze of possible sources it is difficult to reach a firm conclusion; but, as it seems clear that Cubillo knew *El duque de Viseo,* he very likely took the idea for the apparition from that *comedia,* although he may have modified it along the lines of *El caballero de Olmedo.*

Cubillo's indebtedness to Jiménez de Enciso's *El príncipe don Carlos* has been claimed by Schaeffer, who sees in Enciso's Felipe II the model for João II. Both plays deal with pride and ambition set in opposition to authority, and both contain the figure of a king placed in a dilemma because of the conflict between familial ties and the obligations of office; these coincidences, however, are inherent in the subject matter and do not prove that Cubillo drew from Enciso's play, particularly since the parallels noticed by Schaeffer apply to the Portuguese chronicle shown by Avalle-Arce to be Cubillo's principal source. Cubillo may have known *El príncipe don Carlos*,[46] and his familiarity with it may have alerted him to the dramatic possibilities of the chronicle account of Braganza's treason; but that there is a close connection between the two plays is not borne out by a reading of *El príncipe don Carlos*.

Out of the materials from the chronicle Cubillo has constructed a work which, despite its defects, is much superior to his historical plays that continued to be performed well into the eighteenth century. In drawing from the Portuguese chronicle, he acquired an enormous advantage in that his source does not give a bare recital of events; rather, it characterizes Braganza and João vigorously. Thus the playwright had before him the raw materials of tragedy in impressive characters as well as events.

Cubillo makes his selections from the chronicle with discernment, but his arrangement of the material and incorporation of new matter is not always felicitous. In Act I the opening scenes are misleading, for one would assume from them that the play is to be a *comedia de capa y espada*. Even though these scenes are competently plotted, they hold attention too long on secondary matters. After this deceptive start, the main action gets underway with the king's decision to demand a new oath of fealty. As the plot advances, one sees that the purpose of the elaborate opening sequence is to provide a reason for Vasco (a *galán* who has wounded a rival in a duel) to seek refuge on Braganza's estate. His presence there brings into the open the struggle between royal authority and the prerogatives of the nobility. Act I ends on a note of rising interest as the king, who has sensed Braganza's ambition, obliquely warns the duke to exercise restraint in his conduct.

---

[46] Schaeffer says that a line spoken by Cubillo's *gracioso* ("Yo entretendré a Monteñí") is a reminiscence of *El príncipe don Carlos,* in which Montigny is a character.

Act II is the most powerful in the play, since its progress springs mainly from the interaction of character traits of Braganza and the king. Braganza's growing ambition, encouraged by his knowledge of the king's regard, remains unchecked despite repeated warnings: His overconfidence blinds him to the fact that the king is slowly reaching an awareness that duty must supersede ties of blood and affection. In the final scene of Act II, however, in which the interview between Braganza and the king ends in the former's arrest, the melodramatic devices that are so conspicious in Act III begin to appear. From here on, character becomes less important in propelling the action, a defect which may account for the comparative weakness Cotarelo notices in the latter portion of the play. The substance of the interview is taken from the chronicle, but to it Cubillo adds elements of his own devising. For example, when Braganza is ready to deny once more his part in the conspiracy, incriminating letters accidentally fall to the floor. A violent note is added when Braganza unsheathes a dagger to kill the king. That a look from João would stay his hand, however much it may strain the credulity of a twentieth-century reader, may well have been dramatically convincing to a seventeenth-century audience, which could accept the king as a quasi-divine figure.

If Cubillo had delayed the duke's arrest until Act III and then brought the play to a rapid conclusion, he might have sustained the heroic tone that dominates Acts I and II, for as long as the duke and the king are pitted against each other the playwright demonstrates that he can translate character into action. It appears, however, that propagandistic rather than artistic considerations determined the placement of the duke's arrest. An entire act devoted to subsequent events provides a great many opportunities for driving home the doctrine that there can be no justification for rebellion against the divinely ordained institution of monarchy.

The arrangement chosen by Cubillo leaves him with little dramatically viable material to use in Act III, since the main conflict no longer exists. It is fitting that the king's reluctance to order Braganza's execution be shown, and the nobility of the succumbing duke as well; but this material is not sufficient to fill a whole act. In an effort to maintain interest, the playwright resorts to several incidents which have superficial audience appeal. A note of sentimentality is injected into the Duquesa's plea when Braganza's young son accompanies his mother. The appearance of the ghost makes use of an external device to propel action. Until this point, Braganza has retained vestiges of confidence that he will be set free. His realization that he will die does not come, as one might expect from the manner in which Cubillo has characterized him, from within himself but from the specter who announces his fate. The exception that several critics take to this scene may well rest on this incongruity.

The delineation of Braganza is nevertheless convincing proof that the tragic hero was not entirely foreign to Cubillo's talent. It is significant that the term *tragedia* apears in the title of the play; and the seriousness with which the dramatist treats his subject is confirmed by the portrayal of the duke, who is not assigned the showy speeches and exaggerated posturings often associated with the protagonists of Cubillo's historical plays. Here the emphasis is on those traits in Braganza that pervent his talents and lead him to a catastrophic end. He is not portrayed as a victim of others but of his own fatal lack of perception.

At the outset it is the duke's position as defender of the privileges of the nobility that causes him to take the offensive against the crown, a stand that would arouse some sympathy for him, especially since the king has acted in an arbitrary manner. By the time of the first private audience with the king, which is based on the chronicle, it is entirely believable that Braganza is so corrupted by a lust for power that he rejects the king's offer to forget past differences. That the duke's original reason for seeking to dethrone the monarch has been engulfed by his own ambition is transparent, since the concessions the king is willing to make would eliminate most of his grievances.

After this audience, which marks the culmination of Braganza's many errors in judging his adversary, the duke is irremediably fixed on his course. In the second audience it seems likely that Braganza's attempt to murder João is designed to show the final corrupting effect of ambition. Even so, it is arguable that the disintegration of Braganza's character has already been demonstrated and that the attempt at murder is superfluous, not to say turbulent.

Some of the structural weaknesses of Act III which reduce the vigor of characterization have already been pointed out. Yet despite these defects, the act contains a scene that is evidence that Cubillo has not forgotten that he has conceived Braganza as a tragic hero: In prison awaiting execution, the duke reaches a state of self-recognition, which he expresses in a sonnet on the mutability of fortune.

In the king, who is in conflict not only with the duke but also with himself, Cubillo creates a character who is individualized perhaps even more than Braganza. The king's indecisiveness provides a way in which an interplay between his role and Braganza's can be brought about. The sovereign's repeated efforts to give his kinsman every opportunity to turn back advance the plot in that the duke thereby becomes more and more confident of the strength of his position. The king's role retains until the end more vigor than Braganza's, for even after the arrest João is still faced with the choice of sacrificing the duke for the good of his country or pardoning him out of affection. Here Cubillo's fidelity to history did not betray him artistically, for the chronicle tells of the king's anguish over his decision.

No other role in the play approaches those of Braganza and the king in weight or importance. The other male characters are minor figures whose function is to bring into sharper focus the struggle between noble and sovereign. The women's roles are episodic. Violante, a young woman of rank, is introduced to provide the motive for the duel in Act I; the duchess appears in three scenes only.

The poetic style of the play is for the most part direct and dignified, even if it does not achieve grandeur. The verbosity noticed by Cotarelo is confined to a few passages in Act III and is probably the result of efforts to stress the doctrinal message. The Gongoristic images mentioned by Valbuena Prat are found chiefly in Vasco's description of Violante in Act I. A 154-line entreaty for the conspirators to turn back, which is assigned to the duchess, is the only example of the long speech characteristic of Cubillo.

In the final analysis, it may well be that the chief interest of *El duque de Verganza* is as an illustration of what one playwright understood by the term *tragedy*. (It is the only one of his works that Cubillo so designates.) The play gives clear evidence that Cubillo could think in classical terms, no matter how he might diverge from them in practice. While it does not observe the unities of time and place, it adheres firmly to neo-Aristotelian precept in theme, main action, and major characters. Moreover, Cubillo's analytical approach to character — his attention to the motives that underlie action — shows fidelity to a fundamental of tragedy in the classical mold. Nowhere else did Cubillo attempt as much; if he failed to accomplish his purpose fully, *El duque de Verganza* nevertheless stands as a dramatic work that rewards serious study.

10. *Entre los sueltos caballos*

Entre los sueltos caballos does not appear to be a *refundición* but, like *La manga de Sarracino,* an original *comedia* which draws from *romances moriscos* to exploit the appeal of Moorish themes. Although listed in several catalogues of Cubillo's dramatic works, it has not been described by any scholar. La Barrera says that it was printed under Cubillo's name in *Parte cincuenta y siete* of the *Comedias de diferentes autores* (Valencia, 1646) and adds that the only extant copy is in the Library of the University of Bologna. Cotarelo indicates that he had not seen either the Valencia printing or the *suelta* ascribed to Cubillo in Medel's *Índice*. He evidently did not know the undated *suelta* in the British Museum.[47] The date of composition of the play has not been determined.

The plot, in outline, is as follows: Don Pedro Girón, exiled to North Africa, rescues a Christian maiden, Doña Leonor, from abduction by Moorish raiders near Orán. Following an exchange of gallant gestures, Pedro and the Moorish commander, Ceilán, challenge each other to meet later to settle their differences. After reaching Orán, Pedro and Leonor fall in love. Meanwhile, Aureliana, a Moorish maiden, begins to suspect a rival in the beautiful Christian described by Ceilán. Having been asked by the Marqués de Cortes, governor of Orán, to act for him in paying court to Leonor, Pedro seeks to gain time by deceiving him, with the lady's cooperation, into believing that his suit is favored. Called to ward off a Moorish attack, Pedro leaves an inconsolable Leonor behind. After taking Ceilán captive, Pedro sets him free to rejoin Aureliana. Bound by gratitude, Ceilán goes to Orán to pay homage to Leonor's beauty. Aureliana, who has assumed disguise to gain admittance to her supposed rival's house, finds that her suspicions are unjustified. The Marqués, having learned

---

[47] I have not seen the Bologna Library copy mentioned by Cayetano Alberto de la Barrera y Leirado, *Catálogo bibliográfico y biográfico del teatro antiguo español, desde sus orígenes hasta mediados del siglo XVIII* (Madrid: Imprenta y Estereotipia de M. Rivadeneyra, 1860), p. 115. The British Museum *suelta*, which carries Cubillo's name, is the only copy of the play I have been able to locate.

of the love between Pedro and Leonor, magnanimously withdraws his suit.

Several scholars have raised questions concerning the authorship of *Entre los sueltos caballos*. Mesonero Romanos says of it, "Creo sea de Vélez." It may be that Mesonero based his supposition on knowledge of certain satirical verses attacking Luis Vélez de Guevara. As quoted by La Barrera, who also speculates on the validity of the ascription to Cubillo, these verses are as follows:

> Entre los sueltos caballos
> de la mosquetera gente
> que la otra noche silbaron
> entre lo Roque lo Vélez.

Cotarelo conjectures that these lines may mean that the *mosqueteros* hissed a *comedia* by Vélez de Guevara entitled *Entre los sueltos caballos* when it was performed by Roque de Figueroa's company. On the other hand, he says, the verses may be an allusion to the unfavorable reception of another *comedia* by Vélez, and the phrase "entre los sueltos caballos" merely a parody of Góngora's *romance* of the same title.

La Barrera assigns to Vélez two *comedias* on Spaniards in North Africa. Neither *La conquista de Orán,* which deals with the expedition under Cisneros in 1509, nor *Los sucesos en Orán por el marqués de Ardales,* which treats the career of an early seventeenth-century governor of Orán, [48] can be the same play as *Entre los sueltos caballos*. Whether either of the two Vélez *comedias* contains lines from the Góngora *romance* that might have inspired the satirical verses is unknown to the present writer, who has not had access to the text of either *comedia*.

While it does not seem that the verses provide sufficient grounds for assigning *Entre los sueltos caballos* to Vélez, the *comedia* cannot be shown to be indisputably the work of Cubillo. It is true that it

---

[48] For a plot summary of *Los sucesos de Orán por el marqués de Ardales,* see Forrest Eugene Spencer and Rudolph Schevill, *The Dramatic Works of Luis Vélez de Guevara; Their Plots, Sources, and Bibliography,* University of California Publications in Modern Philology, 19 (Berkeley: University of California Press, 1937), pp. 254-57. Spencer and Schevill make no mention of *La conquista de Orán.*

exhibits parallels in style and atmosphere with *La manga de Sarracina,* and the Pedro-Leonor-Marqués intrigue is built around a situation Cubillo was fond of introducing. Then too, the Ceilán-Aureliana courtship is strongly reminiscent of the Ramón-Infanta amours in *La corona del agravio* and the Diego-Galiana intrigue in *La manga de Sarracino.* Moreover, Cubillo uses in other plays fragments of the same ballads that are incorporated here. Nevertheless, these similarities do not furnish incontrovertible evidence.

Two ballads by Góngora, "Servía en Orán al rey" and "Entre los sueltos caballos," suggested the North African setting and the idealized relations between Moor and Christian. Two scenes, moreover, are constructed almost entirely on these *romances.* The beauty of Góngora's verses harmonizes with the poetic style of the rest of the play, which even if it does not attain the same level of excellence, is nevertheless functional and unconstrained.

The two amorous intrigues, the Pedro-Leonor-Marqués triangle in Christian-held Orán and the Ceilán-Aureliana courtship in the Moorish stronghold of Tlemcen, are linked by Pedro and Ceilán's contest to excel each other in prowess at arms and nobility of sentiment. The first of these introduces a situation employed by Cubillo in other *comedias*: a *galán*'s courtship of his own *dama* in the name of a rival suitor to whom he is indebted;[49] the second revolves around an imperious Moorish maiden and her diffident wooer.

Apart from a competently plotted series of incidents at Leonor's balcony, the most engaging scenes are those based on Góngora's *romances.* Since both "Servía en Orán al rey" and "Entre los sueltos caballos" have a strong narrative content, they lend themselves readily to fragmentation into dialogue. The final scene in Act II, Pedro's farewell to Leonor before going off to battle, is constructed almost entirely on lines from "Servía en Orán al rey." Nearly all of "Entre los sueltos caballos" is incorporated into the scene in Act III in which Pedro releases Ceilán in order to allow him to rejoin his lady.[50]

---

[49] In *Perderse por no perderse* and *El señor de Noches Buenas.*

[50] The subject matter of "Entre los sueltos caballos" is essentially the same as that of the first meeting between Rodrigo de Narváez and Abindarráez in *El abencerraje,* which was so aptly dramatized in Lope de Vega's *El remedio en la desdicha.* Góngora's ballad is incorporated almost *in toto* into Act I of Calderón's *El príncipe constante.* Kenneth R. Scholberg, in *La poesía religiosa de Miguel de Barrios* (Columbus, Ohio: Ohio State University Press,

Here, however, the playwright expands his material to include many new lines. For the most part, the passages which supplement the *romance* are designed to elaborate on the content of the model — the expression of noble sentiments by both the Christian and his captive, most particularly the former's magnanimity in freeing his prisoner — since this scene is the high point of the sentimentalized view of relations between the representatives of the two religions.

The competition between Pedro and Ceilán, which dominates the romantic intrigues, lifts the play out of the category of a romantic comedy set in an *ambiente morisco* and gives it the substance as well as the trappings of a *comedia de moros y cristianos*. But to aver that the confrontation receives a treatment going beyond the exploitation of a literary motif is to attribute to *Entre los sueltos caballos* a richness of suggestion that it does not possess. Even so, the incidents are gracefully combined, and the characters are attractive.

11. *La honestidad defendida de Elisa Dido, reina y fundadora de Cartago*

The defense of Dido which Cubillo makes in *La honestidad defendida de Elisa Dido, reina y fundadora de Cartago* reflects a view of the Carthaginian queen that gained wide acceptance in medieval European literature and, in Spain at least, continued until well past the Renaissance. [51] The treatment of Dido as a model of chastity, based on a legend that arose before Virgil composed the *Aeneid*, found its way into several Greek and Roman histories. From there it was taken up by writers seeking to redeem Dido's reputation, which they believed had been unjustly tarnished in Book IV of the *Aeneid*. In

---

n.d.), p. 49, says that Act III of Barrios' *El español de Orán* is basically a gloss of "Entre los sueltos caballos" and "Servía en Orán al rey." Barrios' play was published in *Flor de Apolo* (Brussels, 1665) after the author, a Jew, had left Spain for religious reasons. The plot summary given by Henry V. Besso in *Dramatic Literature of the Sephardic Jews of Amsterdam* (New York: The Hispanic Institute in the United States, 1947), pp. 78-83, does not reveal any notable similarities with the *comedia* ascribed to Cubillo. Cubillo uses fragments of "Entre los sueltos caballos" in *Las muñecas de Marcela* (II) and *El conde de Saldaña, primera parte* (III). Several lines from "Servía en Orán al rey" are in *El conde de Saldaña, segunda parte* (II).

[51] For a study of the literary defense of Dido, see María Rosa Lida, "Dido y su defensa en la literatura española," *Revista de Filología Hispánica*, 4 (1942), 209-52, 313-82.

outline, the pseudo-historical Dido's story is as follows: Elisa, sister of Pygmalion, King of Tyre, flees with some of her followers after her husband is murdered by Pygmalion. At the end of an arduous sea voyage she reaches Lybia, where the inhabitants give her the name of Dido. After founding the city of Carthage, Dido is sought in marriage by the King of Lybia. Under the pretext of ceremonially divesting herself of royal authority before entering upon the marriage her subjects are urging upon her, the queen orders a large pyre to be set up near her palace. After lighting the pyre, she throws herself upon it.

In the Spanish theater, the pseudo-historical Dido appears in two plays antedating *La honestidad defendida*.[52] Cristóbal de Virués' *Tragedia de Elisa Dido* (c. 1580),[53] an attempt at rigid adherence to the precepts of classical drama, unfolds in five somewhat wearisome acts the story of Yarbas of Lydia's efforts to win Dido in marriage, ending with the queen's immolation. The plot follows the account given by the Roman historian Justin, but a number of minor details are drawn from the *Aeneid*. Gabriel Lobo Laso de la Vega's three-act play, *La honra de Dido restaurada,* published in his *Romancero y tragedias, primera parte* (Alcalá, 1587), devotes Act I to Dido's adventures before reaching Africa, Act II to the founding of Carthage, and Act III to the queen's rejection of Yarbas. Although highly episodic and replete with the intervention of mythological and allegorical figures, Laso de la Vega's play has considerably more movement than Virués' tragedy. In the *argumento* Laso de la Vega gives Justin as his source.

Cubillo's *La honestidad defendida de Elisa Dido, reina y fundadora de Cartago,* the third and final Spanish defense of Dido in dramatic form, was first printed in 1654 in *El enano de las musas*.[54] If

---

[52] Besides the Spanish plays glorifying the Dido of the pseudo-histories, there are several dealing with the Virgilian Dido. The first Dido play in Spanish, Juan Cirne's *Tragedia de los amores de Eneas y de la reyna Dido* (c. 1536), belongs to this cycle. Others are Alonso de las Cuevas' *Llegada de Eneas a Cartago* (before 1584), Cristóbal de Morales' *Amor de Dido y Eneas* (period of Calderón) and Antonio Folch de Cardona's *Dido y Eneas* (late seventeenth century).

[53] Although Virués' tragedy was not published until 1609, Cecilia Vennard Sargent, in *A Study of the Dramatic Works of Cristóbal de Virués* (New York: Instituto de las Españas en los Estados Unidos, 1930), p. 31, concludes that it was the first Spanish play on the chaste Dido.

[54] Other editions are: Madrid, 1734; N.p., n.d.

one accepts his statement in the *índice* that it was "nueva, nunca vista ni representada," then it must have been written not long before 1652, when the *aprobación* was granted for *El enano*. An examination of the text discloses nothing that would suggest an earlier date, and no external evidence that would contradict Cubillo has been found.

The several scholars who have studied the *comedia* have made few observations on its purely dramatic and literary qualities. Valbuena Prat sees some stylistic beauties in Elisa's scene at the fountain, with the subsequent appearance of Yarbas as king (II). María Rosa Lida thinks that the appearance of an Athenian philosopher and the shade of Virgil is perhaps "lo mejor y más original de la comedia," but she finds the placing of the funeral pyre on stage a grotesque touch. For the most part, however, investigators have evinced interest in the play because of the place it occupies in the defense of Dido in literature. It would seem that a judgment that the *comedia* has been found wanting artistically is implicit in the fact that Cotarelo, Valbuena Prat, and María Rosa Lida, the scholars who have examined the play in some detail, confine themselves almost exclusively to its associations with the Dido theme.

María Rosa Lida, whose study of the defense of Dido in Spanish literature is the most exhaustive available, maintains that it would be futile to point to any particular work as the source of Cubillo's defense of the queen, since the material was available in an almost infinite number of *silvas, misceláneas,* and *polianteas,* not to mention the plays of Virués and Laso de la Vega. Though Cubillo may have known the earlier plays, a comparison of them with *La honestidad defendida* leads inescapably to the conclusion that neither served as his model. *La honestidad defendida* is closer in subject matter to Virués' tragedy than to Laso de la Vega's in that Dido's misfortunes prior to the founding of Carthage have no place in the action, but otherwise it bears no resemblance to *Elisa Dido*. Besides borrowing from defenses of Dido, Cubillo includes details that reveal acquaintance with the *Aeneid*. The melodramatic sword is from the *Aeneid*, as is Ana, although Cubillo characterizes her as a typical *dama*; the praise of Dido's palace is based on a description of a temple that Virgil's Dido built to Juno.

The plotting of the intrigue that is interwoven with the defense is Cubillo's own, but the devices are commonplaces of the theater of the Golden Age. For example, the incident that gives rise to the complications, Yarbas' assumption of the identity of another in an effort to discover if the queen is as beautiful as her portrait, is used in a number of *comedias*.

Cubillo's decision to graft a trivial intrigue on to the subject matter of the chaste Dido was unfortunate, for it produced neither a convincing treatment of the Dido legend nor a lively *comedia palaciega*. The theme of the Dido legend, the terrible power of love, is inadequately conveyed, because no serious threat is offered to the queen's resolve to remain true to the memory of her late husband. The frivolous intrigue, in which a case of mistaken identity jeopardizes Elisa's reputation, is hardly a fitting substitute for a real conflict. In the legend it was Yarbas who brought about the clash of wills, but surely the amiable Yarbas of *La honestidad defendida,* a typical *galán de comedia,* does not.

If Cubillo considered that the Dido story furnished a pretext for an intrigue that would find favor through the use of mistaken identities, disguises, *equívocos,* and secret meetings, his error lay in not giving himself wholeheartedly to it, for as a comedy of intrigue the play is diminished by the static quality of many of the scenes in which Elisa appears. Had the playwright been less concerned with the polemical features of his material, he might not have devised so many scenes in which the queen speaks at length of her *honestidad* and her determination to preserve it, while other members of the cast stand about praising her moral excellence. Finally having reached the requisite number of lines, he allows Ana to resolve the plot by stepping forward to confess that she had allowed Yarbas to continue in his error when he mistook her for the queen during a nocturnal encounter in the palace garden. The play ends, not with Elisa's suicide, but with her granting permission for Yarbas to continue to pay court to her. Thus Cubillo radically distorts the spirit of the legend of the chaste Dido.

As the foregoing paragraphs imply, the characters of *La honestidad defendida* are colorless. The queen, the character to whom Cubillo gives the greatest attention, does not function dramatically with any degree of success, because there is no interaction on a significant level between her character and the plot. Like many other women characters in Cubillo's historical plays, she is not really attractive as a woman. Perhaps the best description of her is "un mármol de hielo" (II, 73b), a phrase she applies to herself.

Though the reader must perforce judge *La honestidad defendida* harshly, it is entirely possible that the viewer would find that spectacular elements would relieve the tedium of the polemical scenes. The play opens with a procession to the sound of *chirimías* as Elisa, dressed "en vestiduras reales," advances to her palace followed by members of her court. "Por lo alto" appear two soldiers, each bearing a standard displaying the heraldic devices of a bull and a crown. In Act I, 53a, an Athenian philosopher garbed in skins conjures up a view of Virgil composing the *Aeneid*. According to the stage directions, Virgil is revealed when the back curtain is drawn. In Act III a curtained alcove is pressed into use to serve for placement of the funeral pyre. The play closes with a scene almost equal in brilliance to the one that opens it: Servants step forth bearing torches which they present to the assembled cast. Musicians appear and, with castanet accompaniment, a song celebrates Elisa's virtues.

The poetic style of the *comedia*, which one might expact to be inflated, is relatively restrained. The courtier Fabio describes Elisa in *términos cultos* (I, 48b-49a) that include such metaphors as "regia afrenta de Ofir" (Elisa's hair), but aside from this one passage there is no concentration of ornate language. The play contains only one long speech, Elisa's 279-line recital of the events of her life before reaching Africa (I, 57a-60b), but it is relatively straightforward. Nevertheless, the poetic style does not strengthen the play, for in the romantic intrigue the dialogue is not sufficiently sparkling, and in the polemical scenes it is at times decidedly ponderous.

In conclusion, many of the weaknesses of *La honestidad defendida* stem from the same error in judgment that Cubillo makes in *La corona del agravio*. In both *comedias* he attempts to combine historical (or pseudo-historical) subject matter of some gravity with light fictional subject matter; in both instances the disparate material proves resistant to integration. In *La corona del agravio* it has been seen that Ramón de Borgoña provides a link on a very superficial level. Similarly, in *La honestidad defendida* Elisa, depicted as she is in accordance with the tradition of the pseudo-histories, is unconvincing as a figure in the romantic intrigue.

12. *El vencedor de sí mismo*

The Spanish theater of the Golden age offers a number of examples of *comedias caballerescas* inspired by the *Orlando Furioso*, including several which are, like *El vencedor de sí mismo,* based on the Bradamante episode. The obstacles placed to the marriage of Ruggero and Bradamante are treated in Cantos xliv-xlvi of the Italian romance: Rinaldo, not knowing that his father Amone has affianced his sister Bradamante to Leone, son of the Emperor of Byzantium, promises her to his friend Ruggero. Upon appealing to Charlemagne, Bradamante wins from him a promise to award her to the suitor who defeats her in armed combat. Meanwhile, Ruggero sets out to prevent the marriage by slaying Leone. During his search Ruggero leads a Bulgarian army to victory over the Byzantines. Taken prisoner while resting after battle, he is saved from execution by Leone. Having agreed to take his benefactor's place, Ruggero vanquishes Bradamante and then leaves without disclosing his identity. Upon learning that the pledges previously exchanged by the lovers are tantamount to marriage, Leone goes in search of Ruggero. After yielding in his favor, Leone informs Charlemagne of the substitution. Ruggero, who has accepted the Bulgarian crown, then weds Bradamante.

The absence of literary distinction that characterizes the majority of *comedias* based on the *Orlando Furioso* appears to be applicable to those having their origin in the Bradamante episode, beginning with the anonymous *Las bodas de Rugero y Bradamante.*[55] A *farsa caballeresca,* it is described by La Barrera as "insulsa, de pobre inventiva y versificación trabajosa y prosaica." Cubillo's *El vencedor de sí mismo,* which seems to be based directly on the *Orlando* rather than on *Las bodas de Rugero y Bradamante,* was apparently the second full-length Bradamante play in Spanish.[56]

---

[55] A MS of this play in the Biblioteca Nacional (No. 16.111) is in an early seventeenth-century hand. Antonio Portnoy, in *Ariosto y su influencia en la literatura española* (Buenos Aires: Editorial Losada, 1932), p. 212, says that it may be the same as the *Farsa de Rugero y Bradamante,* which was performed at El Pardo in 1593.

[56] Amos Parducci, *La fortuna dell "Orlando furioso" nel teatro spagnolo, Giornale Storico della Letteratura Italiana,* Supplemento No. 26 (Torino: Casa Editrice Giovanni Chiantore, 1937), p. 153. The Bradamante theme on the Spanish stage was not exhausted by *El vencedor de sí mismo,* for the titles of several related *comedias* are known. La Barrera mentions a second *Vencedor de sí mismo,* which he ascribes to Jacinto de Funes y Vallalpando, who was active in the seventeenth century. Parducci lists two other *comedias,* both of which had been lost by the time he was conducting his investigations: *Rugero y Bradamante,* by Luis Calisto Acosta y Faria (1679-1738), and an anonymous *Comedia de Bradamante y Rugero.*

The text of *El vencedor de sí mismo* has survived only in two eighteenth-century printings, both of which carry Cubillo's name. The first of these *sueltas,* printed in Seville (Viuda de Francisco Leefdael), probably dates from the early part of the century. The other, which was issued in Valencia (Hermanos de Orga), is dated 1792. In the latter *suelta,* which is used in the present study, the *comedia* is divided into two acts; this division is, however, probably the result of a compositor's error, since Act II is twice the length of Act I and the total number of lines reaches the normal length for a three-act *comedia.*

Although there is no incontrovertible proof that the play is Cubillo's, it does contain several features that coincide in his feebler works: a clumsily constructed plot, wooden characters, and an excessive use of long speeches and stereotyped figurative language. Several of his favorite stylistic devices — a courtly debate, *culteranista* descriptions of women, and a highly figurative report of a combat — are also employed. No evidence of the date of composition has been found.

Like many other plays ascribed to Cubillo, *El vencedor de sí mismo* has attracted scant attention. Valbuena Prat says that its only good features are a few beautiful images and scenes of "gran aparato teatral." Amos Parducci, who is less severe in his assessment, argues that several situations are skillfully handled: Rugero's renunciation of Bradamonte in her father's presence, his sacrifice of his own future happiness in order to repay his debt of honor to his rival León, and his disclosure to León of his love for Bradamante. It is difficult to subscribe to Parducci's opinion, which may be attributable to a loss of perspective brought about by studying the many lamentable Spanish plays derived from the *Orlando Furioso.*

The *comedia* reveals that its author had a good knowledge not only of the Bradamante episode but also other portions of Ariosto's poem. In the main, he follows his source, but he transposes the order of some incidents and introduces several characters who figure only in other episodes of the poem. Moreover, he adds a few completely new elements. The duel between Rodomonte and Rugero, which in the poem takes place on the last day of the festivities celebrating Bradamante's marriage to Rugero, occurs in the *comedia* well before this event. Bradamante's persuasion of Charlemagne to allow her to wed the knight who defeats her is not given in the order it appears in the *Orlando.* Flordelís, a minor character in *El vencedor de sí mismo,* in the poem is already dead when the Bradamante episode occurs. Rugero's generosity in yielding upon learning that Amón has promised Bradamante to León is not in the poem. The most striking modification, however, is in the role assigned to Doralice, who in the *Orlando* is not loved by Dudón and so does not flee from him. Parducci thinks that Cubillo devised this romantic subplot as a foil to Bradamante's love for Rugero. It is indeed true that the introduction of Doralice leads to many new situations and relationships.

Despite his familiarity with the *Orlando Furioso,* Cubillo does not transfer its aristocratic, elegantly comic spirit to his *comedia.* The high seriousness with which he treats the improbable situations taken from the poem, all the while multiplying the absurd motivations and incidents, is totally at variance with the tone of the *Orlando.* Moreover, long speeches and an overblown style infuse the play with sluggishness. *El vencedor de sí mismo* is clearly a vehicle for a *primera dama* (Bradamonte) and a *primer galán* (Rugero), but their roles are prominent only because of the large number of lines assigned to them.

Obviously a piece of hack work, the play abounds in examples of clumsy technique. A scene which collapses for want of adroitness is the first encounter between Doralice and Bradamonte (Act I). The tension is nullified by a wordy exchange filled with subtleties on the respective merits of *dar* and *pedir.* Furthermore, one can scarcely believe that Bradamante would be willing to renounce Rugero to her rival and act as her advocate. In Act II, after Rugero has received congratulations for having vanquished Rodomonte, he embarks on a metaphor-laden description of the encounter, which is entirely superfluous, since all present are aware of what has happened. Similarly, when Bradamante stands before Charlemagne requesting permission to fight her suitors, she gives an account of all her victories.

When Rugero is taken prisoner by León, he is able, despite his evident distress, to tell his story at much length. León's reply is filled with extended, highly literary similes which no one in such circumstances would utter.

The language of the play is highly figurative, both in the long unfunctional speeches and elsewhere. A typical passage is Rugero's description of Bradamante:

> Venga, dichoso príncipe, y corone
> la frente que del sol ya coronada
> obscurece los rayos que interpone
> crencha de Ofir en nácar dilatada. (I, 3a)

There are some lines of more than passing beauty, as Valbuena Prat says, but they are confined to a few passages. More frequently, the dialogue offers a display of the rhetorical devices of the *estilo culto* accompanied by few indications of a rich poetic imagination.

In regard to the position of *El vencedor de sí mismo* in relation to the other plays attributed to Cubillo, it seems fair to say that it should occupy the lowest level on the scale of literary merit. Surely a few graceful lines do not compensate for the glaring deficiencies that have been pointed out. Because of its derivation from the *Orlando Furioso,* it preserves a certain curiosity value. Considered purely as a dramatic work, it is almost unreadable.

13. *Del engaño hacer virtud*

The legend of Rosimunda, a grisly tale of revenge which unfolds against a backdrop of sixth-century tribal rivalries, reached the Spanish reading public in two sixteenth-century works. The ultimate source of the legend, Paulus Diaconus' *De Gestis Longobardorum* (c. 790), provided Pedro Mexía with material for the version he included in the *Silva de varia lección* (1540). Later in the century Gabriel Lobo Laso de la Vega versified the legend as found in Mexía.[57]

The account given in Laso de la Vega's *romance* is as follows: Alboino, King of the Lombards, after defeating King Chinismundo of the Gepids, has a goblet fashioned from the skull of his victim as a symbol of victory. Having captured Chinismundo's daughter Rosimunda in the same battle, Alboino, "ciego de amor," makes her his wife. Some time after the marriage Alboino arranges a banquet in Verona, at which Rosimunda finds the goblet placed before her. After drinking from the vessel, she is informed of its origin by Alboino. Having resolved to bring about the death of her husband, she appeals to Elmige, one of Alboino's retainers, to serve as the agent of her vengeance. When Elmige agrees to attempt the murder, provided a certain Paradeo can be persuaded to act as his accomplice, Rosimunda applies to the latter, only to meet with his refusal. Knowing that he

---

[57] The text of Laso de la Vega's *romance* is reproduced by Raymond R. MacCurdy, ed., *"Morir pensando matar" y "La vida en el ataúd,"* by Francisco de Rojas, Clásicos Castellanos, 153 (Madrid: Espasa-Calpe, S. A., 1961), pp. xxix-xxxii. MacCurdy apparently did not know *Del engaño hacer virtud*.

is in the habit of spending the night with his mistress, Rosimunda contrives to substitute herself for the lady. After Paradeo has enjoyed her carnally, the queen threatens him with death if he does not carry out her command. Thus compelled, Paradeo joins Elmige, and the two kill the king one day while he is sleeping. After the murder Elmige and Rosimunda flee to Ravenna, where Rosimunda becomes enamoured of a certain Longinos. In an effort to dispose of Elmige, whom she has meanwhile wed, she gives him a poisoned drink. While the venom is taking effect, Elmige forces her to drink from the vessel offered to him. Both expire at the same time, "por paga de sus engaños."

Three seventeenth-century Spanish plays which draw from the legend are known. Two of these are tragedies: *Morir pensando matar,* printed under Francisco de Rojas Zorrilla's name in *Parte treinta y tres* of *Doce comedias famosas de varios autores* (Valencia, 1642), and *La razón busca venganza,* ascribed to Manuel Morchón in *Parte novena* of *Comedias escogidas de los mejores ingenios de España* (Madrid, 1657). The third play, *Del engaño hacer virtud,* reveals no link with *Morir pensando matar,* other than in the use of some of the same legendary material, which was accessible in non-dramatic form. The present writer has not had access to *La razón busca venganza*; however, that it is described as a tragedy would seem to preclude a close connection with *Del engaño hacer virtud.*

As far as can be determined, *Del engaño hacer virtud* has survived only in an undated *suelta* printed under Cubillo's name.[58] Though La Barrera may have known the play, as can be inferred from his supposition that it is the same as *Los casados por fuerza,* a *comedia* ascribed to Cubillo in Medel's *Índice,* there is no evidence that any subsequent investigator has had access to it. The date of composition has not been established, and no record of performance has been found.

A very diluted form of the legend of Rosimunda finds its way into *Del engaño hacer virtud.* Cubillo retains the setting and Rosimunda's marriage to the slayer of her father, but he opens the way for a new treatment by portraying Rosimunda as falling in love with Albuino (Cubillo's name for Alboino) before the marriage. The goblet

---

[58] The only copy I have been able to locate is in the British Museum.

fashioned for Albuino from the skull of his victim is also retained, but the purpose it serves is very different from its function in the legend. In earlier versions Rosimunda determines to kill Albuino when he presents her with the cup at a banquet. In Cubillo's *comedia* Albuino, by his possession of the cup, fails to fulfill the religious requirement of giving burial to his victim; thus he brings down upon himself the wrath of the gods in the form of mental derangement. Since Albuino interprets the disturbances to which he is subject as evidences of divine displeasure at his marriage rather than as punishment for not restoring the skull, he becomes estranged from the bride he loves. Cubillo withholds the banquet episode until after Albuino's madness has been established; hence the cup is ineffective as a means of arousing a thirst for revenge in Rosimunda, who by this time is convinced that her husband is not responsible for his actions. Rosimunda's substitution of herself for her cousin Laura, to whom Albuino turns seeking the tranquility denied him in his marriage, probably has its origin in passages in Mexía and Laso de la Vega telling of Rosimunda's substitution of herself for Paradeo's mistress.

The play contrived out of material from the legend and new elements is an unhappy combination of Senecan turbulence and *intriga novelesca*. The modifications that the playwright imposes on the legend lead to numerous improbabilities and inconsistencies. One is asked to believe not only that Rosimunda would fall in love with her father's murderer but also that she would not be troubled by her husband's failure to give rest to the corpse of his victim. In view of the importance the playwright attaches to the unburied corpse in bringing down the wrath of the gods upon Albuino and in keeping alive in Rosimunda's grandfather, Turisendo, a desire that his son's death be avenged, one can scarcely believe that Rosimunda would remain unaffected.

What little interest the play might evoke would appear to rest on melodramatic episodes — Albuino's narrow escape from death at Turisendo's court, Albuino's dream, the appearance of the ghost of his victim, the grotesque banquet, and the complicated comings and goings in the palace apartments. The playwright's lack of control over his material is apparent not only in the feeble motivations of some of the violent episodes but in the resolution of the plot. After sustaining a Senecan atmosphere until about midway through Act III, he suddenly introduces an episode typical of a *comedia de capa y espada* whereby Rosimunda contrives to take Laura's place in an assignation with Albuino. After what has gone before, it is not dramatically convincing that the king's sleeping with his wife should bring his madness to an end. The fact that the corpse has been laid to rest would be a much better reason for the gods to free Albuino. Yet only in the final lines is it indicated that he has given burial to the murdered prince.

Evidences of clumsy construction can also be seen in the poetic style. The language is not extravagant, yet secondary characters all too often converse at length on matters of no consequence. The *gracioso* Barreno, who is neither amusing nor necessary to the plot, is assigned a large number of lines, chiefly plot-filling observations on seventeenth-century life.

In other *comedias* by Cubillo one finds the same failure to utilize the dramatic potential of sources that is evident in *Del engaño hacer virtud*. A case in point is *La honestidad defendida de Elisa Dido, reina y fundadora de Cartago*. Just as he discards Rosimunda's murder of her husband from the traditional elements considered for inclusion in the first play, so he does not choose to treat Elisa Dido's suicide in the second. In each instance his decision to truncate the legend implies a rejection of its original theme in favor of one that carries much less impact. To his credit, it should nevertheless be recalled that *La tragedia del duque de Verganza* is testimony that he was not always unwilling to come to grips with tragic subject matter.

CHAPTER III

COMEDIAS DE COSTUMBRES

In addition to the *comedia histórica*, Cubillo exploited other kinds of *comedias* that found favor with theatergoers: the *comedia de capa y espada*, the *comedia palaciega*, and the *comedia de figurón*. Each of these has its distinctive tone in the Golden Age theater, yet all are linked by the common feature of a conflict between love and honor that is resolved happily in a setting of contemporary manners and customs. In Cubillo's extant *comedias de costumbres* the society depicted is primarily urban. The action is occasionally set in the countryside, but one looks in vain for the festive evocation of Spanish rural life found in Lope and Tirso.

1. *Añasco el de Talavera*

Añasco el de Talavera, perhaps the most curious of the *comedias de costumbres* ascribed to Cubillo, is known only through two *sueltas* printed under the playwright's name, without date or place of publication. Cotarelo assigns one of these to the late seventeenth century and the other to the early eighteenth. It can be demonstrated by objective evidence that the *comedia* was written during the period when Cubillo was active in the theatrical world, but no conclusive proof of his authorship has been found. On the other hand, the present writer has observed nothing in the play which would dispute the traditional ascription.

The plot concerns the activities of a young lady of Talavera, Dionisia de Añasco, who protests against her female state by engaging in masculine pursuits. After inflicting a wound on Don Diego, a suitor of her cousin Leonor, Dionisia flees to Madrid, where she becomes known as Añasco el de Talavera. Her father, Marcelo, and a rejected suitor, the Conde Enrico, also appear in Madrid, as do Don Juan, Leonor, and Don Diego, a friend of Don Juan. After a series of adventures Dionisia accepts Juan in marriage, and Diego receives Leonor.

The ultimate source of the title of the *comedia* is a *jácara* describing the recollections that pass through the mind of a certain *rufián*, Añasco el de Talavera, as he wanders through the rooms and patios of an abandoned house of prostitution. J. M. Blecua believes that the verses were prompted by a *pragmática* issued by Philip IV on 4 February 1623, ordering the closing of all *mancebías* and *casas públicas*.[1] A 72-line *jácara* on Añasco was published anonymously in the *Primavera y flor de los mejores romances* (Zaragoza, 1636) and was reprinted in the 1659 edition. A 108-line version came out under Quevedo's name in *El parnaso español* (1648). The 16-line fragment inserted in Act II of the play is closer to the version of 1648 than to that of 1636, but since allusions to contemporary events suggest that the *comedia* should be dated before 1648, it may well be that the version ascribed to Quevedo was in circulation some years earlier.

The *comedia* was apparently written during the reign of Philip IV, as indicated by a *romance* on the brilliant character of that monarch's court given in Act II. Moreover, an allusion to the siege of Leucate, first noticed by Cotarelo, would argue for 1637 as a *terminus a quo*.[2] In view of this allusion and one to a campaign near Bayonne which took place in late 1636,[3] it would seem that *Añasco el de Talavera* was written shortly after these events, when they would still have been of topical interest.

On the other hand, some doubts are raised by the allusions to Lope de Vega and Mira de Amescua which Valbuena Prat professes to see. In Act I Dionisia, after disclosing her lack of enthusiasm for

---

[1] José Manuel Blecua, ed., *Obras completas de Francisco de Quevedo*, I (Barcelona: Editorial Planeta, 1963), 1259.

[2]   ¿Cómo? Entréguese Leucata,
       que es su fuerza en extraño reino.   (III)

Leucate, between Narbonne and Perpignan, was besieged by a Spanish force in September 1637.

[3] A ellos, y arda Bayona.   (III)

the Conde Enrico as a suitor, engages in the following exchange with her servant Chacón:

DION.   Nada deso me importa; a quien yo viera
        si algo vencer mi inclinación pudiera
        es a los dos ingenios, que venera
        España por el timbre de su esfera.
CHA.   ¿Quien [sic] son?
DION.   El uno dellos es Belardo.
CHA.   ¡Gran poeta!
DION.   Excelente lo es Lisardo,
        tanto que los ingenios cortesanos
        le han jurado, Chacón, Rey de Romanos.

If 1637 is taken as a *terminus a quo*, would Lope (Belardo) have been praised as a great living poet, when in fact he had died in 1635? If Lisardo is Mira de Amescua, no problem is posed, for Mira lived until 1644. But Lisardo may be Góngora, for Menéndez y Pelayo cites a poem in which he says the names Belardo and Lisardo stand for Lope and Góngora.[4] If Lisardo is indeed Góngora, then attention is directed to an earlier date, for Góngora died in 1627. Certainly it seems more likely that Lope and Góngora would have been praised as the greatest Spanish poets of the time than that Lope and Mira would have been coupled in reputation. So then, if the play was written before Lope's death in 1635, the allusions to military engagements at Bayonne and Leucate must be interpolations. The same would be true if the play was written before Góngora's death in 1627. Yet it may that Belardo and Lisardo do not represent real poets, but only characters in the play, for at the academy meeting in Act II Don Diego makes his poetic offering under the name Belardo, and at the same gathering another member is introduced as Lisardo.

As is not surprising in the case of a play which was apparently printed only twice and is moreover by a minor author, *Añasco el de Talavera* has been little noticed. Schaeffer calls it unoriginal and flatly absurd. Cotarelo, more favorably disposed, describes it as "escrita con mucha soltura y gracejo" and as revealing "una continua ironía y burla de las mujeres literatas y mamirachas." The prison scenes, he says, are "exactamente vistas y dibujadas." Carmen Bravo Villasante, dealing with the *comedia* because it includes a *mujer vestida de*

---

[4] Menéndez y Pelayo, XIII, cxiii-cxiv.

hombre,[5] contends that even if Cubillo is satirizing this convention, he loses his balance in the presentation of Dionisia, "el más desaforado ejemplo de mujer hombruna, de caso contra naturaleza." Bravo Villasante finds Dionisia's declaration of love to her cousin Leonor in Act I tasteless, expecially as each is aware of the other's sex.[6] She finds equally inexcusable that Cubillo should allow the dubious morality of the relationship between Dionisia and Leonor to intervene later, when the former out of jealousy almost kills her cousin's suitor.

In a superficial way *Añasco el de Talavera* recalls *comedias de costumbres* by Tirso and Mira which center around the adventures of a young woman in male disguise. In such plays as Tirso's *Don Gil de las calzas verdes* and *El amor médico* and Mira's *La fénix de Salamanca,* the *dama* dons male attire in order to pursue her lover; that is, the disguise is primarily a convenience that enables her to move about more freely than social conventions would normally permit. She does not, however, acquire a masculine viewpoint when she assumes the dress of the opposite sex. On the contrary, her femininity is frequently enhanced by her costume.

Alongside this type of *mujer vestida de hombre,* there appears on the Spanish stage the warrior maiden who assumes male dress because it is in accord with her unfeminine habits and outlook. It is with this second type that Dionisia's real affinities exist, for even though she moves about in the setting of a *comedia de capa y espada,* she possesses traits which would fit her for the army-leading role of an Amazon. It has been seen in the historical plays that the unfeminine woman of belligerent propensities was no stranger to Cubillo, but in no other play attributed to him does a *mujer hombruna* have so prominent a role.

For the present-day reader, the *comedia* is primarily of interest as an illustration of the extremes to which a playwright would go in responding to the public's demand for *mujeres vestidas de hombres*.[7]

---

[5] Carmen Bravo Villasante, *La mujer vestida de hombre en el teatro español* (Madrid: Revista de Occidente, 1955), pp. 155-57.

[6] The amorous scene in Act II of *El amor cómo ha de ser* between the Duquesa Olimpia and Isabela, who the Duquesa thinks is a man, is also disagreeably suggestive.

[7] In this connection, the lines below are of interest:

DIONISIA. Lindos cuidados por cierto.
CHACÓN. Pues si en toda esta comedia
el poeta lo ha dispuesto

A catalogue of Dionisia's activities bears out the exaggerated nature of her role: She fences with her servant, makes a declaration of love to Leonor, leaves the latter's suitor for dead after a duel, turns an academy meeting into a rout, starts a fight in prison, roams the streets of Madrid with four knives concealed on her person, duels with a captain and two soldiers, takes on an *alguacil* and his assistants, holds off her would-be captors from a tower, slides down a rope from the tower, and duels once again with her cousin's suitor.

Devising a vehicle for a *mujer vestida de hombre* must have been uppermost in Cubillo's mind, for after Act I there is only the feeblest pretense at a plot. The situation when Dionisia arrives in Madrid at the opening of Act II and when she is released from prison at the end of the act is essentially the same. There being nothing in Act II which could give impetus to an additional act, the playwright opens Act III by contriving an insult to Marcelo on the part of Juan in order to furnish a pretext for the succession of duels in which Dionisia subsequently engages. In this act she is, as Bravo Villasante says, "peor que un hombre bravo, es un matón chulo y un pendenciero matasiete."

Two highlights of an otherwise sterile work are a burlesque of a literary academy and a vignette of prison life. In the first of these, the noble patron who presides, the pseudonyms of the members, and the recitations on assigned topics lend an air of authenticity to the proceedings. Academic pedantry comes in for a lively bit of ridicule when one of the members takes exception to Dionisia's failure to describe the nose of the lady who is the subject of her literary portrait. The quickness with which the members cast aside their dignity in defense of a matter of no moment implies a further commentary on the tendency of academicians to attach importance to trifles.

In the prison scene, with its mixed bag of figures from low life, one catches a vivid glimpse of the world of the *hampa*. Contributing to the atmosphere are "un viejo con alforjas al cuello, un valiente, un

---

      de suerte que siempre andamos
      a palos ¿es mucho?
  DIONISIA.   Necio,
      es porque admiran prodigios
      en mujeres destos tiempos,
      unas dando cuchilladas
      y otras escribiendo versos. (III)

ciego con bordón y guitarra, una ciega, un saludador con un crucifijo al cuello," and two women who are presumably prostitutes. The singing of the *jácara* about Añasco el de Talavera, the rough speech of the prisoners, their bullying and squabbling — all lend color.

2. *El amor cómo ha de ser*

El amor cómo ha de ser appears to have been written between 1650, when Adrián López (whose troupe Cubillo says in *El enano de las musas* first performed it) became an *autor de comedias*,[8] and 1652, when the *aprobación* was granted for *El enano*, which contains the earliest extant text.[9] No references have been found in the play to contemporary events, persons, or practices which would permit a reduction of these chronological limits.

The plot deals with the misunderstandings that ensue when the Marquesa Isabela disguises herself as the Conde Claros in order to prevent a marriage between her seducer Don Gastón and the Duquesa Olimpia de Bretaña. (Olimpia, attracted to Gastón, has received permission from the King of Naples to terminate her engagement to the count if he does not appear in Calabria within thirty days.) While on his way to join the duchess, the real Conde Claros encounters the king's sister, the Infanta Rosimunda, in Miraflores and decides to gamble on winning her hand when she obliquely indicates an interest in him. In Miraflores reports of the activities of the false count in Calabria obstruct the progress of the real count's courtship of the Infanta. In Calabria the presence of the false count, coupled with reports concerning the real count, complicates the action. All the principals eventually meet in Miraflores, where the solution of the puzzle leads to announcements of marriages that will be celebrated: the Conde Claros and the Infanta Rosimunda, Gastón and Isabela, and the King of Naples and the Duquesa Olimpia.

Commentary on the play appears as early as 1785, when an anonymous reviewer, writing in the *Memorial Literario* on the occasion of performances in Madrid at the Teatro del Príncipe on April 5-7, says that "[la comedia] parece emendada. Bastante desarreglada en

---

[8] Rennert, p. 506.

[9] Other editions are: Madrid: Doña Teresa de Guzmán, n.d.; in *Comedias escogidas de Álvaro Cubillo de Aragón* (Madrid: Ortega y Compañía, 1826); in BAE, 47 (Madrid: M. Rivadeneyra, 1858).

lugar y tiempo; tiene algunos episodios remotos de la acción, y ésta sólo se halla particularmente tratada en la jornada tercera, en que reina la equivocación, que produce algunas buenas situaciones." [10]

The fullest study comes in 1826 from the anonymous editor of the *Comedias escogidas* of Cubillo, who considers that the chief defect in the play's construction is that after arousing interest in Isabela through her search for her faithless lover, the playwright relegates her to a secondary role. (This occurs after Cubillo introduces Rosimunda, whose amorous relationship with the Conde Claros claims chief attention for the remainder of the play.) Believing that the models for the play are to be found in Tirso's *Don Gil de las calzas verdes* and *El vergonzoso en palacio,* the editor argues that since Cubillo does not equal Tirso as a poet, it is not surprising that *El amor cómo ha de ser* is inferior to its models. Nevertheless, he contends that Cubillo's play "tiene bastante mérito, por la nobleza y verdad de los caracteres, por el interés que inspira, por los diálogos y la versificación, que generalmente es fácil y corriente."

Critical comments by Cotarelo and Valbuena Prat in the main follow previously established lines. Cotarelo adds that "el excesivo miramiento de [Rosimunda] llega a hacerse cansado y aun algo necio y la travesura de [Isabela] es muy poca digna de ser imitada." Valbuena Prat, with his tendency to see traces of decadent super-refinement in Cubillo, says that in this *comedia* the characters are beginning to turn into "muñecos estilizados con los que el autor ha de jugar."

The *comedia,* even if its connection with a previous work is not sufficiently close for it to be called a *refundición,* contains similarities to both *Don Gil de las calzas verdes* and *El vergonzoso en palacio* that appear to be more than coincidental. From *Don Gil* Cubillo may have taken the situation of the young woman who dons male attire in order to court the rival for whom her lover has abandoned her. Tirso's Doña Juana, who becomes Don Gil in order to block her erstwhile lover Don Martín's marriage to Doña Inés, has a counterpart in Cubillo's Doña Isabela, who pretends to be the Conde Claros in an effort to prevent Don Gastón from wedding the Duquesa Olimpia. It will be recalled that in Tirso's play Doña Juana, in assuming the identity of Don Gil, avails herself of the fictitious name under which

---

[10] These are the only documented performances of *El amor cómo ha de ser.*

Don Martín goes to Madrid to court Doña Inés, whereas in *El amor cómo ha de ser* Isabela, in pretending to be the Conde Claros, assumes the identity of one of the other characters in the play. In this way Cubillo links his two plots, the second of which, the Conde Claros-Infanta Rosimunda intrigue, has antecedents in the situation Tirso uses in the Magdalena-Mireno courtship in *El vergonzoso en palacio*: the efforts of a highborn lady to attract and encourage a young man of inferior station without tipping her hand too much. In both plays a subterfuge on the part of the lady keeps the young man near. Doña Magdalena asks that Mireno instruct her in the language of love so that she may declare her affection to her betrothed in suitable terms; the Infanta invents a lady for whom she pretends to speak.

Since character portrayal is secondary to plot complication, one does not find in the *comedia* a penetrating analysis of "el amor cómo ha de ser." Even so, various responses to the opposite sex are presented, albeit superficially, through the principals. Isabela, like Tirso's Doña Juana, pursues her lover not so much for himself as because marriage to her seducer will satisfy the offense to her honor. To Don Gastón, the unworthy object of her pursuit, women are merely a means to worldly advancement, just as they are to Tirso's Don Martín. In contrast, the Infanta's love for the Conde Claros is an innocent emotion, much more thoroughly hedged in by social conventions than is Magdalena's in *El vergonzoso en palacio*. The bold Magdalena eventually compromises herself with Mireno in order to force her father's hand; in the Infanta's case, the solution for a seemingly hopeless love for a social inferior does not present itself until the king decides to take a non-royal mate, thereby opening the way for his sister's marriage to the count. In the latter the transforming power of love is seen as he gradually changes from an opportunist to an adoring, idealistic suitor.

Three dialogues between the Conde and the Infanta go far towards making their courtship the most attractive feature of the play. In these scenes, placed one to each act, one perceives the alterations in their feeling for each other as they verbally advance and withdraw, all the while maintaining the fiction of a mysterious lady. In Act I it is the Infanta who makes the initial advances by inventing the *dama* supposedly in love with the Conde. In Act II it is clear that the Conde is beginning to fall in love with the Infanta, who nevertheless is not sufficiently confident to discard the fiction. By the time of their interview in Act III, the Infanta expresses her love in unmistakable terms, even though she continues to utilize the device of the *dama*.

The scenes between the Conde and the Infanta bring to mind those between the Conde Ramón and the Infanta Urraca in Cubillo's *La corona del agravio*, with the difference that in the latter play the turgid style obscures rather than illuminates nuances of the lovers' attitudes towards each other, a condition which does not prevail in *El amor cómo ha de ser* except in the first dialogue, where a debate on *amar* and *agradecer* is introduced.

The delicacy and charm that characterize the dialogues between the Conde and the Infanta are not apparent in the scenes in which the village maiden Menga and the Duquesa Olimpia become enamoured of the false Conde. In both cases Cubillo upsets the fine balance between good and bad taste that is inevitable in romantic scenes involving a woman disguised as a man. When Menga becomes attracted to the false Conde, there is much embracing between the two, and the dialogue is disagreeably equivocal. In Isabela's scene with the Duquesa the treatment is equally suggestive. Olimpia becomes so eager to enjoy the pleasures of marriage with the supposed Conde that she wants the ceremony performed that very day.

The poetic style of *El amor cómo ha de ser* is typical of Cubillo's *comedias de costumbres* in that it is graceful without being scintillating. Like the *primer galán* in other light works by Cubillo, the Conde Claros uses a great deal of figurative language. The Infanta's hand is an "azucena de cinco hojas" (III, 173c),[11] and her lips are "fruto y cristal fugitivo / que se ve mas no se goza" (III, 173a). Ridiculing prevailing fashions in poetic language, the rustic Bras has this to say:

> ¿No es bobería llamar
> mohatra de luz la luna,
> arbitrista a la fortuna,
> hamaca de nieve al mar,
> carcaj de rayos al sol?
> Pues celebrado esto ha sido;
> que anda agora muy valido
> este lenguaje español. (II, 169a)

---

[11] Citations are to the text in BAE, 47.

As in several other plays, Cubillo inserts a highly stylized description of a woman which he assigns to a character of low station. Usually it is the *gracioso* who describes one of the *damas*; here it is the village girl Menga.

In brief, it can be said that *El amor cómo ha de ser* shows a measure of the competence in treating the conventions of the *comedia de capa y espada* which Cubillo demonstrates more clearly elsewhere. His play has neither the breathtakingly ingenious plot complications of *Don Gil de las calzas verdes* nor characters whose romantic relationship is developed as captivatingly as that of Magdalena and Mireno in *El vergonzoso en palacio*. Nevertheless, the complications proceeding from Isabela's assumption of the Conde Claros' identity are well handled, and several particularly attractive scenes are given to the count and the Infanta Rosimunda.

3. *Perderse por no perderse*

Perderse por no perderse, first printed in *Parte octava* of *Comedias nuevas escogidas de los mejores ingenios de España* (Madrid, 1657),[12] is thought by Cotarelo to have been written after the publication of *El enano de las musas* (1654). Cotarelo adduces no supporting evidence; however, that the play was written after the death on 24 December 1643 of the Italian scenic designer Cosme Lotti[13] appears to be implied in the text. The *gracioso* Merlín, commenting on his master's love for a lady whom he is obliged to court in his sovereign's name, has this to say:

> Ésta es la mayor tramoya,
> porque tocamos, y vemos
> una lealtad hacia fuera,
> y un amor hacia dentro.
> Malos años para el Bacho;
> Cosmelot [sic] fue un zurdo, un necio,
> que para aclarar de un alma
> los encontrados afectos,

---

[12] Other editions are: N.p., n.d.; Valencia: Joseph y Thomas de Orga, 1781.

[13] Emilio Cotarelo y Mori, *Actores famosos del siglo XVII: Sebastián de Prado y su mujer Bernarda Ramírez* (Madrid: Tip. de la "Rev. de Arch., Bibl. y Museos," 1916), p. 112, note.

>   no hay líneas, compases, vigas,
>   maromas, ni carpinteros.[14] (II, 18b)

The plot deals with the efforts of Ruy Gómez de Ávalos, a newcomer at the court of Fernando of Naples, to secure the king's patronage and to win the hand of Estefanía, daughter of Octavio, the king's former *ayo*. The machinations of a courtier, Federico, who is envious of Ruy Gómez' advancement in the king's favor and jealous of the progress of his courtship of Estefanía, pose various obstacles. A more serious complication develops when the king, who is himself attracted to Estefanía, asks Ruy Gómez to pay court to her on his behalf. Dutifully obliging, Ruy Gómez puts aside his own feelings. The king is eventually shamed into withdrawing his suit, and Federico is neutralized as a rival.

Brief observations concerning the play have been made by Schaeffer, Cotarelo, and Valbuena Prat. Schaeffer finds the plot logically and clearly handled and some of the characterizations excellent, especially those of Ruy Gómez and the king. Cotarelo concurs with Schaeffer in regard to the plot and perceives in the versification "la dulce facilidad y grave ternura propias al autor granadino." For Valbuena, who sees in the "ternura y delicadeza" an advance over *La perfecta casada,* the most interesting character is Ruy Gómez, whose "vaivenes de fortuna, ... nobleza y bondad, unidos a la bizarría y bravura de su espíritu, están sabiamente colocados ante la fina psicología de la dama."

Efforts to demonstrate Cubillo's indebtedness to a specific *comedia* by another playwright are likely to prove unprofitable in view of the many instances of kindred situations in the theater of the Golden Age. Valbuena Prat suggests Act I of Luis Vélez de Guevara's *A lo que obliga el ser rey* as a possible source.[15] The germ of the conflict is indeed present in Act I of Vélez' *comedia,* in which King Alfonso el Sabio, whose marriage to Doña Violante de Navarra has been arranged, pays court to Doña Hipólita de Vargas, who seeks to discourage his attentions, since her affection is reserved for Don Ximen

---

[14] Citations are to *Perderse por no perderse* (Valencia: Joseph y Thomas de Orga, 1781).

[15] *A lo que obliga el ser rey,* not printed until 1658, was performed in Madrid by the company of Roque de Figueroa on 28 March 1628 (Spencer and Schevill, p. 6).

de Vargas Manrique. Even so, one can find similar situations in many another play of the period; and in fact the king whose personal inclinations are at odds with the obligations of his office is a recurring figure in plays by Cubillo. Moreover, the situation whereby the king's lack of self-discipline is shown in *Perderse por no perderse,* his obliging a subordinate to act as his proxy in conducting a courtship of a lady he knows the latter loves, is utilized by Cubillo in *El señor de Noches Buenas,* which was very probably written considerably earlier.

The action at the Neapolitan court is set against a background of the French intervention at the end of the fifteenth century. In the presentation of characters and in references to events, the playwright reveals some knowledge of the period, even though several incidents which he places in an explicit historical context are either entirely fanciful or are set in an incorrect chronological sequence. The King Fernando of the play is seemingly Ferdinando II of Naples, who ruled from January 1495 until his death the following year. The fine humanistic education that this king is known to have had is possessed by the Fernando of the play, who excels in all the arts of war and peace. The historical Ferdinando, however, was unpopular with his subjects; Cubillo's Fernando is depicted as basically sympathetic. Ruy Gómez de Ávalos can be linked with a family which produced several colorful figures in both Spain and Italy in the fifteenth and sixteenth centuries. In the play Ruy Gómez identifies himself as a descendant of Ruy López de Ávalos (1357-1428), Constable of Castile, who fled to Aragon in 1422 when his political fortunes suffered eclipse at the Castilian court. In Aragon the constable's several sons gained the protection of Alfonso V, who took them to Italy when he made good his claim to the Neapolitan throne. Among the descendants of Ruy López de Ávalos who made their mark in Italy were Iñigo Lopez d'Avalos (d. 1481) and Ferdinando Francesco d'Avalos, Marquis of Pescara, the victor of Pavia in 1525. Hence the success at court achieved by the Ruy Gómez of the play recalls the *privanza* to which the Avalos family owed much of its prominence, first in Castile and later in Naples.

The historical elements in *Perderse por no perderse* are thus used to introduce elements of the *comedia de privanza,* a subgenre in which may be found portrayals of model *privados* as well as fallen favorites. Ruy Gómez, with his years of loyal military service to the late king, stands in contrast to the untried young Fernando, who for the first time finds himself free to make decisions without the guidance of an *ayo*. The means, however, by which Cubillo shows that it is possible for a man of integrity to survive at court and moreover to become a stabilizing influence on the sovereign would seem to qualify *Perderse por no perderse* for inclusion among his *comedias de costumbres*. It is not in the political sphere but in the king's private life that Ruy Gómez makes the sacrifice that leads the sovereign to recognition of the need for self-mastery. So it is that much of the play offers scope for the playwright to exercise his ingenuity in devising such typical incidents of romantic comedy as assignations and impersonations. The customs and manners reflected are, moreover, emphatically those of seventeenth-century Spain.

The plot construction, while not in any way remarkable, offers a good illustration of the basic precepts set forth by Lope de Vega. Act I, after opening with a standard expository dialogue between master and servant, moves along with an attention-getting incident of a runaway coach, variations on which appear in many a play of the period. The *galán, dama,* and a rival suitor having been brought together here, a further complication is introduced when Ruy Gómez goes to the palace. The pace diminishes somewhat with his recital of his exploits in campaigns against the French, but it quickens by the end of the act when he is asked to court Estefanía in the king's name. The progress of Act II flows principally from overheard conversations, mistaken identities, and *equívocos*. Act III is bolstered by the activities of Federico, whose role as a rival is established early in the play. Federico's part in swordplay at the close of Act II contains the seeds of his intervention in Act III.

The impression of a somewhat frivolous development and resolution is reinforced by the *gracioso* Merlín's propensity for stepping out of his role as a confidential servant and shattering the illusion of the play-world by commenting on theatrical conventions. For example, when the king inquires how he found his way into the royal presence, the *gracioso* replies:

> ¿Cómo?
> Con la ordinaria licencia,
> que ya los graciosos tienen
> en virtud de la comedia. (I, 10b)

Later, when Ruy Gómez remarks that the confusion would have ended if Estefanía's cousin Beatriz had identified herself during a rendezvous at Posillipo, Merlín observes:

> Y se acabara el enredo
> de la comedia, y no hubiera
> más lances, ni más empeños.   (III, 32a)

The dialogue is for the most part functional and free from *culteranismos*. There are some exceptions, however, for three plot-fillers that Cubillo often employs are inserted: a long report of services, culminating in a metaphorical description of an encounter with an adversary (I, 6a-8a); a debate on *amar* and *agredecer*, here between Estefanía and Ruy Gómez (II, 16b-17a); and a highly ornamented description of a woman, spoken as usual by the *gracioso* (III, 27a-27b).

In conclusion, *Perderse por no perderse* is Cubillo's only extant play that can be properly described as a *comedia palaciega*. The basic conflict is interesting, even if its implications are explored within the conventions of a form which relies heavily on contrived incidents. Characterization, notwithstanding the position taken by previous critics, does not seem as vigorous as in *El señor de Noches Buenas,* where much of the action also arises from a *galán*'s being ordered to court his own *dama* on another's behalf. It will be seen that in the latter play Cubillo manages to integrate character and plot much more closely. It may well be that in *Perderse por no perderse* the conflict is robbed of intensity because the underlying didactic aim requires that the king be established as fundamentally good despite his impetuosity. If the *comedia* was first performed in the 1640's, as internal evidence suggests, one wonders what thoughts might have occurred to any spectators who were reminded of the accession of the young Philip IV in 1621.

4. *La perfecta casada: Prudente, sabia y honrada*

From the time of its publication in 1583 Fray Luis de León's little treatise on the obligations of the Christian wife, *La perfecta casada,* met with wide acceptance. Printed twice in 1583, it reappeared five times between 1586 and 1632; a steady output of subsequent reprintings attests to its continuing appeal. The ideal of wifely virtue set forth in this best known of Fray Luis's prose works is reflected in Cubillo's *comedia* of the same title, which is first mentioned in a record of payment made to Alonso de Olmedo on 23 December 1636 for a performance given before Philip IV.[16] The earliest known text came out under Cubillo's name in *Parte doce* of *Comedias nuevas escogidas* (Madrid, 1658), where it carries the title of *Prudente, sabia y honrada*.[17]

The plot of the *comedia* is as follows: The King of Sicily gives a young noblewoman, Estefanía, in marriage to César, commander of the fleet, as a reward for a victory over the Turks. César, who is drawn to a young captive, Rosimunda, who accompanies him to court, accepts his bride reluctantly. After the marriage he remains indifferent to Estefanía and becomes increasingly attentive to Rosimunda. Estefanía meanwhile conducts herself with great forbearance. Her abnegation and devotion finally awaken César's love; Rosimunda is humbled by her mistress' quiet heroism. Just after husband and wife are reconciled, they learn that Rosimunda is César's long-lost sister.

None of Cubillo's *comedias de costumbres*, with the exception of *Las muñecas de Marcela*, has received as much favorable attention as *La perfecta casada*, which has elicited almost unanimous commendation for its characterization of Estefanía. Occasional reservations concerning other features become insignificant when weighed against the rhapsodies over Cubillo's edifying portrait of an exemplary Christian wife. The anonymous editor of the 1826 edition of several of Cubillo's plays dwells at some length on the elevated moral tone that Estefanía gives to the *comedia*, and he praises its construction, style, and versification. The foregoing encomiums are echoed by Schack, who says that "quizás en pocas obras observemos un carácter tan angelical, un corazón y unas costumbres tan puras, que resplandecen

---

[16] Shergold and Varey, p. 233.

[17] Other printed editions are: N.p., n.d.; N.p., n.d. (another edition); Sevilla: Manuel Nicolás Vázquez, n.d.; Valladolid: Alonso del Riego, n.d.; Madrid: Impr. de Antonio Sanz, 1746; Málaga, n.d.; in *Comedias escogidas de Álvaro Cubillo de Aragón* (Madrid: Ortega y Compañía, 1826); in BAE, 47 (Madrid: M. Rivadeneyra, 1858). After the first printing, the title usually appears as *La perfecta casada*, with *Prudente, sabia y honrada* as the subtitle. Two manuscripts of the *comedia* are known. Biblioteca Nacional MS. 15.471 is written in a seventeenth-century hand; Biblioteca Nacional MS. 16.970 is dated later than the first printing, as indicated by the following note (p. 37v°): "En Osuna el 6 dias del mes de agosto de 1668, Jose Thimoteo, residente en esta villa y apuntador maior dela compañia de Francisca Lopez, autora de comedias por su magestad."

siempre serenas hasta en las tentaciones, humillaciones y extravíos." Cotarelo, who regards Estefanía as Cubillo's outstanding female character, says that she is "uno de los primores psicológicos que suelen hallarse en el teatro de [Cubillo]." He sees some inverisimilitude in the expression of the mysterious bond between César and Rosimunda, who turn out to be brother and sister, although he recognizes the difficulty which the treatment of this relationship posed for the playwright if he was to remain within the confines of good taste. Valbuena Prat finds the plot relatively weak, yet despite this qualification, his praise of the portrait of a perfect wife is as unreserved as that of any previous critic.

Although such enthusiasm for *La perfecta casada* seems disproportionate to its merits, the play does represent a higher level of achievement than *La honestidad defendida*, Cubillo's other *comedia* associated with literature in defense of women. Wooden characters, sluggish movement, and an overblown style prevent the latter work from arousing more than academic interest, whereas in *La perfecta casada* the didactic element is embodied in attractive characters, the pace of the action is fairly rapid, and the style is generally graceful.

In both plays the defense of virtue, whether it be of the widowed Dido or the Christian wife Estefanía, is served up with all the paraphernalia of a *comedia de capa y espada*. In *La honestidad defendida* the attempt to harmonize a vindication of Dido with the requirements of a comedy of intrigue is a resounding failure; in *La perfecta casada* the characterization of Estefanía is more closely linked to the progress of the action. Even so, external devices typical of comedies of intrigue, not character, keep the plot moving and bring it to a conclusion. [18]

The portrayal of Estefanía follows the precepts found in the aforementioned work of Fray Luis de León. Fray Luis, after reminding his readers of Christ's injunction to take up the cross, goes on to say that "la cruz que cada uno ha de llevar y por donde ha de llegar a juntarse con Cristo, propiamente es la obligación y la carga que cada

---

[18] Act I is very similar to Act I of *La mayor venganza de honor,* where it will be recalled that Cubillo makes substantial changes in the legend of the Comendadores de Córdoba. In both plays, although the motivations are different, a triangle situation is created when a king arbitrarily awards a woman to one of his commanders. In *La mayor venganza de honor* the wife cannot forget her former suitor; in *La perfecta casada* the situation is reversed in that the husband retains affection for another woman.

uno tiene por razón del estado en que vive; y quien cumple con ella cumple con Dios y sale con su intento, y queda honrado e ilustre, y como por el trabajo de la cruz, alcanza el descanso que merece." [19] Thus "la obligación y la carga" imposed on Estefanía by virtue of her place in life is submission to her husband, as before her marriage it had been acceptance of the will of the other males responsible for her well-being, her father and the king.

Given the fact that the social code prescribed that a married woman should be subservient to her husband and considering that Estefanía knows that César has married her against his will, her patience and tolerance are appropriate to the circumstances in which she finds herself. But however much such essentially passive traits may be applauded, they lend themselves with difficulty to moving a plot. The playwright does indeed provide opportunities for Estefanía to demonstrate the qualities that eventually endear her to her husband, but these scenes result from artificially contrived situations, as in Act I, where Estefanía accidentally finds César making advances to Rosimunda; in Act II, where she suddenly appears to lend aid to her husband just as he is about to duel with the king at the conclusion of an elaborate sequence set in motion by a meddlesome servant; and in Act III, where in *capa y espada* tradition César, concealed behind a curtain, overhears both a servant's confession that satisfies him of his wife's fidelity and Estefanía's offer to provide Rosimunda with a more splendid gift than the one he has chosen. It should be said that the offer places a heavy strain on the credulity of a twentieth-century reader, even if he can accept Estefanía's self-effacement up to this point as being the product of a view of women that was valid in Cubillo's time.

The playwright's inability to set up a serious conflict stemming from character portrayal is seen in Rosimunda, whose delineation is conditioned by the fact that she is ultimately to be revealed as César's sister. That no incestuous passion is to be allowed to develop and thus that Rosimunda's presence poses no real threat is apparent at several points, beginning in Act I with César's presentation of his captive, a girl of about the same age as his sister would be. (She had

---

[19] Fray Luis de León, *La perfecta casada*, in *Obras completas castellanas*, ed. P. Félix García, 2nd ed. (Madrid: Biblioteca de Autores Cristianos, 1951), p. 238.

disappeared years earlier after being captured by the Turks.) In this scene Cubillo takes care to indicate that César has been struck by Rosimunda's *inocencia* and *nobleza*, traits which would predispose an audience to favor her. One might think this to be a false lead when Rosimunda first speaks, because, vexed at César's having agreed to marry Estefanía, she conducts herself like an unsympathetic third party. Such a notion is dispelled before the end of the act with her disclosure of her ambivalent feelings towards César as she confides to the *gracioso* Calvatrueno "que le quiero y no le quiero" (I, 114c). [20] In Act II, after César has left Estefanía to go to see her, it becomes apparent through their mutual confidences that his attraction to her is likewise inexplicably curbed. Moreover, Rosimunda has not changed, for she says to him,

> Solo sé por experiencia
> que si te adoro en ausencia
> presente me das temor. (II, 119a)

So it is that Estefanía's task of neutralizing her supposed rival's effect and winning her husband's love is made infinitely easier because no strong sexual desire draws Rosimunda and César together.

The poetic style, which is for the most part graceful, reveals several features which are encountered repeatedly in Cubillo's *comedias*: a long, ornately phrased report of a battle (I, 112b-113b); elegant language placed in the mouth of a character of low social category, the servant Dorotea (II, 116c); and a discursive *cuestión de amor*, here on *amar* and *agradecer* (I, 111c-112a).

In conclusion, it would seem that *La perfecta casada* has been considerably overvalued by previous critics. It has been shown that their commentary, which is based primarily on moral rather than esthetic considerations, leaves the erroneous impression that the portrayal of Estefanía is much more important in motivating the plot that it in fact is. While it is true that in this play Cubillo contends more successfully with the problem of presenting an exemplary character than he does in *La honestidad defendida de Elisa Dido, reina y fundadora de Cartago*, he nevertheless does not accomplish his two-

---

[20] Citations are to the text in BAE, 47.

fold purpose of entertaining and instructing on as high an artistic level as might be inferred from previous criticism.

5. *Las muñecas de Marcela*

Las muñecas de Marcela, first printed in *El enano de las musas* (1654),[21] where Cubillo says that it had been performed by Tomás Fernández [de Cabredo], is mentioned in a document drawn up in Madrid on 19 February 1636, in which *autores de comedias* were ordered to discontinue performing *comedias, bailes,* and *entremeses* which they had not purchased. Among the works cited is *Las muñecas de Marcela,* listed as the property of the *autor* Tomás Fernández.[22] It seems reasonable to assume that if Fernández took steps to protect his rights to the play in mid-February of 1636, it must have been in his repertory by 1635, if not before.

The plot of the *comedia* is as follows: Don Carlos, while being pursued by Valerio, father of a man he has slain, appeals for asylum to an unknown lady, who proves to be the victim's cousin Marcela. Knowing that Carlos has acted in self-defense, Marcela conceals him in a room holding her collection of dolls. Also living in the house are her sister Vitoria, a rabid defender of the code of vengeance, and her brother Luis, whose support of the code is tempered by his love for Carlos' sister Feliciana. Paralleling Marcela's efforts to keep Carlos safely hidden is the growth of an amorous relationship between the two. Finally the intransigent Valerio dies of grief. Shortly afterwards Feliciana gives birth to a child by Luis. Carlos, mistaken for another *galán,* is entrusted with the infant. Since the insult to Luis's honor represented by Carlos' presence in the house is offset by the latter's possession of the child, the differences can be settled by arranging

---

[21] Other printed editions are: Madrid, 1734; N.p., n.d.; in *Comedias escogidas de Álvaro Cubillo de Aragón* (Madrid: Ortega y Compañía, 1826); in *Tesoro del teatro español,* V (Paris: Baudry, 1838); in BAE, 47 (Madrid: M. Rivadeneyra, 1858); in *Teatro selecto* (Barcelona, 1868); in *Las muñecas de Marcela; El señor de Noches Buenas,* ed. Ángel Valbuena Prat, Clásicos Olvidados, 3 (Madrid: Compañía Ibero-americana de Publicaciones, 1928; rpt. Madrid: Ediciones Alcalá, 1966); in *Teatro español: Historia y antología,* IV (Madrid: M. Aguilar, 1943).

[22] Sánchez-Arjona, pp. 309-10. In 1636 Fernández sent a *poder* to Roque de Burgos, a Sevillian merchant, with instructions that the latter try to prevent plays belonging to Fernández from being performed in Seville. *Las muñecas de Marcela* is mentioned again in the *poder* (Sánchez Arjona, p. 310).

marriages between Carlos and Marcela, Luis and Feliciana, and other characters.

To judge from the length and content of critical commentary, *Las muñecas de Marcela* is Cubillo's *comedia de costumbres* which has found the greatest favor with critics. This is not to say that they have been unstinting in their praise; for the most part they have recognized that the play is not without defects, but that its sprightly action, functional dialogue, and winsome leading character engage attention.

The earliest study appears in 1826 in the *Comedias escogidas* of Cubillo, where the anonymous editor observes that the plot is simple and regular and the characters varied and interesting, although somewhat pale. He calls attention to the portrayal of Marcela but argues that Cubillo's talent did not equip him to show the awakening of love with the subtlety that would have been desirable. Nevertheless, he says, "no debemos ser ingratos a Cubillo; pues al fin inventó lo que los otros no inventaron, y nos dejó un buen bosquejo."

Eugenio de Ochoa, writing in 1838, treats the play at some length, but his analysis is essentially a recasting of the earlier one, with an amplification of the point concerning the relationship between the limitations of Cubillo's talents and the delineation of Marcela.[23] In contrast, Schack expresses no reservations about the characterization of Marcela, for he maintains that "se nos presenta con la mayor delicadeza la aparición del sentimiento del amor en una doncella, casi niña." Cotarelo recognizes that among Cubillo's *comedias de costumbres Las muñecas de Marcela* is "la más celebrada por los críticos," but he voices a doubt that it is the best, "atendiendo a otras circunstancias de más alto valor que el buen desarrollo de una acción privada sin grandes emociones del alma." Nevertheless, he applauds the construction of the plot, the skillful blending of the comic and the serious, and the attention given to metric form and poetic language in the play, which he views as "una de las obras que más deleitan en la lectura entre las del teatro antiguo."

With Valbuena Prat and Sáinz de Robles, the tone of criticism changes in that they place considerable emphasis on a high degree of stylization which they profess to see. Valbuena finds throughout a

---

[23] Eugenio de Ochoa, ed., *Tesoro del teatro español, desde su origen (año de 1356) hasta nuestros días*, V (Paris: Baudry, 1838), 163.

"nota de refinada delicadeza" and contends that Cubillo here is "absolutamente en su propio terreno, en el de un juego delicioso." In Valbuena's opinion, the delicate treatment Cubillo accords his material has a parallel in "la fina labor de orfebre." The same critic adds that *Las muñecas de Marcela* is "una de las comedias del XVII que encierra más fuerte dosis de modernidad, de gracia y de finura." Sáinz de Robles, whose estimate is seemingly derived from Valbuena, terms the work a "modelo de obra de orfebrería. Un auténtico y delicioso juego de salón, al que vendría como anillo al dedo una melodía de Mozart."

A reading of the play brings to mind such model Calderonian comedies of intrigue as *Casa con dos puertas mala es de guardar* and *La dama duende,* where a conflict of love and honor unfolds as an elaborate game of hide and seek. The plot contains little that is new, but the stock situations that are inseparable from comedies of intrigue are manipulated to produce an effect of novelty. Moreover, the fact that the *galán* Carlos' hiding place is a room holding Marcela's collection of dolls is an original touch that delicately suggests her ingenuousness.

Cubillo does not put his characters through their paces with the ingenuity of Calderón at his best, but he does contrive complications in a number sufficient to hold interest. The action gets off to a fast start as Carlos, having eluded his pursuer, finds refuge with the latter's niece. The major characters either appear immediately on stage or are referred to in a phrase which defines their function. After this initial presentation, the problem is to prevent Carlos and his adversaries from encountering each other, all the while making sure that suspense is maintained until the action can be brought to a conclusion. Coincidences and hairbreadth escapes which might be deplored elsewhere are fully admissible here and even constitute much of the appeal of a work in which a tone of a playful romp has been established. There are many examples, all of them effective: in Act I, where the stern Valerio almost searches the room; in Act II, where the equally zealous Vitoria, having obtained a key, almost opens the door before she is prevented by the arrival of Valerio and his nephew Luis; in Act III, where Marcela's suitor Octavio, coming at night with news for Luis about the child the latter has fathered on Carlos' sister Feliciana, tells Carlos the story and gives him the baby.

The *gracioso* Beltrán, to whom Cubillo assigns more lines than he usually does to a comic servant, is not a gross figure, even though he possesses the conventional characteristics of fondness for food and drink. Like many other *graciosos,* he intersperses his speech with a liberal sprinkling of *cuentos* and conducts a love affair with a servant girl. He makes his liveliest contributions in Act I, where he invents a dialogue between Marcela's dolls, and in Act III, where he dreams that he is a valiant warrior against the infidel.

In a *comedia* whose appeal rests so heavily on plot manipulation, attention to character portrayal is unexpected, except as is necessary to establish the *galán* as gallantly dashing and the *dama* as sweetly feminine. Carlos is indeed a stereotyped *galán,* falling in love and then lamenting the hopelessness of his passion. But in presenting Marcela on the threshold of womanhood, still bound to childhood pleasures by her collection of dolls and yet able to be drawn romantically to a member of the opposite sex, Cubillo offers something more than a conventional *dama*. It has been seen that he has been censured for not conveying the awakening of adult responses with more subtlety; yet even if he does not capitalize on the situation to the degree that he might, he devises several graceful dialogues between Marcela and Carlos and introduces them at appropriate points.

The treatment of honor is broadly human and may account in part for the modernity mentioned by Valbuena Prat. The attitude taken towards vengeance aligns the characters into two groups: Valerio, Octavio, and Vitoria *versus* Marcela, Carlos, and Luis. The extremes of the two positions are exemplified in Valerio, the embodiment of intransigence, and Marcela, the challenger of the fossilized code. Valerio's singleminded determination to avenge his son's death is revealed in his attempt to burn down the house where he thinks Carlos is hiding and in his extending the guilt to Carlos' family when he thinks that the *galán*'s reported death has cheated him of his victim. The appalling consequences of resolving the conflict between the principles of Christianity and the code of revenge in favor of the latter is implicit in Valerio's reproach when Luis refuses to undertake to exterminate Carlos' relatives:

> Y creed que os quisiera haber hallado,
> menos cristiano, pero más honrado. [24]   (II, 134c)

---

[24] Citations are to the text in BAE, 47.

The depiction of Valerio as unwavering in his desire for revenge sets off Marcela's function as spokesman for a modification of the code. Knowing that Carlos has killed García in self-defense, she would take this circumstance into account in applying the code. Explaining her viewpoint, she says:

> Teodora, parte me toca
> de la ofensa; pero al fin,
> como ni vida se cobra
> para el muerto don García
> ni el agravio es en la honra,
> toda esa crueldad me ofende. (I, 127b)

She makes clear that mercy can temper her sense of outrage when she tells Carlos that "... no es conmigo / la pasión más poderosa / que la piedad" (I, 128a) and expresses her horror at the thought that vengeance should be taken on someone who cannot defend himself: "... mucho se ofende / quien en un rendido toma venganza ..." (I, 128b).

The poetic style of the play is representative of Cubillo at his best; that is to say, it is lively and graceful. The play contains no long speeches and very little heavily ornamented language, except for a few lines spoken by Carlos and, more inappropriately, by the servant Teodora.

Las muñecas de Marcela, which Cotarelo terms "una de las [comedias] más conocidas" of the Golden Age, has stood the test of time as well as, if not better than, any other of Cubillo's *comedias de costumbres*. In no other light work, except possibly in *El señor de Noches Buenas*, does the playwright so inventively combine incidents and characters. Moreover, he gives an additional dimension by inviting one to look beneath the frothy surface for glimpses of a real society which could exact excessively harsh penalties for infringements upon the code of honor.

In the nineteenth century Cubillo's *comedia* was recast by Félix Enciso Castrillón under the title *El amor por el tejado* (printed 1833).[25] This version was performed in Madrid several times during

---

[25] *El amor por el tejado, comedia nueva en tres actos, formada por el mismo asunto que la que escribió, con el título de las Muñecas de Marcela, el antiguo poeta, Don Álvaro Cubillo*, por Don Félix Enciso Castrillón (Madrid: Cuesta, 1833).

the 1830's.[26] In 1959 several scenes from the original were performed at the University of Barcelona by the Spanish University Syndicate of the University District of Catalonia and the Balearics.[27]

6. *El señor de Noches Buenas*

El señor de Noches Buenas, first published under Antonio de Mendoza's name in *Flor de las mejores doce comedias* (Madrid, 1652), was quickly reclaimed by Cubillo, who included it in *El enano de las musas* (1654).[28] In the dedication Cubillo makes a point of dealing with the question of authorship:

> Y así escogi estas diez [comedias] y entre ellas la del *Señor de Noches Buenas* que por yerro se imprimio en nombre de don Antonio de Mendoza; por cuya reputacion, mas que por la mia, quise deshacer aquel yerro, pues a hombre tan grande y que tan excelentes cosas hizo no era justo atribuirle disparates mios.

Efforts to date the play lead us back several decades before the 1650's. It is known to have been performed before Philip IV by Roque de Figueroa's company on 1 June 1634 and again in April 1635.[29] Cubillo says in the *Enano* that it was also produced by Bartolomé Romero's company, but he gives no date. Since Cubillo, who mentions both *autores*, lists Romero first, it is possible that Romero had the work in his repertory before Figueroa. Within the play itself is an allusion that offers grounds for believing that the *comedia* was written earlier than 1634. In Act III, when the Marqués asks Marcelo to guess what news his agent in Madrid has sent, Marcelo replies:

---

[26] Nicholson B. Adams, in "Siglo de Oro Plays in Madrid, 1820-1850," *Hispanic Review*, 4 (1936), 351, lists two performances in 1831, two in 1832, and eight in 1833.

[27] Jack H. Parker and K.-L. Selig, "A Current Bibliography of Foreign Publications Dealing with the *Comedia*," *Bulletin of the Comediantes*, 12, No. 1 (1960), 10.

[28] Other editions are: N.p., n.d.; in *Comedias escogidas de Álvaro Cubillo de Aragón* (Madrid: Ortega y Compañía, 1826); in BAE, 47 (Madrid: M. Rivadeneyra, 1858); in *Las muñecas de Marcela; El señor de Noches Buenas*, ed. Ángel Valbuena Prat, Clásicos Olvidados, 3 (Madrid: Compañía Ibero-americana de Publicaciones, 1928; rpt. Madrid: Ediciones Alcalá, 1966).

[29] Shergold and Varey, p. 237.

> Escribirá muchas nuevas
> de los sucesos de Italia,
> de Flandes y de las guerras
> de la majestad cesárea
> con el infiel de Suecia. [30]   (III, 156b)

It seems likely that "el infiel de Suecia" is the Protestant Gustavus Adolphus, who, from the summer of 1630, when he brought Sweden into the Thirty Years War by undertaking a campaign in Germany, until his death at the Battle of Lützen on 16 November 1632, was the scourge of the imperial cause supported by Spain. Since the conflict between "la majestad cesárea" and "el infiel de Suecia" is described as still in progress, it appears probable that *El señor de Noches Buenas* dates from sometime between mid-1630 and late 1632.

The plot of the *comedia* is as follows: The poor but admirable Don Enrique, whose presence is a constant irritant to his rich and disagreeable elder twin, the Marqués, agrees to leave Valencia if his brother will help him win the beautiful Porcia in marriage. The Marqués, although he accepts the condition, privately plans to win her for himself. Porcia, upon learning that her father Marcelo has afianced her to the Marqués, sends a message for her betrothed to meet her that night. Unaware of the marriage plans, Enrique goes instead. The lady, believing him to be the Marqués, becomes enchanted with her father's choice. Not until she complains of the younger brother's attentions does Enrique realize that he has been deceived. The following day Porcia's admiration for her betrothed turns to consternation when she meets the real Marqués. Upon accidentally learning that he has sought her hand in order to cause suffering to Enrique, she begs the latter's forgiveness and confesses her love for him. Enrique, after making a show of leaving the city, goes into hiding in her house. When the Marqués urges that the wedding be celebrated without delay, Porcia informs him that they must await the arrival of her relative, Don Enrique del Rincón, Señor de Noches Buenas. The ruse serves to compromise the Marqués, who is obliged to acknowledge the priority of his brother's claim to Porcia's affections.

The play has not been given a great deal of attention by critics, but those who have studied it have conceded that it has considerable

---

[30] Citations are to the text in BAE, 47.

charm. The anonymous editor of the *Comedias escogidas* of Cubillo, writing in 1826, finds that the plot complications are handled with skill and that the best scenes all relate to the final outcome, are well linked, and maintain interest. Schaeffer calls it a fresh and gay work. For Cotarelo, Enrique is one of Cubillo's best creations: "discreto, valeroso, obediente y respetuoso con su hermano mayor y, en fin, cabal en todos sus actos." Valbuena Prat sees the *comedia* as a highly stylized work that moves much more towards the grotesque than Lope's *Las flores de don Juan,* with which some affinities exist. Valbuena chooses Porcia, a "fina y discreta mujer ... de la más delicada sensibilidad," from among the major characters and considers the secondary figures more interesting than would be expected in a light work. Alborg, who calls Cubillo's *comedia* "excelente," challenges Valbuena's opinion concerning elements of stylization; on the contrary, he says, *El señor de Noches Buenas* is very close in spirit to Alarcón's *comedias de carácter*.[31]

Although *El señor de Noches Buenas* is almost entirely original, Cubillo may have taken the basic situation from Lope's *Las flores de don Juan* (dated 1612-1615 by Morley and Bruerton), which also treats the relationship between a *mayorazgo* and his younger brother. The situation at the beginning of Lope's play is essentially the same as in Cubillo's: An older brother (Lope's Don Alonso), having inherited the family property, allows his younger brother (Lope's Don Juan) to live in poverty. Don Alonso, like Cubillo's Marqués, is consumed by envy of his younger brother's uprightness and intelligence and wishes to be free of him. From this point on, however, Lope's plot is different from Cubillo's. In *Las flores de don Juan* Don Alonso loses his fortune at the gaming table; the resourceful Don Juan rises in the world by marrying a rich countess and, after buying the property of his bankrupt brother, demonstrates his magnanimity by restoring it to its former owner.

In *El señor de Noches Buenas* Cubillo turns in the direction of the *comedia de figurón,* but traces of a serious treatment of the relationship between the brothers reveal that he was unable to give himself completely to the demands of caricature. The importance assigned to

---

[31] Alborg, II, 809-10.

the Marqués' ludicrous traits and to artificial devices for advancing the action indicates that the play was designed to provide light entertainment, yet something of the plight of an admirable person who finds himself dependent on a despicable one is conveyed. The plot contains little superfluous material to detract from the Enrique-Porcia-Marqués triangle. The exposition is neatly accomplished by a dialogue between two lackeys and the appearance of the brothers themselves. After this the action gets under way without delay with the Marqués' spiteful decision to steal Porcia from Enrique. Since comic intent is not apparent up to this point, one is not entirely prepared for the light touch that follows in the elaboration and resolution of the intrigue.

The play includes a number of attractive scenes, three of which are particularly successful. A highlight of Act I is Enrique's declaration of love to Porcia, who thinks that the flow of eloquence that rises to her balcony from the darkened street comes from her betrothed. This situation, which brings to mind the famous balcony scene in *Cyrano de Bergerac,* would win an audience, which could take a superior delight in its knowledge of the abyss that separates the real Marqués from the supposed one. In Act II the Marqués' interview with Porcia, who has never spoken with him before, is highly amusing. The effectiveness of this scene is intensified by the implied contrast between the boorishness of the real Marqués and the gallantry of the supposed Marqués the night before. Moreover, spectators would not fail to set the Marqués' social ineptness against Enrique's dignified farewell to Porcia in the preceding scene. In Act III the Marqués' traits again give rise to a diverting spectacle when, on the heels of the maid Aldonza's charge of his lack of manliness, he unwittingly makes remarks which lend support to her insinuations. The irony is enhanced by his belief that he has the situation completely under control.

The Marqués is not, however, entirely a comic figure, even though like many *figurones* he has an exaggerated sense of his own importance, is vain about his appearance, attaches undue regard to rank, is highly materialistic, a physical coward, and insensitive to the feelings of others. Despite the exaggeration of these attributes, the caricature is not pushed to an extreme, for one is never convinced that he is a complete fool, as a genuine *figurón* would be. Besides, he possesses traits — envy and malicious ill will — which Cubillo does not approach in a playful fashion.

Cotarelo's praise notwithstanding, Enrique does not arouse as much interest as the Marqués. Since Enrique's function is to serve as a foil for his older brother, it is fitting that he be depicted as the possessor of the virtues that the other lacks; but he is little more than a stereotype of goodness.

The women characters are not as captivating as those in some of Cubillo's other light works. Even so, Porcia and her cousin Dorotea are engagingly portrayed to complement each other. Anything but frivolous in her attitude towards a prospective husband, Porcia realizes that her future happiness is at stake. In her desire to make the selection herself and in her assertion of independence when her father's choice does not meet her test, she recalls the determined heroine of Rojas Zorrilla's *Entre bobos anda el juego*. Dorotea acts as Porcia's confidante, and her relationship with her betrothed, Leonardo, serves as an example of the ideal relationship which should exist between lovers. She, whose life has been changed by love, stands in contrast to Porcia, who when first introduced has never experienced this emotion.

For the most part, the poetic style is spirited and energetic. No long speeches slow the pace of the action. The playwright employs some metaphorical language in the lovers' dialogues, where it is usually appropriate; he fortunately curbs his tendency to burden a passage with masses of elaborate rhetorical figures, which he sometimes constructs so ponderously.

All in all, *El señor de Noches Buenas* is one of a small number of Cubillo's plays that can survive comparison with better-known works by Golden Age dramatists of greater reputation. It is perhaps the only one of his plays that can be accurately described as serious comedy. In no other *comedia de costumbres* does he make a statement about human nature so successfully in dramatic terms. It has been seen that *El señor de Noches Buenas* has stylized, grotesque elements, as Valbuena Prat says, in that it contains features associated with the *comedia de figurón*; nevertheless, the similarities with the Alarconian *comedia de carácter* noticed by Alborg appear to suggest a more fruitful critical approach in that they imply recognition of the serious purpose that underlies Cubillo's play.

In 1670 *El señor de Noches Buenas* was adapted into French by Thomas Corneille under the title of *La Comtesse d'Orgueil*.[32] Although by this time the number of adaptations of Spanish *comedias* had declined from the high point reached earlier in the century, French playwrights continued to draw fairly steadily from *comedias de figurón* and pseudo-*comedias de figurón*.

7. *El invisible príncipe del Baúl*

A *comedia de figurón* based on *El señor de Noches Buenas*, *El invisible príncipe del Baúl* was first printed in 1654 in *El enano de las musas*.[33] Like its prototype it seems to have been written in the 1630's. Mention of the victory won by imperial troops under the Cardenal-Infante Don Fernando at the Battle of Nördlingen, which took place on 6 September 1634, fixes a *terminus a quo*. Speaking of his master César, the *gracioso* Pedro Grullo has this to say:

> Es bizarro caballero.
> Viene de Flandes; que pasó galante
> en la jornada del señor infante
> Don Fernando, y sirvió con bizarría
> en la batalla de Norlingue, el día
> que fue el duque Veidmar desbaratado.[34]   (I, 179c)

An allusion to a later event may be contained in Pedro Grullo's jesting words to the Príncipe del Baúl that the latter could become a "potente rey de romanos" (II, 190b). The phrase may have reminded spectators of the election of Ferdinand, King of Hungary and brother-in-law of Philip IV, as King of the Romans on 22 December 1636 at Regensburg. Beginning on 15 February 1637, elaborate festivities were held at the Buen Retiro in celebration of Ferdinand's elevation, which was tantamount to recognition as heir to the imperial throne.

---

[32] Lois Strong, *Bibliography of Franco-Spanish Literary Relations until the XIX Century* (New York: Institute of French Studies, 1930), p. 52.

[33] Other printed editions are: Madrid, 1734; in BAE, 47 (Madrid: M. Rivadeneyra, 1858). The only early MS (Biblioteca Nacional No. 16.040) appears to be a late seventeenth-century transcription of the text in the *Enano de las musas*.

[34] Citations are to the text in BAE, 47.

The festivities are described in several contemporary accounts, including a series of newsletters by an anonymous grandee.[35]

According to Cubillo's statement in *El enano de las musas, El invisible príncipe del Baúl* was first performed by [Pedro de la] Rosa, who was an *autor* and *primer galán* by 1636.[36] In view of the internal evidence, it is probable that Rosa had the play early in his career as an impresario, even in 1637.

The plot of the *comedia* is as follows: The Príncipe del Baúl, after purchasing a phoenix feather which he believes will render its wearer invisible, decides to use it to observe two ladies without risking their being dazzled by his presence. The objects of his interest are Rosaura, a cousin, and Matilde, who is loved by César, his worthy younger brother. Eager to make the game of love more exciting and desirous of discomfiting César, he orders his brother to act as his proxy in paying court to Matilde. For a time the prince attaches no significance to Matilde's warm response to César's gallantries, but when he discovers that the two are deeply in love, he orders them to forget each other. After vowing to die together, the lovers arrange to meet in Matilde's garden to carry out their intention. The prince, knowing that they often meet secretly, goes to the garden at the same time. Rosaura, who also finds her way there, mistakes the prince for César, with whom she has long been smitten, and demands marriage. The prince, thinking he is addressing Matilde, accepts. When César and Matilde appear with a light, Rosaura pretends that she had known her companion was the prince and thereby acquires a husband. The prince, taking refuge in his vanity, announces that he will avenge himself on Matilde by forgetting her and ordering her to marry César.

Critical assessment of the *comedia* has varied. Schaeffer calls it, like *El señor de Noches Buenas*, a fresh, gay work and finds especially amusing the scenes in which the prince prances around in his cap adorned with the magic feather. Valbuena Prat, on the other hand, considers that the play marks a descent from *El señor de Noches Buenas*. Without the serious purpose of comparing and contrasting

---

[35] The entertainments are described by J. E. Varey in "Calderón, Cosme Lotti, Velázquez, and the Madrid Festivities of 1636-1637," *Renaissance Drama*, new series, 1 (Evanston, Ill.: Northwestern University Press, 1968), pp. 253-282.

[36] Rennert, p. 585. Rosa, who died in 1675, was active as an *autor de comedias* until the 1670's.

found in the latter play, he says, "la bufonada resulta pálida y sosa. Únicamente la belleza de estilo, cuando se olvida el autor de su propósito grotesco, realza algunas partes de esta comedia."

The play is based loosely on *El señor de Noches Buenas,* but the preoccupation with the serious aspects of the relationship between the brothers has disappeared, leaving only a comic intent. Except for the rivalry between the brothers for the same lady, the similarities between the plays are not great. The only scenes Cubillo lifts directly from the earlier play are the expository ones: A conversation between two minor characters brings out the contrast between the brothers, after which the latter enter and by their behavior corroborate the statements made about them.

The workings of the plot are not especially ingenious, nor is the play studded with scenes that demonstrate Cubillo's talent as a comic writer. To be sure, the sight of the prince strutting around believing the feather makes him invisible would be diverting, but the effectiveness of these scenes would depend in large part on an actor's skill in stage business, since the lines themselves are only mildly amusing. Moreover, by the very nature of the situation, the leading figure is isolated from the other characters. Not once has Cubillo devised a truly clever scene in which the prince furnishes amusement by interacting with the others in the play. (There is of course the episode in the garden in Act III, but it depends on mistaken identities, not on the prince's attributes.)

The prince does, however, qualify as a full-fledged *figurón,* even if he does not have any capital scenes in which to display his traits. Since he acts with none of the calculated malice of the Marqués of *El señor de Noches Buenas,* the contrast between his ludicrous appearance and behavior and the more dignified and decorous *galanes* and *damas* is complete. The audience would be prepared for exaggeration in him by the remarks made by the *gracioso,* as, for example, when the latter says that the prince, instead of following fashion in using a curling iron to make the ends of his mustache curl up, cools his iron with snow so that the ends will droop. The prince's desire to be unique extends beyond personal appearance, however, and leads to his being an easy victim of a sly astrologer's offer of a magic feather. Like other *figurones,* the Príncipe del Baúl is certain that women find him irresistible. He takes excessive pride in his station, and words about his exalted rank and superiority to others are constantly on his lips.

Most of the verbal wit is provided by the *gracioso* Pedro Grullo, who indulges in puns, coins words, tells *cuentos,* and parodies César's elegant language. His love affair with the maid Leonor is a ludicrous imitation of César and Matilde's idealistic courtship. His eminently practical outlook prevails when, upon learning that César and Matilde have determined to die for love, he and Leonor decide that they cannot follow their master and mistress to this extent. In addition, Pedro performs the choral function so often assigned to the *gracioso*: He constantly points out to the prince the errors in the latter's thinking. Pedro's attributes and functions show that he falls within the category of a stereotyped comic servant, but it is rare in Cubillo for a *gracioso* to be equipped with so many devices for making a bid for attention.

The play is free from the long speeches that Cubillo frequently uses. Happily so, for the requirements of caricature would not be served by lengthy declamations. The *comedia* does, however, include a *cuestión de amor,* in this instance on *amar* and *aborrecer* (I, 182b). Metaphorical language is scattered here and there, cropping up most often in the words of the lovelorn César and, to a lesser extent, in Matilde. Even so, no single speech by César can compare in ornamentation with the *gracioso*'s description of Matilde (III, 195c-196a).

Finally, any evaluation of *El invisible príncipe del Baúl* should include at least a brief comparison with other full-fledged *comedias de figurón*. Cubillo's prince does not dominate the action as do the *figurones* of such minor masterpieces as Moreto's *El lindo don Diego* and Rojas Zorrilla's *Entre bobos anda el juego*. On the contrary, it has been seen that he shares much of the comic function with the *gracioso*. While this weakness of focus is readily apparent to a reader of the play, it might nevertheless go undetected in performance, where extra-literary factors count for much. It may well be that in the seventeenth century an actor taking the role of the prince compensated for his somewhat colorless lines through the use of his voice and gestures for comic effect. An actor who succeeded in imposing his presence in this way would have overcome the play's gravest defect, for he thus would have developed the farcical possibilities of a role which Cubillo merely sketches.

Chapter IV

RELIGIOUS PLAYS

The varied subject matter which has been noted in the *comedias* treated in the preceding chapters is also a feature of the eight extant religious plays ascribed to Cubillo. Despite their relatively small number, they include examples of several types of religious drama which found favor with seventeenth-century audiences: the *comedia bíblica*, the *comedia histórico-religiosa*, the *comedia de santos y bandoleros*, and the *auto sacramental*. Separately and as a group, they have attracted little notice, partly because of the rarity of texts and partly, no doubt, because of their unexceptional quality.

1. *El justo Lot*

El justo Lot, which treats the destruction of Sodom and Gomorrah, is ascribed to Cubillo in Medel's *Índice*, where it is first mentioned, and appears under Cubillo's name in the several eighteenth-century printings which are known.[1] Although the present study has produced no evidence that would challenge this ascription, one should nevertheless bear in mind that *El justo Lot* is the only work traditionally assigned to Cubillo which partakes of features of both a *comedia bíblica* and an *auto sacramental*.

The date of the play is unknown; however, several parallels with *La cena del rey Baltasar* suggest a close connection with the Calderonian *auto*, which is thought to have been performed during the

---

[1] Printed editions are: N.p., n.d.; Madrid: Antonio Sanz, n.d.; Sevilla, n.d.; Madrid: 1801.

Corpus Christi celebrations in Seville in 1632.[2] A comparison of the two works offers a convincing case for the priority of the *auto*, which the present writer will attempt to establish in treating the sources of *El justo Lot*.

The plot of Cubillo's play is as follows: Lot, after denouncing the licentious Canaanite court in Sodom, calls upon heaven to punish the king and his subjects for persisting in their wickedness. Abraham, informed that the destruction of the Canaanite cities is imminent, obtains a promise that God will spare them if they can be found to contain ten righteous inhabitants. Some time later, the king and other Canaanites forcibly enter Lot's house, where they attempt to seize for their own lacivious purposes two pilgrims who are lodged there. Before the guests can be harmed, Lot and his house are spirited away. The pilgrims, who reveal that they are angels, announce to Lot that they have been sent to destroy the cities, since ten just persons cannot be found there, but that he and his family will be allowed to leave. His Canaanite sons-in-law, who receive his account of the visit of the angels with pitying disbelief, choose to remain; his daughters, recognizing their husbands' weakness of character, depart with him. While the king is being entertained with an account of Lot's "locuras," darkness descends upon the court. As Lot and his family turn towards a city of refuge, an angel with a flaming sword sets fire to the walls of Sodom.

El justo Lot has been described briefly by Cotarelo, Bell,[3] and Valbuena Prat. Of these, only Cotarelo takes a critical stand — and he somewhat indirectly. Speculating on reasons for the play's apparently not having been printed until the eighteenth century, he says, with perhaps excessive severity, "y ninguna falta hacía."

The outline of the plot is drawn from Genesis 18-19, which tells of Jehovah's decision to destroy Sodom and Gomarrah and of the promise granted to Abraham. The Biblical narrative continues with mention of the attack by the men of Sodom on the two angels lodged in Lot's house and of the opportunity given to Lot and his family to

---

[2] Sánchez Arjona, p. 288. Harry W. Hilborn, in *A Chronology of the Plays of D. Pedro Calderón de la Barca* (Toronto: The University of Toronto Press, 1938), p. 81, dates it 1632.

[3] Aubrey Fitz Gerald Bell, *Castilian Literature* (Oxford: The Clarendon Press, 1938), p. 201.

find safety elsewhere. Lot's failure to dissuade his sons-in-law from their belief that no danger threatens the Canaanite cities is also mentioned.

Superimposed upon this story of divine wrath visited upon a depraved people is the situation which Calderón uses in *La cena del rey Baltasar*: a hedonistic king's refusal to heed the words of a man of God. In adapting this material to fit the story of the destruction of the Cities of the Plain, Cubillo amplifies Lot's role to include the one which Daniel plays in the *auto*, i.e., Divine Judgment, and creates a character, the King of Canaan, unmentioned in the account in Genesis and seemingly modeled on Calderón's Baltasar, to personify the dissoluteness of the inhabitants of Sodom and Gomorrah.

It seems plausible to assume that Cubillo was acquainted with *La cena del rey Baltasar*, for even though he would have known the story of Belshazzar and Daniel from the Biblical account, his handling of the interaction between Lot and the King of Canaan is much closer to Calderón than to Daniel 5. As in Calderón's *auto*, a series of warnings is issued to the king, whereas in the Biblical account Daniel appears before Belshazzar only to interpret the handwriting on the wall. Similarities of execution are also apparent in the lavish court spectacles where the king is seen given over to sensual pleasures. The parallels between the banquet scenes in both works are especially notable. Moreover, as will be seen, some of the characters represent, as they do in *La cena del rey Baltasar*, facets of the king's personality.

The grafting of subject matter and devices from the *auto* on to the material from Genesis produces in *El justo Lot* a work that is midway in form between a *comedia bíblica* and an *auto sacramental*. The three-act division is that of a conventional *comedia*, and the surface story is that of a *comedia bíblica*. At the same time, some of the characters are allegorical, as in an *auto*, and interest is evoked in the lesson conveyed by the relationships among the abstractions.

The structure of the play is carefully ordered, with little extraneous material to disturb the unity of effect. The subject matter from Genesis and that from Daniel 5 by way of Calderón are blended harmoniously, a feat made possible by a theme common to both. The subplot dealing with Lot's daughters and their suitors is not developed enough to detract from the central action; rather, the retention of these characters reinforces the main theme in that the young men represent compromise with evil and so are destroyed too.

As abstractions the characters are successful creations. They bear names that are either taken from the Old Testament or have an Old Testament ring, but most of them are clearly personifications of abstract qualities. The King of Canaan represents "la pompa humana." Attendant upon him are figures who stand for traits he possesses: His courtiers Artemis and Tarso are Vanity; his paramour Irene personifies Carnal Desire; Lot is Divine Judgment. His sons-in-law represent Compromise; his daughters are personifications of Innocence. The shepherd Bato, who provides comic relief, is Cowardice.

Pageantry occupies an important place in the play, not just to delight the eye but also to strengthen the author's didactic purpose. This intent is evident in the scenes at the royal court where, as in *La cena del rey Baltasar,* the pomp and pleasures with which the king surrounds himself point up his enslavement to the things of this world. The opening scene of Act I introduces the opposing forces of the play: the pleasure-seeking king attended by his fawning courtiers and complaisant mistress, and the austere Lot, who, like the Daniel of *La cena del rey Baltasar,* stands out in the midst of the voluptuousness. As the king enters, musicians sing his praises. Later, after Lot has warned him, a song underlines his indifference to divine will:

> La gloria apetezco humana,
> y en ella contento estoy
> gozando del día de hoy,
> y esperando el de mañana.[4]   (I, 3a)

The entertainment offered later in Act I serves to restate the contrast implied between the king and Lot: Black and white masked figures symbolizing night and day, i.e., all of life, perform a dance before the court. As the stage directions state, "pónese enmedio la mujer blanca y echa caños de agua por las plumas." In contrast to this fountain of delights that pours forth for the king is the somber note introduced when Lot's daughters place before the king two covered dishes containing an hourglass and a skull, reminders of the transitory nature of human existence.

In Act II and Act III spectacle continues to serve the didactic aim. In both acts the entire court assembles for the Academia del

---

[4] Citations are to the *suelta,* n.p., n.d.

Gusto, at which the king presents awards to those who have led lives of the greatest self-indulgence. The academy motif further illustrates the king's hedonism, but in an emphatically seventeenth-century fashion. Attention to visual elements continues when the king, accompanied by Irene and his courtiers, sits down at the table of delights, "una mesa con todo servicio y platos cubiertos" (III, 23a). A background song gives the doctrinal message:

> En la mesa del deleite
> la humana pompa se sienta
> henchida del apetito,
> que no hay más Dios en su mesa. (III, 23ab)

In addition to the banquet, its participants, and the circumstances under which it is held, the words of the song offer yet another parallel between *El justo Lot* and *La cena del rey Baltasar*. There is no apotheosis of the Eucharist in *El justo Lot,* as is the case in Calderón's *auto*; nevertheless, the line "que no hay más Dios en su mesa" would seem to be a reminder of the contrast between the Canaanite feast and the sacrament of the Eucharist.

Besides the spectacular elements which enhance the doctrinal message, numerous mechanical devices are employed for purely theatrical effect. An angel who has appeared to Abraham vanishes by means of a rope and pulley, and Abraham and the table at which he is seated disappear "en un bufetón" (II, 11b). At the conclusion of the same act two angels spirit Lot away, and his house disappears. The avenging angel who destroys the city in Act III descends by means of a rope and then vanishes the same way. The noise at this point must have been considerable, for, according to the stage directions, "disparan truenos, rayos y bombas" (III, 24a).

The quality of the verse is sustained at a higher level than is common in Cubillo's *comedias*. The style is vigorous and almost entirely free from bombast, and the resources of poetic language are employed with some artistry to set the tone of a scene, to convey emotions, and to accentuate differences among characters. Lot's directness of speech lends dignity and simplicity to his figure; the king's polished and elegant words befit his hedonism. As is so frequent in Cubillo, the play is not without its long speeches. Lot addresses a 246-line warning to the Canaanite king (I, 7a-9b) and renders to the two angels a 128-line account of the vicious lives of the Canaanites (II, 16a-17a).

The doctrinal character of *El justo Lot,* unlike many Old Testament *comedias* of the Golden Age, and the allusion to the Eucharist suggest that the play may have been written to be performed during festivities celebrating Corpus Christi. No record of performances has been found under the title *El justo Lot*; however, one cannot discount the possibility that *Los dos amigos de Dios Abrahán y justo Loth,* performed at the Caños de Peral on 23 and 26 February 1806 and again on 2 March of the same year,[5] is Cubillo's *comedia.*

2. *El mejor rey del mundo y templo de Salomón*

El mejor rey del mundo y templo de Salomón has been preserved in two *sueltas* printed under Cubillo's name, neither of which bears a date or place of publication. Both of these *sueltas* contain the *primera parte*; the *segunda parte* promised in the final lines is unknown.[6] Cotarelo discovered in Juan Isidro Yáñez Fajardo's *Índice de comedias antiguas* (1717) a reference to a *Quinta parte* of Lope (Madrid, 1634) containing a *comedia* entitled *El mejor rey del mundo y templo de Salomón.* As this volume is unknown, it is impossible to ascertain whether the citation is to a work by Lope or by Cubillo. Cotarelo, who accepts the *comedia* which has survived as an authentic work by Cubillo, doubts that it was written before 1634, "porque no corresponde su estilo ampuloso y desigual al usado entonces por Cubillo." For this reason, moreover, he believes that the *comedia* catalogued by Fajardo is not the same as the one ascribed to Cubillo. Though no evidence fixes the date of composition with precision, one cannot discount the possibility that the play was written earlier than Cotarelo assumes; for there are indications in *La muerte de Frislán,* which the present writer believes was written in 1634, that Cubillo employed an ornate style earlier in his career than Cotarelo thought.[7]

The plot of *El mejor rey del mundo y templo de Salomón* is as follows: Newly invested with kingly rank, Solomon accepts homage from David. The old king advises his son on the responsibilities of his office and reminds him that God has chosen him to erect a great temple. Solomon's bride, Arminda, eager to join her husband, learns

---

[5] Coe, *Catálogo,* p. 76.
[6] .... y así el senado / queda a segunda parte convidado.
[7] See p. 161.

that the building of the temple will delay her entry into Jerusalem. Solomon, told in a dream that he may request a gift, asks for wisdom. Upon awakening, he realizes that God has spoken to him. After David's death, preparations are made to receive Arminda; public audiences make known Solomon's wisdom. Azarías, a captain charged with collecting materials for the temple, reaches Ophir, where the Queen of Sheba expresses a wish to meet the new king. Arminda, united with her royal husband, finds him to her liking; Solomon is equally pleased with her. Moved to describe his amorous experience, he composes the Song of Songs. Just after completion of the temple is announced, Azarías reports on his voyage. Solomon, desirous that the Queen of Sheba see the achievements of his reign, orders suitable preparations made. Afterwards, all go off to inspect the temple.

The play has been the subject of comments by Schaeffer, Cotarelo, and Valbuena Prat. Schaeffer, who terms it worthless, contends that its poorly handled plot and stiff poetic diction are real tests of the reader's patience. Cotarelo points out that it does not have "verdadera acción dramática." Valbuena, who also gives it only perfunctory attention, remarks on the visual appeal of the costumes and scenery.

The scant attention which the *comedia* has attracted is explicable in view of its highly undramatic quality. Devoid of a conflict of even the most elementary kind, it consists of a series of episodic scenes loosely held together by the figure of Solomon, who is shown in situations which illustrate very statically that he is endowed with traits which justify the appellation of "el mejor rey del mundo." The Biblical subject matter [8] is thus used to exalt the ideal of divinely inspired monarchy rather than to arouse purely religious feelings. [9] Even so, the theme can scarcely be said to receive adequate treatment in a work which has neither a cohesive plot nor significant dialogue. Instead, it is through eye-filling pageantry, often employed as an end in itself, that the dramatist seemingly attempts to capture and hold his audience.

---

[8] I Kings 1-10. Solomon and the Queen of Sheba also figure in Calderón's *La sibila de Oriente,* with which Cubillo's *comedia* exhibits a few parallels. Among these are Solomon's dream and the detailed descriptions of materials for the temple.

[9] The court fool Momo, whose capers occasionally quicken the slow pace of the *comedia,* makes a number of observations which would serve to link kingship in Solomon's time with the monarchical ideals of seventeenth-century Spain.

The impressive visual effects sought by the playwright are implicit in the detailed directions for costumes, stage properties, music, and dances. The chief device used to evoke pomp and splendor is the court procession, used once in Act I and twice in Act II. The first of these gets under way just after the *comedia* opens. Escorted by members of his court, including "Banaías, capitán general de Juda, Azarías, capitán, Sadoc, sacerdote, de barba y vestido al uso de los sacerdotes de aquel tiempo, bien adornados," the newly crowned Solomon "debajo de palio ... al traje judaico, manto arrastrando, significación de púrpura real, cabello largo, corona real puesta, cetro y espada desnuda en las dos manos," enters the room where David awaits him. Act II opens with another procession as the funeral cortege of David passes before the spectators: "Entran por palenque en orden de entierro funerales pompas militares, al son de roncos instrumentos, estandarte delante, en él las armas de David, y él en media caja armado, coronado, y manto puesto, la espada desnuda sobre el cuerpo, encima las manos y Salomón detrás, dan vuelta al teatro y éntrase." Equal in magnificence is the entourage of the Queen of Sheba: "Tornan a tocar y sale la reina Sabá con gente, ella y ellos negros, bizarramente adornada, manto arrastrando y coronada con arco grande y flecha en las manos o con espada y daga y bastón."

In addition to court processions, Solomon's vision in Act II and his writing of the *Cantar de los cantares* in Act III also contribute to the visual appeal. The first of these scenes is of some interest for the use made of the curtained rear alcove, the upper stage, and mechanical contrivances. After the rear curtain opens to reveal the king sleeping on "una cama muy bien adornada," "descubren cortina y nube arriba y detrás de un velo de rosa o de plata se ve una visión de blanco." Music then sounds, and the bed on which Solomon is lying rises as the vision descends "siempre echado el velo." When they are side by side above the stage, they stop moving. After Solomon has received his promise of wisdom, riches, and fame, "suena música y baja la cama y sube la visión."

Mechanical devices are again brought into use when the king receives divine inspiration to compose the *Cantar de los cantares*. Seated at a table with pen in hand, he hears music as an angel appears in *lo alto*. Inspired by the heavenly messenger, he begins to write the words that he hears sung (in Latin). Then the chair in which the king is sitting rises into the air to make room for El Esposo, who "sale muy galán," and La Esposa, who follows him "despavorida." After the lovers complete their dance, the chair slowly descends, and the angel rises until it disappears.

The richness of the spectacle finds a stylistic counterpart in passages describing the fine materials to be used in the temple, the magnificent gifts presented by the Egyptian ambassador, and the dazzling equipage which the Queen of Sheba will bring. Some *culteranismos* are employed here, as elsewhere in the play, but it is principally through enumeration of gorgeous objects that showy effects are achieved. Yet even if an atmosphere of opulent exoticism is created by the exploitation of verbal as well as visual resources, these very prolix descriptions, which are frequently in *octavas reales*, are in no way an adequate substitute for dialogue with dramatic content.

It has already been seen that in two other *comedias*, *La honestidad defendida de Elisa Dido, reina y fundadora de Cartago* and *La perfecta casada*, Cubillo takes an exemplary figure as his central character. While his efforts to construct a play around an undynamic character are not entirely successful in either instance, he nevertheless attempts to solve the problem in dramatic terms. In contrast, he very nearly abdicates his function as a playwright in *El mejor rey del mundo*, since he uses visual effects to fill a vacuum created by the absence of significant action.

Whether the promised *segunda parte* was written is an open question, but it presumably would have dealt with the Queen of Sheba's visit to Solomon's court. Cubillo clearly anticipates this subject matter when he closes the first play with mention of preparations for her arrival. He very likely intended for manner as well as content to link the two *partes*, for the queen's visit would have afforded many opportunities for the use of spectacle.

3. *Los desagravios de Christo*

Los desagravios de Christo, which treats the destruction of Jerusalem by the Romans in A.D. 70, is ascribed to Cubillo in *Parte treinta y dos, con doce comedias de diferentes autores* (Zaragoza, 1640). It appeared again in the seventeenth century when Cubillo included it in *El enano de las musas* (1654).[10] The only known manuscript is an

---

[10] Other editions are: N.p., n.d.; Sevilla: Francisco Leefdael, n.d.; Madrid: Imprenta de la Calle de la Paz, 1735; Madrid: Antonio Sanz, 1751;

acting copy dated after Cubillo's death.[11] In *El enano* the playwright says that it was performed by Alonso de Olmedo. Cotarelo adds that Olmedo's company first acted it c. 1637, but he offers no documentation. No evidence that would corroborate Cotarelo's statement has been found.

The plot of the *comedia* is as follows: The Roman general Vespasian, in Palestine with his sons Titus and Domitian to crush a rebellion of the Zealots, captures Josephus, leader of the insurgents. When Josephus declares that he believes Christ was innocent of the charges brought against him by the Jews, he is supported by Titus, who tells his father of the Savior's ministry on earth. Vespasian, who has meanwhile learned of his election as emperor, resolves to avenge the Crucifixion by destroying Jerusalem. He then names Titus co-emperor and announces that the imperial standard will bear an image of the Crucified Christ as a symbol of the Roman mission. In the city two young women, Berenice (Cubillo's Veronice) and Rachel (Cubillo's Raquel), rouse the Jews to action. Josephus, paroled by the Romans, returns to his people, who accuse him of having betrayed them and cast him out when he argues that their plight is God's punishment for their misdeeds. Thus prevented from giving direct aid, Josephus decides to write an account of the events. After the city falls, Domitian takes Berenice prisoner. When Titus disputes his claim — a claim which both brothers have desired to exercise since glimpsing her during the siege — Vespasian takes her into his keeping. Shortly afterwards, the Romans seize the Jew who has captured the symbolic banner. Unmoved by the discovery that it has preserved him from the effects of a shower of arrows, he offers to sell it for thirty pieces of silver. Vespasian, marveling at this display of hardheartedness, decrees that all the Jews will perish as punishment for their guilt in the Crucifixion. When Josephus pleads for him to show clemency, the emperor orders the carnage to cease and the miraculous standard to be raised. Josephus will be spared; Berenice and Rachel will accompany the victors to Rome; the other Jews will be sold into slavery.

Valencia: Viuda de Joseph de Orga, 1765; Alcalá: Imprenta de Don Isidro López, n.d.

[11] Folio 40 of the MS (Biblioteca Nacional No. 15.997) contains a note to the effect that the MS belonged to the *autor* Jerónimo de Sandoval and that it was copied in Gerona on 7 October 1672. At the end of the MS are *aprobaciones* given in Madrid on 30 January and 1 February 1675.

Until recently, scholars studying Cubillo's dramatic works have taken little notice of *Los desagravios de Christo*. Schaeffer devotes a few lines to a summary of the plot and adds that Titus and Domitian impress the reader as Romans rather than, as one might expect, seventeenth-century Spaniards. For Valbuena, who classifies the work as a "comedia heroica ... de historia extranjera," its distinctive feature is "escultural dignidad." Cotarelo, who also gives a brief synopsis, censures Cubillo for presenting a Roman army in the time of Vespasian carrying an image of Christ on its standard.

The only significant study comes from Edward Glaser, who shows that *The Jewish Wars* of the historian Josephus served as Cubillo's principal source.[12] Glaser contends that the true significance of the *comedia* eluded earlier investigators because they overlooked the role assigned to Josephus. Because of this role, he says, the *comedia* comes near to being a dramatized Christian apologetic. On the grounds that the deeds of Vespasian and his sons and the amours of Titus and Berenice are secondary to the theme of the Passion of Christ and the punishment of his murderers, he argues that the play should be classified as religious rather than historical.

Reflected in *Los desagravios de Christo* is Josephus' thesis that the capture of Jerusalem and the destruction of the Temple were divine retribution for the wickedness of the Jews. Josephus portrays Titus and Vespasian as instruments of God's will and implies that his own defection before the siege was justified by a conviction that God was on the Roman side. Cubillo, going a step further than attributing the calamities that befell the Jews to their having ceased to be a God-fearing people, ascribes their misfortunes to their guilt in one specific instance, the Crucifixion. Thus it is that in the play Vespasian and

---

[12] Edward Glaser, "Álvaro Cubillo de Aragón's *Los desagravios de Christo*," *Hispanic Review*, 24 (1956), 307. Josephus, after being active as a leader of the Zealots in their rebellion against the Romans in Palestine, went over to the enemy and served as adviser to Titus at the siege of Jerusalem. *The Jewish Wars*, which covers the period from 170 B. C. to A. D. 70, and the *Antiquities*, which treats the history of the Jews to A. D. 66, took on new importance with the triumph of Christianity. They came to be regarded as a kind of introduction to the Gospels, since they cast light on the times in which Christianity arose. Spanish translations of *The Jewish Wars* were published in 1492, 1532, 1536, 1557, 1608, 1616, and 1657. The text used in the present study is *Josephus*, with an English translation by H. St. J. Thackeray, The Loeb Classical Library (London: William Heinemann; New York: G. P. Putnam's Sons, 1926-1943), II-III.

Titus are converted into champions of Christianity; Josephus becomes a choral figure who underscores their mission by speaking out in support of the righteousness of their cause. Though this christianization of materials does violence to the modern reader's view of Roman history, the modification probably did not represent to Cubillo a significant departure from his source, since *The Jewish Wars* had already been invested with Christian significance by previous generations.

The playwright's dependence on Josephus is apparent not only in the broad scheme of *Los desagravios de Christo* but also in a number of details: Vespasian's capture of Josephus while in Palestine to quell a revolt of the Zealots, Josephus' prediction that Vespasian will become emperor, Vespasian's acclamation as emperor while in the East, Josephus' return under parole to his own people, and his futile exhortation to the Jews. The various unfavorable omens disregarded by Berenice, including a sword of fire, may also have been suggested by a passage in Josephus where it is told that portents of the fall of Jerusalem, including a star resembling a sword which hung over the city, were ignored by the Jews.

In the main action the most notable addition to the material from Josephus is the banner emblazoned with an image of the Crucified Christ. In view of the role assigned to the Romans, the attempts of the Jews to gain possession of the standard take on added meaning as a symbol of the struggle between Church and Synagogue. The refusal of Tomás, the Jew who captures the banner, to attribute his preservation from deadly arrows to its miraculous powers, symbolizes the unregenerate persistence of the Jews in their error and thus justifies the destruction of Jerusalem and the enslavement of its inhabitants.

For the secondary actions, the playwright seems to have drawn from Suetonius' *Lives of the Caesars*.[13] Suetonius' biographical sketches of the Flavian emperors tell of Domitian's envy of his brother Titus, the latter's generosity to all, his tireless efforts to win Domitian's friendship, Domitian's uneasy relations with Vespasian, and Titus' love

---

[13] A Spanish translation, *Las vidas de los doze Césares*, appeared in Tarragona in 1596.

for Berenice.[14] The incidents that illuminate these relationships are of Cubillo's own devising, but the germ for many of them is in Suetonius.

It is in the secondary action — that is, where Cubillo gives comparatively free rein to his powers of invention — that much that is trivial and even absurd appears. The treatment given the Titus-Domitian rivalry and the Titus-Berenice-Domitian triangle is not on a level which harmonizes with the dramatization of the struggle between Church and Synagogue, which, however discomfiting its implications may be to readers today, is a theme of some power. Moreover, the subplots occupy so much of the play that the main line of action is frequently obscured.

One can, however, perceive a link with the central theme in that many of the subordinate incidents seem designed to exalt Titus, who is also the chief defender of Christianity. The doctrinal aims serve the purely dramatic aims badly, for Titus is depicted as a model of perfection. Thus a wholly good Titus is placed against a wholly bad Domitian. The strained relations between the two lead to little more than a series of unimpressive scenes in which Titus is shown turning the other cheek to Domitian.

The rivalry for Berenice gives rise to some of the more wearisome devices sometimes employed by Cubillo, as when the brothers embark upon a lengthy debate on "el dulce imperio de amor" near the end of Act II. Courtly discourse is unconvincing at this juncture, when Domitian and Titus should be concerned about the progress of the siege. In Act III the contest of wills between the brothers after Domitian captures Berenice is far from heroic, for courtly subtleties on *dar* and *pedir* occupy their attention at a critical moment in the assault on the city. Because of these features, the present writer does not find Domitian and Titus as Roman in spirit as does Schaeffer.

Berenice herself is a typical *mujer vestida de hombre* who, like her counterparts in other *comedias* by Cubillo, inspires strong passions

---

[14] *Suetonius,* with an English translation by J. C. Rolfe, The Loeb Classical Library (London: W. Heinemann; New York: G. P. Putnam's Sons, 1920), II, 281-385 *passim.* There is no historical basis for placing Vespasian and Domitian among the besiegers of Jerusalem. Cubillo would have known from Josephus that Vespasian returned to Rome after his acclamation as emperor, leaving Titus in charge of the Palestinian operations. Both Josephus and Suetonius are silent on the whereabouts of Domitian and Berenice during the siege; other sources, however, disclose that Domitian was never in Palestine and that Berenice joined the Romans before the siege.

even though neither her actions nor her words indicate the presence of qualities which would attract the opposite sex. She rallies an army of females, leads the defenders of Jerusalem, fights in hand-to-hand combat with the Romans, and rides boldly into their camp.

The poetic style of the *comedia*, although somewhat rhetorical, displays few *culteranismos* except in one passage, Titus' emotion-charged account of the Life and Passion of Christ (Act I). The only long speech in the *comedia*, it is of particular interest for its description of the Savior, in which the playwright utilizes terms usually reserved for idealized descriptions of women. Glaser, who sees in this passage a reflection of the polemics on the physical appearance of Christ, says that "Cubillo resolutely sides with those theologians who, like Francisco Suárez, uphold the *pulchritudo carnis Christi*."

In conclusion, it should be borne in mind that while Glaser enables one to see *Los desagravios de Christo* in fresh perspective, he gives little attention to the subplots which greatly diffuse the impact of the subject matter taken from Josephus. Indeed, it may well be that the arrangement of the material is responsible for the failure of scholars before Glaser to perceive the importance of the religious theme. This explanation appears very likely in view of the fact that in plot structure and character portrayal *Los desagravios de Christo* is closer to Cubillo's *comedias históricas* on Bernardo del Carpio and Mudarra than to his other religious plays.

Among Cubillo's *comedias*, *Los desagravios de Christo* seems to have been surpassed in popularity only by the two *partes* of *El conde de Saldaña* and the two of *El rayo de Andalucía*. In the records of performances which the present writer has examined, the title appears as early as 1691 and from then on recurs fairly frequently until 1794.

4. *Ganar por la mano el juego*

That banditry was a literary theme which responded to the prevailing climate of taste among Spanish audiences of the Golden Age is attested by an impressive number of *comedias*. The popularity of such works does not seem to have been restricted to a brief period but to have continued from the time of Lope and his contemporaries to that of the Calderonian decadents. As in *El condenado por desconfiado* and *El esclavo del demonio,* banditry was often associated with *comedias* containing a doctrinal message, for the bandit's life became a symbol of the life of the hardened sinner. Thus if God's mercy could be extended to a bandit if he sincerely repented, so it could to other erring mortals. [15]

Ganar por la mano el juego, which, together with *El bandolero de Flandes*, makes up Cubillo's contribution to literary *bandolerismo*, has come down only in *Parte veinte y nueve* of *Comedias nuevas escogidas* (Madrid, 1668). The date of composition has not been determined, nor is it known when the play was first performed. Cotarelo, basing his supposition on the final *redondilla* in Act III, thinks that it may have been Cubillo's last dramatic work:

> Y aquí da fin la comedia
> pidiendo perdón y aplauso
> Álvaro Cubillo, en quien
> serán los últimos rasgos. (III, 273b)

Valbuena Prat, who considers that this passage is too vague to be taken as a farewell to the theater, contends that the overabundant action and the strong influence of Mira de Amescua are clear signs that the play belongs to Cubillo's early period. It may well be that the lines are too ambiguous to risk conclusions, yet one would hesitate to place the *comedia* with Cubillo's early works merely on the strength of the arguments advanced by Valbuena. In the first place, the chronology of Cubillo's plays is not sufficiently well-established for a clear-cut pattern of evolution towards plot simplification to be detected. Furthermore, action-packed *comedias de santos y bandoleros* are not confined to the period when Cubillo was beginning his career. And as will be seen, the strong influence of Mira is debatable.

In brief, the plot of *Ganar por la mano el juego* is as follows: Arnesto, a victorious general, gives León, a Persian captain taken in

---

[15] For a discussion of banditry in the *comedia*, see Alexander A. Parker, "Santos y bandoleros en el teatro español del Siglo de Oro," *Arbor*, 13 (1949), 395-416. Parker sees, in addition to the treatment of the problem of the criminal's capacity for repentance, two other fundamental elements: (1) The majority of bandits rebel against society in order to avenge a "deshonra injusta" that prevents them from continuing to be respected. (2) In most of the *comedias* the father is the embodiment of social authority, hence rebellion against society is often linked to rebellion against parental authority. Parker argues that banditry in the *comedia de santos y bandoleros* is used as an illustration of misdirected vital energy — the same vital energy, he says, that is indispensable to the making of a saint.

battle, to King Ascanio of Memphis. Isidoro, a hermit of the Thebaid, upon seeing the captive, predicts that he will wear a crown. The holy man predicts also that a high destiny, which will not be found in marriage, awaits Lidora, the king's elder daughter. When Ascanio decides to keep Lidora unwed, Arnesto arranges an elopement. That night in the palace garden Lidora encounters León, who she thinks is Arnesto, and flees with him. After recognizing her abductor, who convinces her of Arnesto's duplicity, she promises her hand to him if he will observe two conditions: deliver Arnesto to her so that she can take revenge, and respect her virtue until, through marriage to her, he becomes king. The two then join a band of brigands. Some time later Lidora shoots León and leaves him for dead. Miraculously spared, he prays for forgiveness; but when he captures both Lidora and Arnesto, he forgets his vow to begin anew. Holding both of them, he ravages the countryside with his band. After being crowned King of the Thebaid, he confesses that Arnesto has not deceived her. Overcome by this disclosure, yet bound by her promise, Lidora severs her hand and gives it to León. She then retires to a cave to expiate her sins; León does likewise. The severed hand is then miraculously restored.

Critical observations concerning the *comedia* have been made by Schaeffer, Cotarelo, and Valbuena Prat, all of whom take an unfavorable view. Schaeffer finds that the play is characterized by extreme exaggeration degenerating into crudeness. Cotarelo calls it "una de las más desaforadas" of Cubillo's *comedias*. Valbuena, who terms it "desgarrada," does concede that the bandit scenes are of "una plasticidad perfecta." They form, he says, "un cuadro con todos los elementos de la España romántica a lo Mérimée y Bizet." Presumably he means that the bandit scenes anticipate the Romantic exaltation of anti-social types.

The chief source of *Ganar por la mano el juego* is *El prodigio de Etiopía*,[16] a *comedia de santos y bandoleros* based on Pedro de Ribadeneyra's account (*Flos Sanctorum*, 1599) of the lives of San Moisén, an Ethiopian Negro, and Santa Teodora of Alexandria. Cubillo retains the basic plot and the Egyptian setting of *El prodigio de Etiopía*, although he changes the names of some of the characters.

---

[16] *El prodigio de Etiopía* has been attributed to Lope de Vega; Morley and Bruerton, however, doubt that it is by Lope.

The Ethiopian Filipo of the first play becomes the Persian León of *Ganar por la mano el juego*. Teodora is Cubillo's Lidora; Alejandro is Cubillo's Arnesto. Leopoldo, Teodora's father, becomes Ascanio, aged ruler of Memphis. Cubillo's Act I ends at the same point as does Act I of *El prodigio de Etiopía*: the leading woman character's flight with a man she erroneously believes to be her lover. Act II of *Ganar por la mano el juego*, like that of its model, deals chiefly with incidents in the career of banditry taken up by the two principals. Act III begins with the crowning of León as king, just as Act III of *El prodigio de Etiopía* opens with the crowning of Filipo.

By ending his *comedia* with the repentance of León and Lidora, who, unlike the Filipo and Teodora of *El prodigio de Etiopía*, have no connection with identifiable saints, Cubillo is able to add some new material. (The model contains several scenes after the repentance of the main characters.) It cannot be said, however, that his selections represent any notable advance.

Among the innovations is setting the opening scene in the Thebaid, to which Ascanio and his court have retired in order to visit the hermit Isidoro. The mood, which is set by dialogue heavy with *culteranismos*, sounds of a harp, and dancing to a song filled with color symbolism, is aristocratically bucolic rather than ascetic. Other new elements — the intervention of bandits in Act I, the more elaborately contrived confusion in the garden of Ascanio's palace, and Lidora's attempts to kill León — crowd an already busy plot. At the same time, this new material is utilized in such a way that León is depicted somewhat more sympathetically than Filipo before falling victim to a "loco amor," and Lidora becomes more of a monster than Teodora. In addition, in Act II, León's miraculous preservation from death by gunfire foreshadows the mercy extended to the sinners at the end of the play.

The influence of *El esclavo del demonio*, while not so marked as that of *El prodigio de Etiopía*, is also discernible. Valbuena Prat, who goes so far as to say that of all Cubillo's plays *Ganar por la mano el juego* shows the most direct influence of Mira, points out that the scene of León's conversion is a direct imitation of Don Gil's in *El esclavo del demonio*, even to the detail of a gloss in double quintillas of the song "Esclavo soy pero cuyo. . . ." One might add that Cubillo seemingly takes the detail of the prophecy that Lidora will become a saint from the one about Lisarda in Mira's *comedia*. The placement of the prophecy in Act I, as in *El esclavo del demonio,* is unlike *El prodigio de Etiopía,* in which no prophecy is made until Act III, when Teodora is already on the point of achieving sainthood.

Even though these details, especially the gloss, point to Cubillo's acquaintance with *El esclavo del demonio,* the extent of Mira's influence is difficult to assess in view of the fact that much of what strikes one as reminiscent of *El esclavo del demonio* is also present in *El prodigio de Etiopía,* which is clearly the principal model for Cubillo's *comedia.* Moreover, *Ganar por la mano el juego* differs strikingly from Mira's play in the relative weight given to the religious theme. In Cubillo's play, as in *El prodigio de Etiopía,* the religious theme is only faintly perceptible under a mass of *intriga novelesca,* whereas in *El esclavo del demonio* it is evident throughout.

The poetic style of *Ganar por la mano el juego* displays excesses comparable to the extravagances of the plot. Arnesto's report to Ascanio in Act I is Cubillo's standard battle account, moving from a description of opposing armies to the encounter between their two leaders. The inevitable description of a horse here contains such metaphors as "Vesuvio portátil," "monte de azabache," and "volcán de humo." Although Arnesto's report is the only long speech, the accumulation of highly stylized language is considerable in the course of the three acts. Passages that might be mentioned are the lines spoken by Lidora in Act II, 146a-146b and the inappropriately *culto* words of one of the *bandoleros* in Act II, 251b.

In brief, *Ganar por la mano el juego* appears to have been rightly termed a *comedia* without artistic distinction. Its tumultuous action and clumsy linking of scenes produce a chaotic effect; its overblown language adds yet another element of disharmony. Together with its model, it is a good illustration of a dramatist's inability to meet the challenge imposed by the *comedia de santos y bandoleros.*

El prodigio de Etiopía, and hence the subject matter of *Ganar por la mano el juego,* was recast by Juan Bautista Diamante as *El negro más prodigioso.* This latter *comedia,* which follows the plot of its model closely, exhibits a lack of restraint in poetic style even more deplorable than Cubillo's play.

5. *El bandolero de Flandes*

El bandolero de Flandes, which deals with a character whose career of wrongdoing is followed by repentance and salvation, has survived in both manuscript and printed form. The only known manuscript (Biblioteca Nacional No. 17.065) is written in a late seventeenth-century hand and carries Cubillo's name as author. The three extant printings, all of which are undated *sueltas,* also carry his name. [17] The *comedia* is ascribed to Cubillo in Medel's *Índice* (1735) and in García de la Huerta's *Catálogo alphabético* (1785), where a *segunda parte* is mentioned. [18] This *segunda parte* is unknown.

Nothing is known of the history of the *comedia* on the stage, but it attracted some attention in the eighteenth century, since the inquisition of Granada in 1787 issued an order prohibiting its performance. The censor, Fray Andrés de Herrera, based his decision on "las llanezas que se dicen y tienen los graciosos, con voces torpes y aun acciones, en las conjeturas contra la estimación de algunas familias, al suponer que D. Fernando Osorio, secretario del virrey de Flandes, era judío y de linaje de judíos, y finalmente en el hurto de una hostia por precio de 30 dineros, y en algunos versos sacrílegos." [19]

Although *El bandolero de Flandes* has been traditionally ascribed to Cubillo, no incontrovertible evidence for his authorship has been adduced. William Macas, in support of his opinion that the play is by Cubillo, points out that its strong anti-Jewish bias is also found in *Los desagravios de Christo,* which is unquestionably by Cubillo. Macas mentions also an etiquette for the reception or presentation of royal documents (the kissing of the document, which the recipient then places above his head), which is found not only in *El bandolero de Flandes* but also in writings indisputably by Cubillo. [20] (Diplomatic historians would challenge Macas' assertion that this procedure was unusual in the seventeenth century.) In short, while the internal evidence for Cubillo's authorship is not impressive, the play appears to contain nothing that argues for assigning it to another dramatist.

---

[17] Sevilla: Francisco de Leefdael, n.d.; Salamanca: Francisco Diego de Torres, n.d.; Salamanca, Imprenta de la Santa Cruz, n.d.

[18] Antonio García de la Huerta, *Theatro Hespanol. Catalogo alphabetico de las comedias, tragedias, autos, zarzuelas, entremeses y otras obras correspondientes al Theatro Hespanol* (Madrid: Imprenta Real, 1785), XVI, 29.

[19] Quoted by Paz y Melia, I, 54-55, who had seen a copy of the order attached to "el texto de la comedia impresa en Salamanca." Paz y Melia does not indicate which of the two Salamanca printings he examined.

[20] William Macas, "A Critical and Annotated Edition of Álvaro Cubillo de Aragón's *El vandolero de Flandes,*" unpubl. diss. (New Mexico, 1967), pp. xli-xlii.

The date of composition of *El bandolero de Flandes* has not been determined. It would appear that the playwright knew Calderón's *La devoción de la cruz*, which Hilborn dates c. 1633.[21] Macas, however, does not discount the possibility that Calderón and Cubillo drew independently from a legend concerning San Pedro Nolasco: The aged saint is carried in the arms of two angels to receive the sacrament and then returned to his cell. Since Pedro Nolasco was canonized in 1628, it may well be, says Macas, that both *comedias* should be dated c. 1628.

The plot of *El bandolero de Flandes*, taken from the manuscript version, is as follows: Don Jaime Formach, struck by an unknown man whom he sees leaving his house, accuses his daughter Laura of receiving the visits of a lover. Protesting that she has guarded her virtue, Laura gives her father a letter containing a promise of marriage from Don Cosme Brunsuic (Brunswick), a friend of her brother Paulo. Charged with avenging the insult to his father, Paulo mortally wounds Cosme in a duel. Afterwards he takes the severed hand of his victim to the Viceroy of Flanders. Upon discovering that the viceroy is Cosme's cousin, Paulo takes flight. The viceroy sends his Jewish secretary Osorio to arrest Jaime, who refuses the escort of so unworthy a person. Jaime later goes alone to the viceregal court, where he is taken into custody. Paulo, who has meanwhile acquired notoriety as a brigand, steals a consecrated host for Osorio, who is plotting with his co-religionists. Having learned of his father's imprisonment, Paulo waylays the viceroy, who tells him that he has become enamoured of Laura. After wounding the viceroy, Paulo takes refuge in a hermitage. There the ghost of Cosme urges him to repent and to return the severed hand. Paulo then surrenders to the viceroy, who gives him the hand of Cosme in exchange for a promise to return after restoring it to the corpse. Meanwhile Osorio has decided to resort to magic in an effort to inspire hatred of Laura in his master. As he stabs a sacramental wafer (the wafer procured for him by Paulo), blood splashes upon his face. The viceroy, who has witnessed the miracle, gives orders for his secretary's execution. After Paulo returns the hand to Cosme's ghost, he surrenders to the authorities. Unable to decide whether the prisoner should be released or executed, the viceroy defers to Jaime. The latter covers his eyes, shuffles the papers, and affixes

---

[21] Hilborn, pp. 73-74.

his signature — to the death sentence. Paulo's corpse is displayed; Llorente, a peasant holding a grievance, voices his satisfaction that justice has been done.

The printed texts follow the plot of the manuscript version closely except towards the end of Act III. Macas believes that the changes made in the *sueltas* were designed to explain what happened to Gila, a peasant bride abducted by Paulo, and to attentuate the harshness of the final scene. In the *sueltas* Gila, who has been thrown into prison, is brought before the viceroy, to whom she reveals her identity. She then wins the forgiveness of Llorente, her husband, who has come to the court to demand that Paulo be punished. The viceroy obtains the hand of Laura in marriage; Llorente's words of satisfaction upon viewing Paulo's body are no longer included.

The *comedia* has been studied by Gossart, Cotarelo, Valbuena Prat, and Macas. Gossart, who includes it in a 1914 survey of *comedias* on Spaniards in Flanders,[22] gives a plot summary and suggests possible sources. Among his few critical comments is the observation that the characters seem Spanish in their outlook, even though they are identified as Flemish in the *comedia*. Cotarelo calls the *comedia* "bien escrita" and goes on to say that the situations, despite their diversity, are well ordered. The village scenes, he says, are "muy lindas y graciosas."

The closest study of the play comes from Macas, who sees it as a propaganda work written in support of the anti-*converso* attitudes of ordinary Spaniards. Thus the dramatist attempts to show, through Osorio, that Jews are filled with hatred for all things Chrsitian, even though they may have formally accepted Christianity. Macas contends that the play reveals "as much envy and fear of the social and economic pre-eminence of the New Christian as conventional religious prejudice" and that because it contains so much racial bigotry, it cannot be taken seriously as a religious work.

Macas shows that an important source for the play is the story of a sacrilegious act committed by some Jews of Brussels in 1370: A Jew persuades a convert to Christianity to steal some consecrated wafers from a church. After acquiring the hosts, the Jew takes a

---

[22] Macas, pp. lxviii-lxix, mentions the comments made in Ernest Édouard Gossart, *Les Espagnoles en Flandre: Histoire et poésie* (Brussels: Henri Lamertin, 1914).

perverse delight in subjecting them to mockery. Some time later he is found stabbed to death. His widow then gives the hosts to some other Jews, who assemble in Brussels at Easter to profane them. As they stab the wafers, blood gushes forth. When the miracle becomes known, the Jews are arrested and put to death.

No printed account of the Brussels story is known to have circulated in Spanish during Cubillo's lifetime, but Macas thinks that the playwright may have heard the story from travelers from the Spanish Netherlands. Indeed, this conjecture appears plausible, for one of the glories of Brussels is the splendid chapel constructed in the cathedral church of Saint Michael and Saint Gudule in the 1530's as a shrine for the wonder-working hosts. Moreover, the chapel would have had special significance for Spaniards, since its magnificent stained glass windows bear portraits of Charles V and several of his kinsmen.

Macas argues that Cubillo dramatizes the Brussels host story under the inspiration of *El condenado por desconfiado*: The *converso* Osorio is thus modeled on the hermit Paulo, whose Christianity is merely outward; Paulo of *El bandolero de Flandes* is derived from Enrico, the bandit who undergoes spiritual regeneration. Macas holds that the influence of the Brussels story, however, leads to a very different contrast between the two sinners in *El bandolero de Flandes*. Whereas in the earlier play Paulo and Enrico have an equal opportunity to repent, the *converso* is not allowed a real chance in *El bandolero de Flandes*. The playwright's bias against Jews thus leads to a static demonstration of why Osorio should be damned and Paulo saved.

While Macas argues convincingly about the effect of the Brussels story on the way in which Paulo and Osorio are contrasted, he is less convincing when he takes the position that Cubillo was heavily influenced by *El condenado por desconfiado*. It may well be that Cubillo knew this play, but the similarities pointed out do not, in the opinion of the present writer, constitute evidence of the preponderant influence of one play; what they do show is that *El bandolero de Flandes* is dependent on the conventions of an established dramatic form, the *comedia de santos y bandoleros*.

Even so, certain parallels with specific *comedias*, notably Calderón's *La devoción de la cruz*, are to be noted. The similarities between Calderón's *comedia* and *El bandolero de Flandes*, which are found more in plot than in spirit, are especially evident in Act I of the two plays. It will be recalled that in *La devoción de la cruz* Lisardo, who has found papers involving his friend Eusebio with his sister Julia, accuses the former of an improper relationship with the young woman and reproaches him for not being open with her father about his interest in her. Lisardo wishes to settle the matter with a duel, but Eusebio forestalls him by giving his version of the courtship. The account having failed to produce the desired reaction, a duel ensues in which Lisardo is mortally wounded. Upon asking for confession, he is taken by Eusebio to a nearby hermitage. Before he expires, Lisardo promises that if he reaches heaven he will ask that his slayer not die without an opportunity for confession.

It would appear that the parallels between the two plays are more than coincidental. In Cubillo's play it is the brother who kills the lover and then becomes a brigand, rather than vice-versa, but otherwise the pattern of incidents is close. From this point on, however, the similarities are not strong, other than in the *bandolero*-redemption theme, although one might mention the scene in Act II of *La devoción de la cruz* in which Eusebio's ghost frightens the rustic Gil. In *El bandolero de Flandes* some peasants are similarly frightened by the specter of Cosme.

Among the reminiscences of other *comedias* are several which have been pointed out by Valbuena Prat. The name Paulo and the bandit scenes, he says, may have been inspired by *El condenado por desconfiado*. Jaime's testing of his son's courage by gripping his hand brings to mind Guillén de Castro's *Las mocedades del Cid*. A scene of a singing *correo* is also in *El tejedor de Segovia, segunda parte*.

It is the present writer's opinion that there is little to admire in *El bandolero de Flandes*. Although its poetic style is relatively restrained, its action is crudely melodramatic and sensational, with one *coup de théâtre* following another in an almost feverish succession — outrages to family honor, duels to the death, severed hands, ghosts, kidnappings, plots against the Catholic religion, magic, acts of sacrilege, and headless corpses. It is, in short, an appalling example of abuse of the freedom accorded dramatists in the Golden Age.

The responsibility for meretricious effects in the play is ultimately Cubillo's, yet the linking of *bandolerismo* with the doctrine of grace, which had already occurred in the Spanish theater before his time, would seem to present greater difficulties to a playwright of limited talent than would certain other kinds of material. On the one hand, it is self-evident that the Christian belief in the infinite mercy of God can be forcefully presented if that mercy is extended to a creature who has committed acts that would be readily recognizable as enormities. That banditry can furnish opportunities for illustrating man's capacity for evil — and thus the conflict between natural impulse and the Christian ethic — it undeniable; nevertheless, it would seem that coupling *bandolerismo* with a religious theme is an invitation to cheap theatrics, for it can only too easily tempt a playwright into sacrificing a logical pattern of incidents for situations contrived for their shock value.[23] When this striving for thrills at the expense of plot and character is carried to extremes, the consequence can be an intellectually and artistically vulgar work like *El bandolero de Flandes*.

6. *Los triunfos de San Miguel*

Los triunfos de San Miguel is known only through the text in *El enano de las musas,* where Cubillo describes it as "nueva, nunca vista, ni representada."[24] A reference by the Diablo Cojuelo, a character in the *comedia,* to a book in which his adventures have been set down, establishes 1641 as a *terminus a quo*:

> Con letras góticas anda
> mi nombre escrito en un libro,
> que un ingeniazo de chapa,
> de mis inauditos hechos,
> sacó a luz y dio a la estampa.   (I, 131a)

The play then must have been written between 1641, the date of the publication of Vélez de Guevara's *El diablo cojuelo,* and 1652, when the *aprobación* was issued for the *Enano*.

The plot of *Los triunfos de San Miguel* is as follows: Luzbel, having rebelled in heaven, is defeated and cast out by San Miguel. After his stratagems in the Garden of Eden prove successful, he becomes confident that he will hold everlasting control over mankind.

---

[23] In this connection it is well to recall that Parker's reappraisal of the *comedia de santos y bandoleros,* in which he draws attention to underlying psychological and social truths which he believes earlier critics failed to perceive, is based on those dramas which he terms "los mejores." (p. 396).

[24] Cotarelo says that a 1734 printing is listed in a catalogue of Cubillo's works which appears at the end of the 1734 printing of *Las muñecas de Marcela*. This second printing of *Los triunfos de San Miguel,* presumably a *suelta,* has disappeared, if indeed it ever existed.

Assisted by the Diablo Cojuelo, he causes Cain to murder Abel. San Miguel, unwilling to concede that mankind is irremediably lost, prophesies that a Son of God will be born from the seed of Adam.

In the depraved city of Nineveh, Luzbel, still accompanied by the Diablo Cojuelo, gains ascendancy over the self-indulgent king and causes the prophet Jonah to turn from his mission of warning that only a return to God can save the city. Upon Jonah's return, festivities celebrating his removal come to a halt. The prophet, whose punishment of being swallowed by a whale has caused him to see his duty clearly, utters his warning. Lending support, San Miguel identifies himself to the king, who is moved to repent and to banish Luzbel.

Discouraged by his defeats, Luzbel arrives with the Diablo Cojuelo in strife-torn Visigothic Toledo. Upon hearing San Miguel predict that the accession of Bamba, a simple farmer, will restore peace, Luzbel resolves to prevent his election. This he fails to do, but after taking on the appearance of a Visigoth, he is named a royal councillor. San Miguel then assumes Luzbel's Visigothic identity and instructs the new king in statecraft. Although confounded to see Bamba ruling wisely, Luzbel acknowledges only a temporary defeat. Spain will be his, he announces, when he brings about the Moorish conquest. San Miguel, in an attempt to lessen the effect of these words, promises a line of great kings. Upon beholding a vision of Spain's greatness under the Habsburgs, Bamba names San Miguel patron of the kingdom.

A few observations by Cotarelo and Valbuena Prat constitute the chief critical commentary on the play. Cotarelo finds merit only in Act III, where he singles out the contribution made by the "gracias y sátiras" of the Diablo Cojuelo. In contrast, Valbuena holds that interest decreases with each act. For him, Act I is "muy curiosa y llena de sugerencias"; Act II has "algo de ironía y de ambiente de buen auto bíblico"; and the value of Act III is "casi nulo." Valbuena deems the *comedia* superior to *La creación del mundo y primera culpa de Adán*, a play attributed to Lope de Vega, which is the model for Act I. He thinks that "las escenas de Cubillo entre el diablo y Caín, como la adivinación deslumbrante de la civilización a los ojos del primitivo es una maravilla de ironía y encanto."

At least three *comedias* seemingly provided material for *Los triunfos de San Miguel*. Cubillo appears to have taken from *La creación del mundo y primera culpa de Adán* not only the treatment of the Cain-Abel theme but also the outlines of the contest between San Miguel and Luzbel. For Act II the playwright takes his subject matter from the Biblical account of the prophet Jonah; however, the atmosphere of this act, with its lavish court scenes, pleasure-bent king, and fulminating prophet, is strongly reminiscent of Calderón's *La cena del rey Baltasar* and also Cubillo's *El justo Lot*. Act III recalls Act II of Lope's *Comedia de Bamba*. Since material on King Wamba was available elsewhere, one might hesitate to identify this *comedia* as the playwright's source. Cubillo, however, incorporates an incident which apparently was original with Lope: the naming of the reluctant Bamba as *alcalde*. Moreover, Cubillo follows Lope in calling the king Bamba; more often he is known as Wamba.

The *comedia* is a dramatization of San Miguel's function as champion of mankind against Satan, an office assigned to the archangel by Christian tradition. Although, as Valbuena Prat has pointed out, the play is really a trilogy, with each act independent of the others, the contest between San Miguel and Luzbel gives thematic unity. That the action is laid in three different ages — a feature likely to scandalize admirers of the dramatic unities — would emphasize to a Catholic audience that San Miguel's advocacy is not conditioned by time. Although, as Valbuena says, "el elemento plástico se sobrepone a la acción dramática desde el principio," the play does not rely overwhelmingly on spectacle. Each act has a concentrated plot, and the dialogue is functional. Hence the *comedia* does not have the static quality of such a play as Cubillo's *El mejor rey del mundo*.

The attention given to visual and auditory effects is to be noted in the use of distinctive — and frequently symbolic — dress, music, dances, impressive assemblages, and mechanical devices. In the opening scene of Act I, Luzbel and San Miguel come out attired as angels carrying swords. After Miguel vanquishes Luzbel, a chorus of angels formed of "todas las mujeres y niños que pudieren, haciendo un escuadrón vistoso," chants praise of the archangel. Luzbel, after his fall, wears "plumas negras." Cain and Abel also wear colors that define their roles: Cain appears in black skins and Abel in white. Luzbel's temptation of Cain brings in a mechanical device: "Arranca un monte y múdase a la otra parte del teatro, y descúbrese Abel con un cordero blanco que va al sacrificio." Afterwards, "vuelve el monte a su lugar y cúbrese Abel." The act closes with a brilliant spectacle as angels take lighted torches and go off stage "acompañando a Adán y Eva en forma de entierro."

Act II, which opens with the entrance of the Diablo Cojuelo "vestido de loco," continues the pageantry. The attire of the King and Queen of Nineveh is not specified, though presumably it would have suggested opulence. As the two appear, a chorus sings a song which underscores the voluptuousness of their court. Later in the act "salen cuatro máscaras con hachas," and another song is sung for the king's entertainment. The revels are interrupted by Jonah, who puts in an appearance under truly remarkable conditions: "[A]parece la ballena y sale por la boca Jonas cubierto de ovas."

In Act III, as Luzbel and the Diablo Cojuelo approach Toledo, they receive a warning that San Miguel is contesting their presence: "Aparece el alcázar y encima de la puerta San Miguel con la espada." Then "desaparece el alcázar y San Miguel." The play closes with an apotheosis of the House of Austria as defender of the faith: A tree is disclosed "con Felipe el I, el II, el III, Carlos V, y Felipe IV en el pimpollo, con una hacha encendida."

The *comedia* abounds in anachronisms, many of which are concentrated in Luzbel's temptation of Cain. Parading in the attire of a *galán,* Luzbel points to the plumes, rich cloth, silk hose, and beribboned garters that Cain will never have the pleasure of wearing and describes wonders that he will never see. The Diablo Cojuelo contributes a zestful enumeration of items of food and drink that were esteemed in seventeenth-century Spain. A seventeenth-century note is also evident in Act II, in which the Diablo Cojuelo, the personification of vanity, relates with relish his success in converting his victims into slaves of modish dress and youthful appearance. The above-mentioned anachronisms are engagingly integrated into the *comedia*; however, the modern reader cannot fail to be mildly disconcerted to discover that Jonah's warning to the King of Nineveh is issued in the form of a gloss of lines from Jorge Manrique's *Coplas por la muerte de su padre* (I, 122a).

The program for the conduct of the affairs of the Visigothic kingdom brings to mind the interest in reform evinced by Cubillo in *Curia leónica* and *Las cortes del león y del águila*. San Miguel proposes that the king distribute important posts among learned men of the kingdom, without their soliciting them, in order to ensure that they be under obligation to no one but the monarch. Royal justice should be dispensed without regard to rank; provision should be made for the care of the indigent and the elderly; and pensions should be granted to those who have served their country.

As a religious play, *Los triunfos de San Miguel* is addressed primarily to the popular mentality. The playwright does not explore deeply the problem of evil; on the contrary, he gives a somewhat simplistic demonstration that belief in San Miguel's advocacy should sustain the Christian. The saint is not portrayed as an awe-inspiring battler but as a gentle protector; as an adversary, Luzbel is inept rather than formidable. Thus San Miguel's victories are all too easily won. Moreover, the fact that Luzbel's companion is the Diablo Cojuelo, a folkloric figure viewed almost affectionately by the ordinary Spaniard, indicates further that the religious thesis of the play is developed on the level of the comfortably familiar.

Little is known about the history of *Los triunfos de San Miguel* on the stage. Cotarelo did not think that it had ever been performed. The present writer has seen no record of a performance in Spain but has found documentation for one in Lima in 1669.[25]

7. *Ciento por uno: Auto de Nuestra Señora del Rosario*

In classifying the one-act allegorical dramas written for performance at Corpus Christi, one should distinguish between the *autos sacramentales*, which allude to the Eucharist, and the *autos sacramentales marianos*, which allude to the Virgin. Concerning the latter category, Nicolás González Ruiz observes that "la que pudiéramos llamar sagacidad teológica española percibe muy pronto la altísima y trascendental significación de la Virgen, y sabe perfectamente que no comete error ni incongruencia al celebrar solamente a María en la festividad del Santísimo Cuerpo de Cristo."[26]

The cult of the Virgin which finds expression in the *autos sacramentales marianos* is also evident in a number of non-allegorical one-act dramas that relate a miraculous intercesión of the Virgin in favor of one of her devotees. Such plays, among which can be included

---

[25] Guillermo Lohmann Villena and Raúl Moglia, "Las representaciones teatrales en Lima hasta el siglo XVIII," *Revista de Filología Hispánica*, 5 (1943), 323.

[26] Quoted in Bruce W. Wardropper, *Introducción al teatro religioso del Siglo de Oro* (Madrid: Revista de Occidente, 1953), p. 27.

Ciento por uno, are in Wardropper's opinion more properly termed *comedias divinas en un acto,* since they are neither allegorical nor related to the Eucharist.[27]

Ciento por uno is known only through the printing in *Navidad y Corpus Christi, festejados por los mejores ingenios de España* (Madrid, 1664), where it carries Cubillo's name. A statement on the title page describes the *autos, loas,* and *entremeses* in the volume as "representados en esta corte." One would surmise from its subject matter that it was commissioned for performance at the feast of Nuestra Señora del Rosario (October 7). The year of its first performance is unknown; the text provides no clues to a date. It has not been described by any scholar; Cotarelo makes only the observation that it "no ofrece nada de particular."

The *auto* is an unpretentious work which elucidates Matthew 19:29 [28] in accordance with Catholic teaching by affirming through a tale of a miraculous conversion that good works are a condition for attaining salvation: Iris, a rich pagan of Messina married to María, a Christian, is moved by avarice when his wife, confident that God returns "ciento por uno," urges him to distribute his wealth to the poor. The Demonio, who has assumed the form of Iris' steward, resolves to cause them to endure such need that María will lose her faith and Iris will never accept Christianity. After they undergo many privations, the Ángel Custodio, who has been sent by the Virgin, gives María a small sum of money, with the assurance that it will increase a hundredfold. Just as Iris and María are about to buy a fish, they receive one as a gift from a beggar they have earlier assisted. Upon opening the fish, they find a precious stone inside. A jeweler searching for a jewel for a royal wedding tries to purchase it, but he finally acknowledges its value is so great that only the king should set a price on it. After telling the king how he acquired his treasure, Iris announces that the miracle has made him desire to become a Christian. He expresses also a wish to become a Cofrade del Rosario. The king and queen offer him a governorship and ask to sponsor his baptism. The Demonio, having lost his opportunity to destroy Iris, now

---

[27] Wardropper, p. 311. In this category Wardropper places Tirso's *La madrina del cielo* and Luis Vélez Guevara's *La abadesa del cielo.*

[28] "And every one that hath forsaken houses or brethren, or sisters, or father, or mother, or wife, or children, or lands, for my name's sake, shall receive an hundredfold, and shall inherit everlasting life."

beholds Christ and María witnessing his baptism. The Ángel Custodio summarizes the lesson of the play.

To achieve his doctrinal aim, Cubillo does not construct an imposing edifice of scholastic subtleties; rather, he reduces the theological lesson to the simplest terms and focuses attention on his plot, which is spun out with the directness, simplicity — and naiveté — of a medieval exemplum. The doctrinal message implicit in the action becomes explicit in the closing lines, where the Ángel Custodio addresses the audience directly:

> Señores, si a un demonio
> le dice el mismo Dios que se convierta,
> bien claro testimonio
> es éste, que jamas cerró la puerta
> a un alma arrepentida,
> llorando culpas de una amarga vida.
> ... ...
> Opinión es de santos,
> que quien rezare y caridad tuviere,
> de los eternos llantos
> no ha de participar, donde se infiere,
> que bien quiere mirarse,
> que quien lo hiciere, no ha de condenarse.   (p. 391)

That the play was designed to commend a particular form of prayer, the saying of the rosary, is plain not only in the intercession of the Virgen del Rosario, in María's offer of protection to the beggars who have rosarios, and in Iris' announcement of his intention of entering a Cofradía del Rosario, but also in the exhortation that the Ángel Custodio makes at the conclusion:

> Salga el amor ardiente
> de nuestros pechos, porque el bien nos sobre,
> y muera el vil contrario
> teniendo devoción con el rosario.
> De nuevo encargar quiero
> aquesta devoción por justa y santa,
> y que lo haréis espero.   (p. 391)

There is no evidence that *Ciento por uno* was conceived as a brilliant spectacle, as were many one-act religious dramas of the Golden Age. The opening scene, in which "salen Iris de gentil y María, cristiana, su esposa, dadas las manos, cantando y bailando con acompañamiento, y el demonio de gentilhombre" (p. 375), would capture attention by its movement, music, and varied costumes, yet it would scarcely require elaborate accessories. The tableau of Iris' baptism is apparently the only instance in which striking visual effects were sought: "Tocan la música, descúbrese Cristo y María sentados, un ángel con una fuente y un jarro echando agua a Iris, estando de rodillas en camisa, calzón de lienzo, y a los lados rey y reina" (p. 390).

In sum, *Ciento por uno* is an unassuming little play that conveys something of the same spirit that one finds in medieval collections of miracles of the Virgin. Its message, directed to simple hearts, is stated in terms that even the most humble among the devout would be able to grasp.

8. *La muerte de Frislán*

La muerte de Frislán, an *auto sacramental histórico,* has as its principal character Albrecht von Wallenstein, Duke of Friedland (1583-1634), the brilliant commander of the armies of Emperor Ferdinand II in the Thirty Years War. While he held command, Wallenstein for a time had the support of Spain, but in 1633, when he repeatedly refused to detach troops to reinforce an army that Spain wished to station in Alsace, Spanish hostility began to make itself felt. Castañeda, the resident Spanish ambassador, and the Conde de Oñate, a special envoy sent from Madrid in the fall of 1633, worked tirelessly at the court of Vienna to undermine his position. An edict placing Wallenstein under the ban of the empire was signed on 24 January 1634 and promulgated on 18 February. The general was assassinated at Eger, in Bohemia, on 25 February 1634 by an Irish dragoon, Devereaux, who had joined a plot with three other officers, Butler, Gordon, and Leslie.[29]

On the Spanish stage in the 1630's Wallenstein was hailed as a champion of Catholic might and then vilified as an arch-traitor. In a report dated 4 March 1634, Serrano, the Florentine ambassador in Madrid, gives a brief description of a *comedia* on Wallenstein written by Calderón and Coello. He comments on the favorable reception of

---

[29] Francis Watson, *Wallenstein* (New York, London: D. Appleton-Century Company, 1938), chap. xiv *passim.*

the battle scenes, particularly those showing the defeat of the King of Sweden, and the manner in which both the king and Wallenstein were portrayed. Serrano mentions explicitly that the play was approved by the Consejo de Estado before performance. [30]

The lost *comedia* by Calderón and Coello appears to be the same Wallenstein play that a German traveler, Hieronymus Welsch, says was performed during his sojourn in Madrid in early 1634. Welsch says that it opened with Wallenstein's exploits after the Bohemian War and the reconstitution of the Union of the German Protestant States and included his defeat of the Swedes. He adds that when the news of Wallenstein's death reached Madrid, the play was withdrawn with such dispatch that the performance announced for the following day was cancelled. [31]

Černý infers from Serrano and Welsch that the action of the *comedia* encompassed Wallenstein's career from 1625 to 1632. He concludes that the *comedia* had its first performance towards the end of February 1634 and that it must have remained on the stage for about four weeks, since Wallenstein's death was first reported in Madrid on 25 March 1634. Černý points to a paradox implicit in the performance of the play: The Consejo de Estado allowed a play glorifying Wallenstein to be performed in early 1634, although on 25 September 1633 it had voted to recommend to the emperor that the general be arrested or put to death if it could be proved that he had broken faith. Černý believes that the Consejo authorized the *comedia* because it was not prepared to risk alerting the public to a change in policy. A further paradox noticed by the same scholar is that, because of the interval between the date of Wallenstein's assassination and the date the news reached Madrid, the *comedia* was being performed after its hero had died a traitor's death. [32]

---

[30] Václav Černý, "Wallenstein, héros d'un drame de Calderón," *Revue de Littérature Comparée*, 36 (1962), 179. The title of the *comedia* described by Serrano is unknown. La Barrera, p. 242, states that Barbosa Machado said that a *comedia* entitled *La vida de Frislán* was published in a *suelta* under Matos Fragoso's name. Barbosa Machado, says La Barrera, had reservations about its authorship.

[31] Černý, pp. 184-86.

[32] There is no proof that Wallenstein figured in Spanish plays before 1634, although he may have been a character in a lost *comedia*, *La muerte del rey de Suecia*, performed in February 1633, since he was in command of the imperial forces at Lützen, where Gustavus Adolphus lost his life.

La muerte de Frislán, which is testimony to the existence of intense anti-Wallenstein sentiment in Spain after the general's death had become known, has been preserved in two almost identical seventeenth-century manuscripts (Biblioteca Nacional MSS. 15.143 and 15.327), both of which carry Cubillo's name. There is no evidence that it was ever printed, and it has not been described by any scholar. The topical interest that the subject matter would have aroused at Corpus Christi in 1634, only a few months after Wallenstein's death, strongly suggests that it dates from that year. Alonso de Olmedo had it in his repertory before 25 March 1637, when he listed it as one of several plays that had been performed without his authorization.[33]

The plot can be summarized as follows: The Duque de Frislán, sword unsheathed, overtakes a muffled figure, who identifies himself as the Duque de Sajonia. When Frislán expresses astonishment, Sajonia replies that since he is La Herejía, who has given Frislán (El Demonio) so many victories, their friendship should remain concealed. At Sajonia's request, Frislán reports on the state of his affairs: Having been raised to eminence by the emperor (Dios), he now aspires "al celeste imperio / y la húngara corona / de ése que es hombre y es Dios." After being temporarily checked by the squadrons of the Conde de Galaso (El Arcángel Miguel), Frislán has now reached Pilsen, where he has learned that the Queen of Hungary (La Iglesia) is raising an army to protect the empire. To counter this move, Frislán-El Demonio has determined to attack the key city of Eger with the aid of Sajonia's troops. Finding the plan acceptable, Sajonia-La Herejía offers support. The colonel (El Hombre) in command of Eger, having informed the King of Hungary (Cristo) and his queen that Frislán has moved into the city, receives permission to undertake his assassination. As Frislán-El Demonio, his face covered with blood, makes a final stand against El Coronel-Hombre, Sajonia's army of heretics arrives. El Coronel-Hombre invokes the aid of Christ and the Church; Frislán-El Demonio calls for the death of man. Music is heard, and La Reina-Iglesia is revealed enthroned. Frislán-El Demonio, still defiant, argues that just as Adam yielded to hunger, so will El Coronel-Hombre; the queen maintains that one mouthful of food from her will sustain him. An altar is revealed, before which El Rey-Cristo stands holding a chalice and a host. Frislán-El Demonio and Sajonia-La

---

[33] Pérez Pastor, *Nuevos datos,* 1.ª serie, pp. 204-05.

Herejía present arguments against the efficacy of the Eucharist; La Reina-Iglesia explains the doctrine of transubstantiation. Provoked by Frislán's taunts, El Coronel-Hombre deals him a final blow. After Frislán staggers off, El Coronel-Hombre announces a victory over the forces of darkness. El Rey-Cristo then reminds him of the importance of a contrite approach to the sacrament of the Eucharist. La Alegría seeks to drive away El Pesar, but he, the burden of man's sin, remains.

All the characters in the *auto*, with the exception of La Alegría and El Pesar, who are pure abstractions, are historical figures who are assigned allegorical roles. "El demonio, que es el duque de Frislán," is Wallenstein; "Cristo, que es el rey de Hungría," is Ferdinand, son of Emperor Ferdinand II and first cousin of Philip IV of Spain; "la iglesia, que es la reina de Hungría" is the Infanta María, sister of Philip IV and wife of Ferdinand, King of Hungary; "el duque de Sajonia, que es la herejía" is Franz Albrecht of Saxe-Lauenburg, one of Wallenstein's few supporters in the final months of his life; "el coronel, que es el hombre" is Walter Butler, an Irish officer who was one of the conspirators in the assassination plot. That Cubillo had some idea of the colonel's name is evident from the following passage: "El coronel Budel [sic], el hombre, hechura / soy de tu majestad" (7v°).

Two historical figures who do not appear on stage are also referred to in allegorical terms. Emperor Ferdinand II is God; Matthias Gallas, a Tyrolese who rose to a generalship under Wallenstein and succeeded him as commander of the imperial armies, is the archangel Michael, called Miguel, Conde de Galaso by Cubillo.

Cubillo's characterization of Wallenstein and his knowledge of the final episodes in the life of the general are seemingly derived from a propaganda tract which circulated in Spain in 1634, the *Relacion verdadera, que contiene la gran traicion que auia maquinado el Duque de Fritlandt contra la Magestad Cesarea del Emperador, y destruicion de los Estados de la potentissima Casa de Austria.*[34] The pamphleteer, who describes Wallenstein's rise to prominence, the suspicions that gathered around him in the summer of 1633, the confirmation of

---

[34] A Madrid edition (Imprenta de Francisco Martínez, 1634) has been used in this study. Other editions are known to have appeared in Sevilla and Valencia in the same year.

reports of his conspiracy (with particular emphasis on the role of the Conde de Oñate in exposing his treasonable aims), his fall from favor, and his assassination at Eger, sees the general as an ambitious tyrant intent upon using his power to turn upon his imperial master, destroy the House of Austria, and set himself up as an independent ruler.

As dramatized in the *auto*, the final episodes of Wallenstein's life follow the *relación* closely. From it Cubillo would have known of the edict ordering that Wallenstein be taken dead or alive and also that Gallas had promulgated an edict whereby the emperor absolved officers from their oath of loyalty to Wallenstein.[35] The *relación* tells also of Wallenstein's presence in Pilsen, the arrival there of the "Duque Francisco Alberto de Saxonia" to treat with him concerning treasonable activity, and his departure for Eger "no se teniendo por seguro en Pilcen, por no tener por tan fuerte aquella Ciudad, como era menester para estar tan cerca de la gente Imperial."[36]

In dealing with the assassination Cubillo gives to Butler the prominence which he has in the *relación*: "El Coronel Budler [sic] Irlandes (que era el Gouernador de Egra) y el Coronel de Dragones Gordon Olandes," upon learning that an army under the Duke of Saxony was within three hours' march of the city, decided to assassinate Wallenstein. After slaying his chief subordinates, Butler and Gordon "se fueron a palacio, donde estaba Fritlandt acostado por el mal de la gota, y entraron rompiendo las puertas. Fritlandt se levantó en camisa, y procuró echarse por la ventana; y no lo pudiendo hazer por estar cerrada boluio el rostro, y hizo cara al Coronel Budler Irlandes, el qual le dio con una arma enhastada, que le derribo, y todos tantas cuchilladas, que no le dexaron forma de hombre."[37] The changes which Cubillo makes are slight. For purposes of concentration, he eliminates the character of Gordon. In the *auto* the Duke de Saxony arrives before Wallenstein expires, whereas the *relación* tells that he reached Eger a few hours after Wallenstein's death and was arrested there.

A drama in which the House of Austria is exalted and its enemies are denounced, *La muerte de Frislán* is clearly propagandistic in aim.

---

[35] The "Vando que el Conde Galaso publico, para que Fritlandt no fuesse obedecido, ni tenido por General del Emperador" is reproduced in the *Relación verdadera*, p. 3r°. In the *auto* Frislán says, "Mas el Conde de Galaso / un bando imperial promulga..." (3v°).

[36] *Relacion verdadera*, p. 3v°.

[37] *Relacion verdadera*, p. 3v°.

Writing at a time when troops of the Spanish Habsburgs were active in many parts of Europe in support of the Austrian branch, Cubillo seeks to impress on spectators that they were engaged in a just cause: that the political and religious goals of the House of Austria were inseparable and that its preservation was tantamount to preservation of the Catholic faith. That this was the playwright's intent is patent in that Wallenstein's alleged conspiracy against the empire is equated with rebellion against God and also in that his assassination by an officer supported by the ruling house is equated with man's ability to overcome evil through the sustaining power of the Eucharist.

That Wallenstein is assigned the allegorical role of Satan is indicative of the astounding impact of the final actions of his life. When the *auto* begins, he has already risen against the Emperor Ferdinand and suffered reverses inflicted by the Conde de Galaso, just as on the allegorical level Satan has rebelled in heaven and been driven out by the armies of the archangel Michael. Hence the Christian theme of the *auto* is the problem of evil at large in the world; Wallenstein, then, is the form in which evil manifests itself at a particular historical moment. The outline of Cubillo's characterization of the general is implicit in the *relación*. A debt is also evident to the literary tradition of the fallen favorite as well as to the theological tradition of Satan. By emphasizing Wallenstein's heroic traits — courage, resolution, and capacity for leadership — Cubillo shows the powerful attraction that evil can exert on man. In religious terms Wallenstein's death represents but one victory in the never-ending struggle against evil: The weight of original sin renders man vulnerable for all time, but he can arm himself for combat by partaking of the sacrament of the Eucharist.

Even though the *auto* is loftily conceived and the abstract and the concrete are impressively articulated, in some respects its execution leaves much to be desired. The subject matter and theme require grandeur of language, and Cubillo attempted to supply this when he composed it in the *estilo culto*. Yet the fact remains that he was not a master of this style, and the *auto* shows that his poetic imagination was unequal to the demands he placed on it.

As a Wallenstein play, *La muerte de Frislán* should command the attention of the literary historian, for it is one of the earliest dramatic works in any language to treat the circumstances of the general's death. It is indeed the only seventeenth-century Spanish play known to have been written on the subject.[38] Although, for Cubillo, Wallenstein is not an enigma, as he is for many historians, who find inexplicable contradictions in his actions, the manner in which he is portrayed reveals something of the same attraction that he afterwards held for imaginative writers and historical scholars alike.

---

[38] For a brief survey of seventeenth-century plays on Wallenstein, see Theodor Vetter, *Wallenstein in der dramatischen Dichtung des Jahrzehnts seines Todes* (Frauenfeld: J. Huber, 1894).

Chapter V

CONCLUSION

After confronting the problem of the authorship and the chronology of the dramatic works attributed to Cubillo, the present writer must acknowledge that some of the results of this survey may be open to revision. Objective evidence of Cubillo's authorship has not been found for several of the plays, and the application of stylistic criteria has proved inconclusive. Only one of the extant plays, *El hereje,* can be indisputably assigned to a specific year, although some can be shown to have been written within the limits of a relatively short period. Others have proved singularly resistant to yielding any useful clue to their chronology. All this, of course, is true to a considerable extent of other playwrights of the Golden Age.

Such chronological data as has been assembled, however, supports Valbuena Prat's position that Cubillo should be regarded as a transitional dramatist eventually dominated by the Calderonian mode, but who sometimes wrote in the Lopean manner even after he had begun to come under Calderón's influence. Moreover, it appears very likely that a closer dating of the plays would not radically alter the view of Cubillo as a playwright who vascillated between the two modes instead of moving steadily towards the second.

That Cubillo was alert to material in earlier *comedias,* historical writings, the Bible, prose fiction, narrative verse, and contemporary events is shown in his sources. A facile versifier rather than a true poet, moderately inventive rather than profoundly imaginative, he was a follower of literary trends rather than an innovator. His extant dramatic production is thus extremely uneven in literary merit. Yet because he essayed many types of dramatic works that were popular in seventeenth-century Spain, the study of his plays is perhaps more rewarding than would be those of certain other minor dramatists.

Cubillo has frequently been taken to task for his lack of originality, but in fact the recasting of earlier plays was a common practice among nearly all playwrights of his generation. A more justifiable criticism, however, would be that he often did not improve substantially on his models. When he reworked a *comedia,* he usually removed extraneous episodes and characters and thus produced a *refundición* that was more regularly constructed than the original, but he rarely expanded the main action in a significant way. Rather, he frequently had recourse to plot fillers, principally lengthy declamations and extended courtly debates.

The plays based on subject matter from history and legend, the largest category of his extant works, present considerably less uniformity than do either the *comedias de costumbres* or the religious dramas. *La tragedia del duque de Verganza,* his most ambitious play, is testimony that he recognized tragedy as a separate dramatic form and, moreover, that he had more aptitude for serious drama than he usually evinced; *La mayor venganza de honor* survives comparison with all but a few Golden Age dramas of conjugal honor. In contrast, *El vencedor de sí mismo* and *El conde de Saldaña, segunda parte* are so clumsily executed than an attempt to analyze them as dramatic literature is largely an exercise in frustration. Midway between these two poles are such *comedias* as *El conde de Saldaña, primera parte* and *El rayo de Andalucía y genízaro de España, primera parte.* In these latter *comedias* the playwright's ability to give dynamism to characters from the national past in some measure counterbalances their structural flaws. Other *comedias* that should probably have a place in the middle range are *Entre los sueltos caballos* and *La manga de Sarracino,* which have fewer pretensions to the heroic.

Without exception, Cubillo's least ambitious plays, his *comedias de costumbres,* show that he was at ease with the conventions of the *comedia de capa y espada* and its related forms. Relatively free from the *culteranismos* which he sometimes introduces so mechanically, they contain few long speeches designed as histrionic vehicles and are original in the sense that they do not appear to be recastings of plays by other dramatists. Although they pale beside the best light works by Lope, Calderón, and Tirso, they are nonetheless sprightly and actable. Two, in particular, should be mentioned: *Las muñecas de Marcela,* which shows Cubillo as an adroit manipulator of plot complications, and *El señor de Noches Buenas,* which stands as evidence of his awareness of the moral function of comedy.

Taken as a group, Cubillo's *comedias religiosas* are probably his least satisfying works. When dealing with questions of Catholic belief and theology, he frequently seems to have experienced difficulty in achieving harmony between theme and structure. In *El bandolero de Flandes* and *Ganar por la mano el juego,* for example, an accumulation of incidents reduces the impact of the religious message; in *Los desagravios de Christo* a trivial subplot weakens the doctrinal thesis; in *El mejor rey del mundo y templo de Salomón* the religious theme is inadequately conveyed because of a reliance on spectacle at the expense of plot development.

Cubillo's activity as a writer of *autos sacramentales* is attested by biographical data and titles of lost works; however, it would be hazardous to speculate on his achievements on the basis of the two *autos* examined here, which differ greatly in subject matter and method of treatment. It has been seen that *Ciento por uno* is a work of extreme simplicity, a pious tale retold for the edification of the devout. On the other hand, *La muerte de Frislán,* which was probably written earlier, is intellectually and structurally a work of some complexity. And while one cannot tell exactly what stage it represents in the playwright's career as a writer of *autos,* it may well be that it served as preparation for a secular play, *La tragedia del duque de Verganza.* It appears likely that in the early 1640's, when Cubillo portrayed the Duke of Braganza as a tragic hero, he recalled that in the mid-1630's he had depicted Wallenstein with some of the same attributes.

In conclusion, Cubillo set no new directions, and within the framework of established modes he composed only a few works of real literary distinction. Nevertheless, a number of his plays bear the mark of a competent artisan, and even the weakest nearly always include an isolated scene, a minor character, or a lyric passage that surprises and delights. Indeed, his career serves as a reminder that the Spanish theater of the Golden Age is one of the great European national theaters not only because it produced such major figures as Lope, Calderón, and Tirso, but also because it gave rise to an impressive number of secondary writers who demonstrated a grasp of the principles of dramatic craftsmanship.

BIBLIOGRAPHY

A. Manuscripts of Cubillo's Plays

Bandolero de Flandes, El. Biblioteca Nacional, Madrid, MS. 17.065. "El vandolero de Flandes."
Conde de Saldaña, El, primera parte. Biblioteca Nacional, Madrid, MS. 16.720. "El bastardo de Castilla."
Conde de Saldaña, El, segunda parte (Los hechos de Bernardo del Carpio). Biblioteca Nacional, Madrid, MS. 15.121.
———. Biblioteca Nacional, Madrid, MS. 15.387.
Conde Dirlos, El. Biblioteca Nacional, Madrid, MS. 16.823.
Desagravios de Christo, Los. Biblioteca Nacional, Madrid, MS. 15.997.
Invisible príncipe del Baúl, El. Biblioteca Nacional, Madrid, MS. 16.040.
Muerte de Frislán, La. Biblioteca Nacional, Madrid, MS. 15.327. "Auto del santissimo Sacram[to] dela muerte defrislan."
———. Biblioteca Nacional, Madrid, MS. 15.142. "Auto Sacramental, dela muerte de Frislan."
Perfecta casada, La: Prudente, sabia y honrada. Biblioteca Nacional, Madrid, MS. 16.970.
———. Biblioteca Nacional, Madrid, MS. 15.471.
Rayo de Andalucía y genízaro de España, El, primera parte. Biblioteca Nacional, Madrid, MS. 16.555. "El genízaro de España."
———. Biblioteca Nacional, Madrid, MS. 17.208.

B. Printed Texts of Cubillo's Plays

Amor cómo ha de ser, El. In *El enano de las musas,* Madrid: María de Quiñones, 1654; rpt. Hildesheim: Georg Olms, 1971; Madrid: Doña Teresa de Guzmán, n.d.; in *Comedias escogidas de Álvaro Cubillo de Aragón,* Madrid: Ortega y Compañía, 1826; in BAE, 47, Madrid: M. Rivadeneyra, 1858.
Añasco el de Talavera. N.p., n.d.; N.p., n.d. [another edition].
Bandolero de Flandes, El. Sevilla: Francisco de Leefdael, n.d.; Salamanca: Francisco Diego de Torres, n.d.; Salamanca: Imprenta de la Santa Cruz, n.d.
Ciento por uno. In *Navidad y Corpus Christi, festejados por los mejores ingenios de España,* Madrid: Joseph Fernández de Buendía, 1664.

Conde de Saldaña, El, primera parte. N.p., n.d.; Madrid: Juan Sanz, n.d.; Sevilla, n.d.; Salamanca, n.d.; Madrid: Antonio Sanz, 1751; Barcelona: C. Sapera, 1769; Valencia: Joseph y Thomas de Orga, 1776; Barcelona, n.d.; Barcelona, n.d. [another edition]; Madrid: Quiroga, 1791; Valencia: Laborda, n.d.; in BAE, 47, Madrid: M. Rivadeneyra, 1858.

Conde de Saldaña, El, segunda parte. In *Comedias nuevas escogidas, parte trece,* Madrid: Mateo Fernández, 1660; Sevilla: Imprenta Real, n.d.; Madrid: Antonio Sanz, 1738; Madrid: Antonio Sanz, 1751; Salamanca, n.d.; Barcelona, n.d.; Valencia: Imprenta de Joseph y Thomas de Orga, 1776; Murcia: Juan López, n.d.; Madrid: Librería de Quiroga, n.d.; Valencia: Ildefonso Mompié, 1822; La Habana: Imprenta de R. Oliva, 1840; in BAE, 47, Madrid: M. Rivadeneyra, 1858.

Conde Dirlos, El. N.p., n.d.

Corona del agravio, La. N.p., n.d.

Del engaño hacer virtud. N.p., n.d.

Desagravios de Christo, Los. In *Parte treinta y dos, con doce comedias de diferentes autores,* Zaragoza: Diego Dormer, 1640; in *El enano de las musas,* Madrid: María de Quiñones, 1654; rpt. Hildesheim: Georg Olms, 1971; N.p., n.d.; Sevilla: Francisco Leefdael, n.d.; Madrid: Imprenta de la Calle de la Paz, 1735; Madrid: Antonio Sanz, 1751; Valencia: Viuda de Joseph de Orga, 1765; Alcalá: Imprenta de Don Isidro López, n.d.

Entre los sueltos caballos. In *Comedias de diferentes autores,* Valencia: 1646; N.p., n.d.

Ganar por la mano el juego. In *Comedias nuevas escogidas, parte veinte y nueve,* Madrid, 1668.

Honestidad defendida de Elisa Dido, reina y fundadora de Cartago, La. In *El enano de las musas,* Madrid: María de Quiñones, 1654; rpt. Hildesheim: Georg Olms, 1971; Madrid, 1734; N.p., n.d.

Invisible príncipe del Baúl, El. In *El enano de las musas,* Madrid: María de Quiñones, 1654; rpt. Hildesheim: Georg Olms, 1971; Madrid, 1734; in BAE, 47, Madrid: M. Rivadeneyra, 1858.

Justo Lot, El. N.p., n.d.; Madrid: Antonio Sanz, n.d.; Sevilla, n.d.; Madrid, 1801.

Manga de Sarracino, La. N.p., n.d.

Mayor venganza de honor, La. In *Nuevo teatro de comedias varias de diferentes autores, décima parte,* Madrid: Imprenta Real, 1658.

Mejor rey del mundo y templo de Salomón, El. N.p., n.d.; N.p., n.d. [another edition].

Muñecas de Marcela, Las. In *El enano de las musas,* Madrid: María de Quiñones, 1654; rpt. Hildesheim: Georg Olms, 1971; Madrid, 1734; N.p., n.d.; in *Comedias escogidas de Álvaro Cubillo de Aragón,* Madrid: Ortega y Compañía, 1826; in *Tesoro del teatro español,* V, Paris: Baudry, 1838; in BAE, 47, Madrid: M. Rivadeneyra, 1858; in *Teatro selecto,* Barcelona, 1868; in *Las muñecas de Marcela; El señor de Noches Buenas,* ed. Ángel Valbuena Prat, Madrid: Compañía Ibero-americana de Publicaciones, 1928; rpt. Madrid: Ediciones Alcalá, 1966; in *Teatro español: Historia y antología,* IV, Madrid: M. Aguilar, 1943.

Perderse por no perderse. In *Comedias nuevas escogidas de los mejores ingenios de España, octava parte,* Madrid: Andrés García de la Iglesia, 1657; N.p., n.d.; Valencia: Joseph y Thomas de Orga, 1781.

Perfecta casada, La. In *Comedias escogidas, parte doce,* Madrid, 1658; N.p., n.d.; N.p., n.d. [another edition]; Sevilla: Manuel Nicolás Vázquez, n.d.;

Sevilla: Imprenta Castellana y Latina de Hermosilla, n.d.; Valladolid: Alonso del Riego, n.d.; Madrid: Imprenta de Antonio Sanz, 1746; Málaga, n.d.; in *Comedias escogidas de Álvaro Cubillo de Aragón*, Madrid: Ortega y Compañía, 1826; in BAE, 47, Madrid: M. Rivadeneyra, 1858.

Rayo de Andalucía, El, primera parte. In *El enano de las musas*, Madrid: María de Quiñones, 1654; rpt. Hildesheim: Georg Olms, 1971; Barcelona, n.d.; N.p., n.d.; Madrid: Antonio Sanz, 1734; Madrid, 1747; Madrid, 1747 [another edition]; Salamanca, n.d.; Valencia: Imprenta de la Viuda de Joseph de Orga, 1770; Salamanca: Imprenta de la Santa Cruz, 1792; Barcelona: Francisco Suriá y Burgada, n.d.; Sevilla: Imprenta del Correo Viejo, n.d.

Rayo de Andalucía, El, segunda parte. In *El enano de las musas*, Madrid: María de Quiñones, 1654; rpt. Hildesheim: Georg Olms, 1971; N.p., n.d.; Salamanca: Imprenta de la Santa Cruz, n.d.; Madrid: Antonio Sanz, 1734; Madrid: Antonio Sanz, 1747; Valencia: Imprenta de la Viuda de Joseph de Orga, 1770; Barcelona: Francisco Suriá y Burgada, n.d.

Señor de Noches Buenas, El. In *Flor de las mejores doce comedias* [under Antonio de Mendoza's name], Madrid, 1652; in *El enano de las musas*, Madrid: María de Quiñones, 1654; rpt. Hildesheim: Georg Olms, 1971; N.p., n.d.; in *Comedias escogidas de Álvaro Cubillo de Aragón*, Madrid: Ortega y Compañía, 1826; in BAE, 47, Madrid: M. Rivadeneyra, 1858; in *Las muñecas de Marcela; El señor de Noches Buenas*, ed. Ángel Valbuena Prat, Madrid: Compañía Ibero-americana de Publicaciones, 1928; rpt. Madrid: Ediciones Alcalá, 1966.

Tragedia del duque de Verganza, La. In *El enano de las musas*, Madrid: María de Quiñones, 1654; rpt. Hildesheim: Georg Olms, 1971; Salamanca: Francisco Diego de Torres, n.d.; N.p., n.d.

Triunfos de San Miguel, Los. In *El enano de las musas*, Madrid: María de Quiñones, 1654; rpt. Hildesheim: Georg Olms, 1971.

Vencedor de sí mismo, El. Sevilla: Viuda de Francisco de Leefdael, n.d.; Valencia: Imprenta de los Hermanos de Orga, 1792.

C. BOOKS AND ARTICLES

Adams, Nicholson B. "Siglo de Oro Plays in Madrid, 1820-1850." *Hispanic Review*, 4 (1936), 342-57.

Alborg, Juan Luis. "Dramaturgos menores del ciclo de Calderón: Álvaro Cubillo de Aragón." *Época barroca*. Vol. II of *Historia de la literatura española*. Madrid: Editorial Gredos, S. A., 1967.

Alonso Cortés, Narciso. "El teatro en Valladolid." *Boletín de la Real Academia Española*, 8 (1921), 571-84; 9 (1922), 366-86, 471-87, 650-55; 10 (1923), 55-71. Pertinent sections of a longer study.

Avalle-Arce, J. B. "Dos notas a Lope de Vega." *Nueva Revista de Filología Hispánica*, 7 (1953), 426-32.

Barrera y Leirado, Cayetano Alberto de la. *Catálogo bibliográfico y biográfico del teatro antiguo español, desde sus orígenes hasta mediados del siglo XVIII*. Madrid: Imprenta y Estereotipia de M. Rivadeneyra, 1860.

Bell, Aubrey Fitz Gerald. *Castilian Literature*. Oxford: The Clarendon Press, 1938.

Besso, Henry V. *Dramatic Literature of the Sephardic Jews of Amsterdam.* New York: The Hispanic Institute in the United States, 1947.
Blecua, José Manuel, ed. *Obras completas de Francisco de Quevedo.* Vol. I. Barcelona: Editorial Planeta, 1963.
Bravo Villasante, Carmen. *La mujer vestida de hombre en el teatro español.* Madrid: Revista de Occidente, 1955.
Carrasco Urgoiti, María Soledad. *El moro de Granada en la literatura (del siglo XV al XX).* Madrid: Revista de Occidente, 1956.
Castro, Américo. *La realidad histórica de España.* México: Editorial Porrúa, 1954.
―――. *The Structure of Spanish History.* Translated by Edmund L. King. Princeton University Press, 1954.
Černý, Václav. "Wallenstein, héros d'un drame de Calderón." *Revue de Littérature Comparée,* 36 (1962), 179-90.
Coe, Ada M. *Carteleras madrileñas, 1677-1792, 1819.* México, 1952.
―――. *Catálogo bibliográfico y crítico de las comedias anunciadas en los periódicos de Madrid desde 1661 hasta 1819.* The Johns Hopkins Studies in Romance Literatures and Languages, Extra Vol. 9. Baltimore, Md.: The Johns Hopkins Press, 1935.
Cotarelo y Mori, Emilio. *Actores famosos del siglo XVII: Sebastián de Prado y su mujer Bernarda Ramírez.* Madrid: Tip. de la "Rev. de Arch., Bibl. y Museos," 1916.
―――. "Dramáticos españoles del siglo XVII: Álvaro Cubillo de Aragón." *Boletín de la Real Academia Española,* 5 (1918), 3-23, 241-80.
―――. *Ensayo sobre la vida y obras de don Pedro Calderón de la Barca.* Madrid: Tip. de la "Rev. de Arch., Bibl. y Museos," 1924.
―――. *Isidoro Máiquez y el teatro de su tiempo.* Madrid: Impr. de J. Perales y Martínez, 1902.
―――, et al., eds. *Obras de Lope de Vega, publicadas por la Real Academia Española.* Nueva edición. 13 vols. Madrid: Tipografía de la Revista de Archivos, Bibliotecas y Museos, 1916-1930.
Cubillo de Aragón, Álvaro. *Comedias escogidas.* Madrid: Imprenta de Ortega y Compañía, 1826.
―――. *Curia leonica.* Compvesta Por Aluaro Cubillo de Aragon, vezino de Granada, y Alcayde perpetuo de la carcel Real de Calatraua. Dirigido al Exmo. Sr. Don Gaspar de Guzman, Conde de Oliuares, Sumiller de corps del Rey nuestro Señor, su Cauallerizo mayor, y de su Consejo de Estado, Alcayde perpetuo de los Reales Alcaçares de Sevilla, etc. Impresso con licencia, en Granada, Por Martin Fernandez, Año 1625.
―――. *El Enano de las Musas. Comedias y obras diversas, con vn poema de las Cortes del Leon, y del Agvila, acerca del bvo gallego.* Sv Avtor Alvaro Cvbillo de Aragon. Dedicado a Don Sebastian Lopez Hierro de Castro, Cauallero del Orden de Calatraua, del Consejo de Su Magestad en la Tribunal de la Contaduria Mayor de Quentas, y Su Secretario de la Iunta de millones, Tesorero general de la Santa Cruzada, etc. Con privilegio. En Madrid, por Maria de Quiñones, año de 1654; rpt. Hildesheim: Georg Olms, 1971.
Cueva, Juan de la. *Comedias y tragedias.* Vol. I. Sociedad de Bibliófilos Españoles. Madrid: Imprenta Ibérica, 1917.
Durán, Agustín, ed. *Romancero general o colección de romances castellanos anteriores al siglo XVIII.* 2 vols. Biblioteca de Autores Españoles, 10, 16. Madrid: Librería de los Sucesores de Hernando, 1924.

Enciso Castrillón, Félix. *El amor por el tejado, comedia nueva en tres actos, formada por el mismo asunto que la que escribió, con el título de las Muñecas de Marcela, el antiguo poeta, Don Álvaro Cubillo*. Madrid: Cuesta, 1833.
Franklin, Albert B. "A Study of the Origins of the Legend of Bernardo del Carpio." *Hispanic Review*, 5 (1937), 286-303.
Gallego Morell, Antonio. *Sesenta escritores granadinos con sus partidas de bautismo*. Granada: Caja de Ahorros de Granada, 1970.
———. "Treinta partidas de bautismo de escritores granadinos." *Boletín de la Real Academia Española*, 34 (1954), 263-84.
García de la Huerta, Vicente. *Theatro Hespanol: Catalogo alphabetico de las comedias, tragedias, autos, zarzuelas, entremeses y otras obras correspondientes al Theatro Hespanol*. Madrid: Imprenta Real, 1785.
Gil y Zárate, Antonio. *Manual de literatura: Resumen histórico de la literatura española*. 3 vols. Madrid: Boix, 1844.
Glaser, Edward. "Álvaro Cubillo de Aragón's *Los desagravios de Christo*." *Hispanic Review*, 24 (1956), 306-21.
Hilborn, Harry Warren. *A Chronology of the Plays of D. Pedro Calderón de la Barca*. Toronto: The University of Toronto Press, 1938.
Josephus. With an English translation by H. St. J. Thackeray. 6 vols. The Loeb Classical Library. London: William Heinemann; New York: G. P. Putnam's Sons, 1926-1943. II, III.
Juliá Martínez, Eduardo, ed. *Obras de don Guillem de Castro y Bellvís*. 3 vols. Madrid: Imp. de la "Rev. de Arch., Bibl. y Museos," 1925-1927.
———. "El teatro en Valencia." *Boletín de la Real Academia Española*, 13 (1926), 318-41.
Leavitt, Sturgis E. *The "Estrella de Sevilla" and Claramonte*. Cambridge, Mass.: Harvard University Press, 1931.
León, Fray Luis de. *Obras completas castellanas*. Edited by P. Félix García. 2.ª edición, corregida y aumentada. Madrid: Biblioteca de Autores Cristianos, 1951.
Leonard, Irving A. "El teatro en Lima, 1790-93." *Hispanic Review*, 8 (1940), 93-112.
Lida, María Rosa. "Dido y su defensa en la literatura española." *Revista de Filología Hispánica*, 4 (1942), 209-52, 313-82.
Lista y Aragón, Alberto. *Lecciones de literatura española*. 2 vols. Madrid: Nicolás Arias, 1841.
Lohmann Villena, Guillermo, and Moglia, Raúl. "Las representaciones teatrales en Lima hasta el siglo XVIII." *Revista de Filología Hispánica*, 5 (1943), 313-43.
López Estrada, Francisco, and Keller, John Esten, eds. *Antonio de Villegas' "El abencerraje."* University of North Carolina Studies in Comparative Literature, No. 39. Chapel Hill: The University of North Carolina Press, 1964.
Luzán, Ignacio de. *La poética, o reglas de la poesía en general, y de sus principales especies*. Corregida y aumentada por su mismo autor. 2 vols. Madrid: Imprenta de D. Antonio de Sancha, 1789.
———. *La poética, o reglas de la poesía* [Text of the first (1737) edition]. Con un estudio de Luigi de Filippo. 2 vols. Barcelona: Selecciones Bibliófilos, 1956.
Macas, William. "A Critical and Annotated Edition of Álvaro Cubillo de Aragón's *El vandolero de Flandes*." Diss. New Mexico 1967.

McCready, W. T., and Molinaro, J. A. "La *Relación breve* de Cubillo de Aragón y la Paz de los Pirineos." *Bulletin Hispanique*, 62 (1960), 438-43.

MacCurdy, Raymond R., ed. *"Morir pensando matar"* y *"La vida en el ataúd,"* by Francisco de Rojas. Clásicos Castellanos, 153. Madrid: Espasa-Calpe, S. A., 1961.

María y Campos, Armando de. *Guía de representaciones teatrales en la Nueva España: Siglos XVI al XVIII.* México: B. Costa Amic, n.d.

Mariana, Juan de. *Historia general de España.* Vol. I. Biblioteca de Autores Españoles, 30. Madrid: M. Rivadeneyra, 1854.

Medel del Castillo, Francisco. *Indice general alfabetico de todos los titulos de comedias que se han escrito por varios autores antiguos y modernos, y de los autos sacramentales y alegoricos, assi de D. Pedro Calderon de la Barca, como de otros autores clasicos.* Ed. J. M. Hill. *Revue Hispanique*, 75 (1929), 144-369.

Menéndez y Pelayo, Marcelino, ed. *Obras de Lope de Vega, publicadas por la Real Academia Española.* 15 vols. Madrid: "Sucesores de Rivadeneyra," 1890-1913.

Menéndez Pidal, Ramón. *La leyenda de los infantes de Lara.* 2nd ed. Madrid: Centro de Estudios Históricos, 1934.

Mesonero Romanos, Ramón de, ed. *Dramáticos posteriores a Lope de Vega.* Vol. I. Biblioteca de Autores Españoles, 47. Madrid: Librería de los Sucesores de Hernando, 1924.

Morley, S. Griswold, and Bruerton, Courtney. *The Chronology of Lope de Vega's "Comedias."* Modern Language Association of America, Monograph Series, No. 11. New York: Modern Language Association of America, 1940.

Ochoa, Eugenio de, ed. *Tesoro del teatro español, desde su origen (año de 1356) hasta nuestros días.* Vol. V. Paris: Baudry, 1838.

Orozco Díaz, Emilio: "Unas páginas desconocidas de Cubillo de Aragón," *Boletín de la Universidad de Granada*, 10 (1938), 21-28.

Par, Alfonso. "Representaciones teatrales en Barcelona durante el siglo xviii." *Boletín de la Real Academia Española*, 16 (1929), 326-46, 492-513, 594-614.

Parducci, Amos. *La fortuna dell' "Orlando furioso" nel teatro spagnolo.* Giornale Storico della Letteratura Italiana, Supplemento No. 26. Torino: Casa Editrice Giovanni Chiantore, 1937.

Parker, Alexander A. "Santos y bandoleros en el teatro español del Siglo de Oro," *Arbor*, 13 (1949), 395-416.

Parker, Jack H., and K.-L. Selig. "A Current Bibliography of Foreign Publications Dealing with the *Comedia.*" *Bulletin of the Comediantes*, 12, No. 1 (1960), 10.

Paz y Melia, Antonio. *Catálogo de las piezas de teatro que se conservan en el departamento de manuscritos de la Biblioteca Nacional.* 2nd ed. 2 vols. Madrid: Blass, S. A. Tipográfica, 1934-1935.

Pérez Pastor, Cristóbal. *Noticias y documentos relativos a la historia y literatura españolas.* 4 vols. Madrid: Imprenta de la Revista de Legislación, 1910-1926.

———. *Nuevos datos acerca del histrionismo español en los siglos XVI y XVII.* 1.ª serie. Madrid: Imprenta de la Revista Española, 1901.

———. *Nuevos datos acerca del histrionismo español en los siglos XVI y XVII.* 2.ª serie, publicada con un índice por Georges Cirot. Bordeaux: Feret et Fils, 1914.

Pina, Rui de. *Crónica de el-rei D. João II.* Nova edicão com prefacio e notas de Alberto Martins de Carvaljo. Coimbra: Atlântida, 1950.
Portnoy, Antonio. *Ariosto y su influencia en la literatura española.* Buenos Aires: Editorial Estrada, 1932.
Primera crónica general de España. Vol. I. Nueva Biblioteca de Autores Españoles, 5. Madrid: Bailly-Bailliere e Hijos, 1906.
Relacion verdadera, que contiene la gran traicion que auia maquinado el Duque de Fritlandt contra la Magestad Cesarea del Emperador, y destruicion de los Estados de la potentissima Casa de Austria. Madrid: Imprenta de Francisco Martínez, 1634.
Rennert, H[ugo] A[lbert]. *The Spanish Stage in the Time of Lope de Vega.* New York: The Hispanic Society of America, 1909.
―――, and Castro, Américo. *Vida de Lope de Vega.* Madrid: Imprenta de los Sucesores de Hernando, 1919.
Sáinz de Robles, Federico Carlos. *Teatro español: Historia y antología.* 7 vols. Madrid: M. Aguilar, 1942-1943.
Sánchez Arjona, José. *Noticias referentes a los anales del teatro en Sevilla desde Lope de Rueda hasta fines del siglo XVII.* Sevilla: Imprenta de E. Rasco, 1898.
Sargent, Cecilia Vennard. *A Study of the Dramatic Works of Cristóbal de Virués.* New York: Instituto de las Españas en los Estados Unidos, 1930.
Schack, Adolfo Federico, Conde de. *Historia de la literatura y del arte dramático en España.* Translated by Eduardo de Mier. 5 vols. Madrid: Imprenta y Fundición de M. Tello, 1885-1887.
Schaeffer, Adolf. *Geschichte des spanischen Nationaldramas.* 2 vols. Leipzig: F. A. Brockhaus, 1890.
Scholberg, Kenneth R. *La poesía religiosa de Miguel de Barrios.* Columbus, Ohio: Ohio State University Press, n. d.
Shergold, N. D. *A History of the Spanish Stage from Medieval Times until the End of the Seventeenth Century.* Oxford: The Clarendon Press, 1967.
―――, and Varey, J. E. "Some Palace Performances of Seventeenth-Century Plays." *Bulletin of Hispanic Studies,* 40 (1963), 212-44.
Spencer, Forrest Eugene, and Schevill, Rudolph. *The Dramatic Works of Luis Vélez de Guevara: Their Plots, Sources, and Bibliography.* University of California Publications in Modern Philology, No. 19. Berkeley: University of California Press, 1937.
Strong, Lois. *Bibliography of Franco-Spanish Literary Relations until the XIX Century.* New York: Institute of French Studies, 1930.
Subirá, José. "Repertorio teatral madrileño y resplandor transitorio de la zarzuela (años 1763 a 1777)." *Boletín de la Real Academia Española,* 39 (1959), 429-62.
Suetonius. With an English translations by J. C. Rolfe. Vol. II. The Loeb Classical Library. London: W. Heinemann; New York: G. P. Putnam's Sons, 1920.
Ticknor, George. *History of Spanish Literature.* 3 vols. New York: Harper and Brothers, 1849.
Valbuena Prat, Ángel, ed. *Las muñecas de Marcela; El señor de Noches Buenas,* by Álvaro Cubillo de Aragón. Clásicos Olvidados, 3. Madrid: Compañía Ibero-americana de Publicaciones, 1928; rpt. Madrid: Ediciones Alcalá, 1966.

Varey, J. E. "Calderón, Cosme Lotti, Velázquez, and the Madrid Festivities of 1636-1637." *Renaissance Drama.* New series, 1. Evanston, Ill.: Northwestern University Press, 1968. Pp. 253-82.

Vélez de Guevara, Luis. *El diablo cojuelo.* Edición y notas de Francisco Rodríguez Marín. Clásicos Castellanos, 34. Madrid: Espasa-Calpe, S. A., 1941.

Vetter, Theodor. *Wallenstein in der dramatischen Dichtung des Jahrzehnts seines Todes.* Frauenfeld: J. Huber, 1894.

Wardropper, Bruce W. *Introducción al teatro religioso del Siglo de Oro.* Madrid: Revista de Occidente, 1953.

Watson, Francis. *Wallenstein.* New York, London: D. Appleton-Century Company, 1938.

Wilson, E. M. "The Four Elements in the Imagery of Calderón." *Modern Language Review,* 31 (1936), 34-47.

Wolf, Fernando José, and Hofmann, Conrado. *Primavera y flor de romances.* 2 vols. Berlin: A. Asher y Comp., 1856.

The Department of Romance Studies Digital Arts and Collaboration Lab at the University of North Carolina at Chapel Hill is proud to support the digitization of the North Carolina Studies in the Romance Languages and Literatures series.

www.ingramcontent.com/pod-product-compliance
Lightning Source LLC
Chambersburg PA
CBHW020416230426
43663CB00007BA/1192